DogLife ❧ Lifelong Care for Your Dog™

CHIHUAHUA

tfh

Debra J. White

CHIHUAHUA

Project Team
Editor: Stephanie Fornino
Indexer: Elizabeth Walker
Design: Angela Stanford
Series Design: Mary Ann Kahn, Angela Stanford

T.F.H. Publications
President/CEO: Glen S. Axelrod
Executive Vice President: Mark E. Johnson
Publisher: Christopher T. Reggio
Production Manager: Kathy Bontz

T.F.H. Publications, Inc.
One TFH Plaza
Third and Union Avenues
Neptune City, NJ 07753

Printed and bound in China

10 11 12 13 14   1 3 5 7 9 8 6 4 2

White, Debra J.
  Chihuahua / Debra J. White.
      p. cm.
  Includes bibliographical references and index.
  ISBN 978-0-7938-3605-5 (alk. paper)
  1. Chihuahua (Dog breed) I. Title.
  SF429.C45W48 2011
  636.76--dc22

                          2010010128

The Leader In Responsible Animal Care for Over 50 Years!®
www.tfh.com

CONTENTS

Introducing the Chihuahua 6

PART I:PUPPYHOOD

1: Is the Chihuahua Right for You? 18

2: Finding and Prepping for Your Chihuahua Puppy. 30

3: Care of Your Chihuahua Puppy. 44

4: Training Your Chihuahua Puppy 56

PART II:ADULTHOOD

5: Finding Your Chihuahua Adult 74

6: Chihuahua Grooming Needs 82

7: Chihuahua Nutritional Needs 96

8: Chihuahua Health and Wellness .110

9: Chihuahua Training. 132

10: Chihuahua Problem Behaviors. .142

11: Chihuahua Sports and Activities 154

PART III:SENIOR YEARS

12: Finding Your Chihuahua Senior .172

13: Care of Your Chihuahua Senior. .178

14: End-of-Life Issues 192

50 Fun Facts Every Chihuahua Owner Should Know 198

Resources 200

Index 204

INTRODUCTION

INTRODUCING THE CHIHUAHUA

Nearly everyone recognizes the Chihuahua. Some say that Chihuahuas are like potato chips—one is not enough. Famous Chihuahuas grab our attention in television commercials, Broadway plays, and major motion pictures. Super-sharp Chihuahuas score big during obedience trials at major dog shows. Some serve as therapy dogs, providing comfort to sick and dying patients in hospitals, long-term care facilities, and nursing homes. The average Chihuahua, though, is a cherished family pet, loved and pampered by all.

Despite their popularity in Hollywood and among average Americans, Chihuahuas are not for everyone. Loyal and devoted to their families or individual owners, Chihuahuas can also be pushy. They are pint-sized dogs with giant attitudes. If you already live with a Chihuahua or have in the past, you love their sense of humor, endless curiosity, and need for affection. For the newcomers, read further here about the Chihuahua to make sure that this is the dog for you.

THE DOMESTICATION OF THE DOG

Scientists say that all dogs *(Canis familiaris)*, including the small, perky Chihuahua, descend most likely from the gray wolf, *Canis lupus*). When you look at a wolf and then at a Chihuahua, it may be hard to believe, but it is true. We will never know exactly how or when the long domestication process began hundreds of thousands of years ago, but several theories exist.

Recent DNA evidence links the gray wolf with today's canine. Some researchers suggest that domestication started as early as 130,000 years ago, while other researchers place the date later, at 10,000 to 15,000 years. Regardless of the timeline, it is thought that prehistoric men invited wolves into their caves, perhaps so that the animals could escape the cold or rain. It is also possible that people wanted the wolves for warmth or protection from other animals or human enemies.

Other scientists say that the wolf experienced a gradual transition before living with man because the wolf has always been wild, not known for its coziness to humans. Wolves still do not approach humans. Why would they have approached man so many years ago?

Scientists suggest that gradual changes predisposed the wolf to man's environment because wild animals like wolves would have been hard if not impossible to live with. Maybe harsh weather, wars, or crop disease caused famine, so wolves started hanging around man's encampments to scavenge for food, thus making them dependent on humans for handouts. As man moved from one place to another, wolves followed the food source to prevent starvation.

Alternatively, man could have intruded upon the wolf, perhaps destroying its habitat. Out of survival instinct, the wolf then relied on man for food. So the wolf learned to start sharing space with man, thus beginning the domestication process.

In short, no one knows exactly what happened all those years ago. The aforementioned are only theories based on available evidence. Modern dogs were selectively bred to hunt, herd, and guard. Some dogs, such as the toy breeds, were bred as companion animals. Royalty in earlier times considered the toy breeds as lapdogs. Chihuahuas are examples of toy dogs.

Theories exist about the Chihuahua's ancestry, but the truth may never be known. It is buried with history. Our knowledge is based on a mixture of folklore, history, and speculation. A few possible origins are discussed in this chapter.

THE CHIHUAHUA IN MEXICO

Various civilizations rose up and seized power through Mexico's long history. They ruled for a time and then perished because of war, disease, or famine. Mayans, Toltecs, and Aztecs are

It may be hard to believe, but the tiny Chihuahua descended from wolves.

believed to have shared their empires with dogs.

A small dog called the Techichi lived among the Toltecs (the Aztec word for skilled artisan). Historical evidence suggests that the Toltecs, who originated in northern Mexico but expanded southward, cherished and honored the small dog known as the Techichi. Some Techichis joined priests in their temples. The priests believed that the little dog possessed spiritual powers to predict the future.

Archeological evidence suggests that the dog lived among the Mayans too, as far back as the 5th century. Dog ownership in Mayan culture represented wealth, and slaves often cared for the dogs in addition to their other chores and duties. But not all Mexican dogs or Techichis lived comfortably. Some were hunted and killed for food; others were sacrificed to the gods along with other animals. Toltecs believed that the Techichi would guide the spirit to the afterlife, a belief evidenced by the fact that graves excavated in Mexico in later years reveal the skeletons of tiny dogs—most likely the Techichi.

Depicted in stone carvings, especially in the pyramids of Cholula and the Monastery of Huejotzingo, the Techichi bears a fairly strong resemblance to the modern-day Chihuahua, with erect ears, a bony head, and short, delicate legs.

Another potential theory holds that the Techichi was mixed with a feral Mexican dog, called the Perro Chihuahueno, who lived in the mountains. These dogs allegedly had short pointy noses, skinny legs, large pointed ears, long toenails, and a wild streak, traits

that are similar to those found in the modern Chihuahua. But wait—some say that the Techichi was not a dog at all but a large rodent. That would be one huge rat!

Whether the Techichi was a dog or a rat, a major upheaval altered the indigenous society in the 16th century. Hernando Cortez and the Spaniards invaded the New World, virtually wiping out the Toltecs' society. Nothing more was heard about the Techichis. Some suggest that they survived on rodents and other small animals, but history says that the Spaniards also hunted them for food. The Techichis probably lost their position of spiritual importance. Little else was heard about them.

CHIHUAHUAS IN THE MEDITERRANEAN
Another theory says the Chihuahua originated on the Mediterranean island of

The Chihuahua may have originated in Mexico.

Chihuahuas were first registered by the AKC in the early part of the 20th century.

Malta, far away from Mexico. A small dog with a molera, a slight indentation on the head, allegedly lived there. History says that early traders introduced the dog to continental Europe via ship.

Some European artists depict a small dog in their work. A fresco in the Sistine Chapel that dates around 1482 has a small dog with a round head, large erect ears, and a smooth coat. Could it be a Chihuahua? The painting was supposedly done before Columbus arrived in the New World, thus shattering the myth that the Chihuahua originated in Mexico. The presence of this small dog in European paintings leads some to believe that the Chihuahua was introduced to Mexico by Spanish invaders who destroyed the civilization they found.

Alternatively, it is possible that traders brought the Chihuahua to Mexico from Malta. Reverse migration would create an entirely different scenario about the dog's origins. There is ample evidence that small dogs lived among the Aztecs, the Toltecs, and other societies in Central America and what is now known as Mexico.

CHIHUAHUAS IN CHINA

Yet another theory suggests that the Chihuahua originated in China and followed tribes across the Bering Strait to the American continent. Little archeological evidence backs up the Chinese connection, though.

CHIHUAHUAS IN NORTH AFRICA

An even less popular theory holds that the Chihuahua is a descendant of an African fox, *Fennecus zerda*. The African fox supposedly had large ears, big round eyes, and a small body. Sound like a Chihuahua? But how did the fox dog get to the United States? No reasonable explanation is offered other than the physical resemblance of the two animals.

CHIHUAHUAS IN THE UNITED STATES

Small dogs were discovered around 1850 in the Mexican state of Chihuahua. These dogs became quite popular along the border states of Arizona, New Mexico, California, and Texas, where poor Mexican peasants sold them, probably to earn money. Known then as Arizona or Texas dogs, they appealed to tourists because of their small size. Later they were called Mexican Chihuahuas after the part of Mexico in which they were found.

James Watson, an American dog lover, purchased his first Arizona dog in 1888 for a few dollars. It is said that he loved the Arizona dog, or the Chihuahua, so much that he bought several more. Neutering was not popular then, so he probably ended up with a family of Arizona dogs. Perhaps he gave some to family or friends or began selling the Arizona dog too.

The Chihuahua Club of America encourages and promotes quality breeding of pedigree Chihuahuas.

RECOGNITION BY MAJOR CLUBS

Founded in 1884, the American Kennel Club (AKC) is a non-profit organization that speaks for purebred dogs like the Chihuahua by promoting their well-being, safety, and welfare. The AKC advocates for canine health and the rights of dog owners, and advances responsible dog ownership so that purebred dogs become valued family members. More than 500 breed clubs in the United States belong to the AKC. Each club is represented by a delegate who votes on AKC rules and club directors. The AKC maintains a list of purebred Chihuahua breeders who are expected to follow the organization's guidelines, rules, and regulations. Penalties apply to those who do not. The AKC keeps a vast registry of purebred dogs, and it publishes a monthly magazine, books, and other educational material, including pamphlets about responsible dog ownership.

Midget, owned by H. Raynor of El Paso, Texas, was the first Chihuahua to be registered with the AKC. He was born in 1903. There are no records that James Watson registered his dogs with the AKC. In either 1915 or 1916, the AKC registered a mere 30 Chihuahuas. Very likely, more Chihuahuas existed in the United States, particularly in the Southwest. They just were not registered with the AKC because of either the fees or unfamiliarity with the process. By 1967, the breed was much more popular. Registration hit 37,000. In 2008, the AKC registered 150,000 Chihuahuas, making it the 12th most popular dog that year. That is a lot of Chihuahuas!

The Chihuahua Club of America (CCA)

Established in 1923, the Chihuahua Club of America encourages and promotes quality breeding of pedigree Chihuahuas. Members are expected to follow and promote AKC standards of excellence and responsibility. Further, members protect and further the interests of the Chihuahua by educating the public through brochures, pamphlets, seminars, and maintaining an up-to-date library data bank, in print and online. The club conducts sanctioned dog shows and obedience trials in accordance with AKC rules and regulations. Membership is composed of individual breeders, Chihuahua owners, and local Chihuahua clubs that abide by the national rules. Breeders who do not adhere to CCA standards face sanctions. Repeated sanctions or failure to abide by the rules could lead to expulsion or suspension of privileges.

The British Kennel Club

The British Kennel Club recognized the Chihuahua with the breed's first official registration in 1907. Another dog was not registered until 1924. The upheaval of World War I in British society may have been one of the reasons. Barely 100 dogs were registered by the onset of World War II. The nightmarish devastation of years of war halted interest in purebred dog registries. In 1949, only eight Chihuahuas remained listed with the club. The fate of those dogs and their owners is not known. As a way to recover from the cruel and crushing aftermath of a world war, British citizens took in dogs, especially small ones like the Chihuahua, who were easy to care for. As the country slowly rebuilt, the Chihuahua registry started to rebound. By 1953 there were 111 Chihuahuas registered with the British Kennel Club. In 2007, the numbers had risen dramatically. There were 1,728 long-coated Chihuahuas and 1,143 smooth-coated Chihuahuas listed with the British Kennel Club. Perhaps the cool, damp weather influences decision making, because the British clearly seem to prefer the long-coated Chihuahua.

FAMOUS CHIHUAHUAS AND THEIR PEOPLE

Most Chihuahuas are ordinary house pets and never appear on the silver screen. A few Chihuahuas, though, blazed their way to fame and fortune, starring in television commercials, hit movies, and Broadway plays.

Gigdet

This Chihuahua earned fame as the Taco Bell dog in the 1990s. She appeared in hundreds of TV commercials, uttering a simple Spanish phrase, "Yo quiero Taco Bell" which translates into English as "I want Taco Bell." For three years (1997 to 2000) Gidget was a familiar face on nightly television commercials. After retirement from show business, Gidget lived leisurely with her trainer. At the age of 15, Gidget died on July 22, 2009 from a stroke.

Chihuahuas are popular for use in films and advertising.

Barely 100 dogs were registered by the onset of World War II in England.

Bruiser

Named Moonie in real life, Bruiser starred in the 2001 silver screen hit *Legally Blonde*, along with actress Reese Witherspoon. The movie was so popular that a sequel and a Broadway musical soon followed, all starring a Chihuahua.

Other Famous Chihuahuas

Coco, a Chihuahua, starred on the Disney television series *That's So Raven*.

Another Chihuahua, also named Coco, appeared on Cesar Milan's TV series *The Dog Whisperer*. Pancho, a Chihuahua, had a role in the movie *Big Mama's House 2*.

Wheelchair Willy, a paralyzed Chihuahua found as a stray in Southern California, got a set of wheels from his adoptive family. He later became a therapy dog and the subject of two popular children's books. Tito the Chihuahua had a part in Disney's animated film Oliver and Company.

Famous Hollywood personalities such as Paris Hilton, Scarlett Johansson, Hilary Duff, and Sharon Osborne all have had or currently own Chihuahuas. Some such as Duff and Hilton are often photographed in popular magazines holding their Chihuahuas. Duff and her Chihuahua Lola appeared on the cover of the now defunct magazine *Hollywood Dog*.

Beverly Hills Chihuahua, a 2008 Disney movie, featured none other than Chloe, a Chihuahua, in a major role.

Dr. Papidies, a three-year-old Chihuahua, is so cute and adorable that he recently won a $1 million dollar prize in the Cutest Dog Competition, sponsored by All American Pet Brands. But Dr. Papidies lives a good life with Dr. Leslie Capin, a Denver area dermatologist, and her husband, Dr. Natalio Banchero. Recognizing that other dogs are not so fortunate, Dr. Capin donated the prize money to local animal charities. Paid out in 30 annual installments, the Denver Dumb Friends League (DDFL) and the Max Fund will benefit from Dr. Capin's generosity.

The withering economy sliced into shelter donations, so the prize money helps more than ever, says Bob Rohde, executive director of the Denver Dumb Friends League. The shelter takes in thousands of unwanted dogs and cats every year. So does the Max Fund.

Dr. Capin's love for animals even reached unwanted Chihuahuas dumped in California shelters. To help save them from euthanasia, Dr. Capin covered expenses to fly 170 Chihuahuas from southern California shelters to the DDFL for a special adoption event in January 2010. Rohde says the event went very well and nearly all of the Chihuahuas found good homes.

Dr. Capin is quite the humanitarian. A powerful earthquake rocked the poverty stricken island nation of Haiti on January 12, 2010, leaving millions homeless, hungry, and hurt. Thousands perished under the rubble of collapsed buildings. To aid the sick and injured, Dr. Capin flew to Haiti. She treated dozens of patients desperate for health care.

Dr. Papidies, meanwhile, reports to work every day with Capin. The Chihuahua meets and greets patients at her dermatology clinic. In March, the perky Chihuahua will join her at the annual meeting of the American Academy of Dermatology and rub noses with other hundreds of doctors. Dr. Capin and her husband have no children, so Dr. Papidies is their "son." His prize money will give other unwanted animals the chance for the fabulous

PART I

PUPPYHOOD

CHAPTER 1

IS THE CHIHUAHUA RIGHT FOR YOU?

Chihuahuas can be wonderful companions. They greet you with tail wags and kisses, even if your trip to the mailbox took a mere two minutes. No one else may be glad to see you, but your dog always is. Their devotion is unwavering. That kind of loyalty is hard to beat. Dogs can break a lonely senior citizen's isolation or help soothe hurt feelings after a bitter divorce. Your boss scolded you for being five minutes late, but your dog sees you as royalty.

Dog breeds are different, however. Each one has special qualities such as size, type of coat, length of ears, and temperament that sets them apart. Is the Chihuahua the most appropriate dog for you? We will help you decide.

GENERAL BREED CHARACTERISTICS

Chihuahuas are smart, intuitive, and shrewd. Besides being intelligent, they are scrappy little dogs with lion-sized attitudes. Do not mess with a Chihuahua. Their loud, shrill bark will scare off any intruder, be that intruder human or animal. Size does not matter either. The intruders could be a gang of armed thieves and the Chihuahua would still do his best to scare them away.

But Chihuahuas are also tender, loyal, and cuddly. They are happiest snuggled up next to their owners in the warmth of the family room or enjoying a belly rub stretched out on their favorite pillow. Chihuahuas are loaded with plenty of love and sassy attitude.

Space requirements for the compact Chihuahua are considerably less than for a Great Dane or a Saint Bernard. They adjust quite well to apartment, condominium, or mobile home living. They are great company for a senior citizen in assisted living. Chihuahuas have no need for a roomy back yard, but if you have the outdoor space they enjoy occasional visits to snoop around or take in fresh air. Most Chihuahuas, however, do not romp through the grass or fly through the air chasing after a flying disc.

A low-maintenance dog, the Chihuahua can live almost anywhere as long as he has his comfort. With an owner to fuss over him, home could be a Vermont dairy farm, a gleaming Manhattan high-rise, or a San Francisco houseboat. Exercise requirements are modest. Grooming is uncomplicated, and the Chihuahua has a small appetite. He travels light; just add love and affection.

A Chihuahua's yapping will alert you when someone rings the doorbell, knocks at the door, or stands by your window. He knows whether an intruder lurks in the back yard or inside the bushes. Chihuahuas are protective of their owners and their turf. Even when no danger exists, Chihuahuas can be persistent and bark long after your guests are inside. The Chihuahua eventually calms down, especially if the owner encourages him to meet and greet guests. Some Chihuahuas are more reserved than other dogs. They usually do not throw themselves at Uncle Joe but approach him cautiously. Once a Chihuahua gives your company the once-over, he decides whether he wants petting or not. Chances are that he'll favor the stroking and generous belly rubs.

Encourage your friends or family members to bend down so that they are more nearly on his level as they approach your Chihuahua. Eye-to-eye contact makes the Chihuahua feel safer. Like dogs of most other breeds, Chihuahuas are especially delighted if your friends arrive with dog biscuits or a tiny sliver of chicken or cheese.

Chihuahuas are toy dogs who enjoy a long life span, which averages 12 to 17 years. With proper veterinary care, good wholesome food, and indoor living, some live even longer. Are you prepared for a lengthy commitment that involves money, time, and hard work? If so, then look closer at the characteristics of a Chihuahua.

PHYSICAL CHARACTERISTICS

The American Kennel Club (AKC) sorts purebred dogs into seven groups: Hound, Sporting, Working, Terrier, Non-Sporting, Toy, and Herding. The Chihuahua is among the toy breeds. All toy dogs are small, but each breed has traits that make it unique.

General Body Structure

Graceful yet elegant, the Chihuahua's slightly arched neck rolls smoothly into his small shoulders. (The Chihuahua should have a level back.) He has straight legs and round ribs. Measure a Chihuahua from the pointy piece that sticks out under the neck to the buttocks and you'll see that he is a little longer than he is tall. His feet are tiny and delicate.

By the Numbers

Are you ready to be a responsible dog owner? You love your brother's Chihuahua puppy. He is sweet and adorable, and he sleeps next to you every time he visits. But are you ready for responsible pet ownership yourself? Here are six things you'll have to do:

- clean up waste
- teach obedience skills
- pay the annual license fee
- abide by leash laws
- not let your dog breed carelessly
- assume full financial responsibility for his care

If you are ready for all of this, then pursue further steps to acquire a Chihuahua puppy from a conscientious breeder or an animal shelter/rescue. You will be thrilled, delighted, and maybe challenged with a Chihuahua. Most of all, nothing can replace the genuine love and affection from a dog.

Chihuahuas have either a short coat (called a smooth coat) or a long coat.

Size

Ideally, a Chihuahua should range from 6 to 9 inches (15 to 23 cm) tall when measured from the ground to the top of his shoulders (withers) according to the AKC breed standard and generally weigh no more than 6 pounds (2.5 kg). Chihuahuas who tip the scales at more than 6 (2.5 kg) pounds or are taller than 9 inches (23 cm) fail to qualify for the show ring, but they can still be fabulous house pets. Neither size nor weight diminishes a Chihuahua's capacity for love. Chunky Chihuahuas, however, may have health problems, so it is best to keep your pet slender and lean. A further discussion about Chihuahua health and wellness can be found in Chapter 8.

Coat Type

Two different coat types exist in Chihuahuas: smooth (short) and long.

Smooth Coats

Smooth coats are the most popular, with fur that is short and smooth and clings to the body. The fur should be silky and shiny. Some smooth-coated Chihuahuas are born with an undercoat. If that is the case, their coats appear thicker. There should be a light ruff around the neck but without fringes. Smooth-coated Chihuahuas are easy to groom. The tail should be curly and furry. Short-coated Chihuahuas still shed, although not as much as long-coated Chihuahuas. They still need to be brushed regularly.

Long Coats

Breed experts say that in earlier years short-coated Chihuahuas were mixed with Papillons. That resulted in the long-coated Chihuahua, now recognized as a separate type. Born with long, soft fur about 1.5 (4 cm) inches long, the coat can be flat or fluffy. Feathering surrounds the ears. There is an ample ruff about the neck.

Two-month-old Chihuahua puppies are smart enough for you to start the housetraining process. Begin training as soon as you bring your puppy home from the breeder. For example, take him outside after he has had his first meal. As soon as he has eliminated, bring him back inside. That is the first housetraining step. Housetraining is discussed further in Chapter 4.

A long-haired plume covers the tail. Wispy hair stretches along the hind legs. The fur is silky, soft, and shiny. Long-coated Chihuahuas shed more often, so be prepared to brush them regularly to keep their coats healthy and clean. Regular brushing also keeps excessive fur from collecting on furniture and clothes.

Color

Chihuahuas are bred in several different colors. Cream, fawn, red, and white are popular in the show ring, but there are a lot of people who like brown or black-and-tan Chihuahuas. Blue Chihuahuas are rare.

Head and Neck

A piece of fruit? Yes, a Chihuahua's head should be round like a juicy apple, according to breed experts. That is part of what makes Chihuahuas special. Many Chihuahuas are born with a molera, a slight indentation on the head. A molera is like a soft spot on a baby's skull. In some Chihuahuas, the molera closes on its own by age three. Never press or hold down on the molera, but otherwise it poses no health concerns for a Chihuahua.

Eyes

The eyes are nearly always dark yet perky and inquisitive. Some light-coated Chihuahuas may have light-colored eyes. A well-bred and healthy Chihuahua has expressive eyes that are set equally apart, shiny but not protruding. They should not bulge or be too small.

Ears

Chihuahua ears are pointy and erect. The inside should be pink. Chihuahuas' ears are large for such a small dog, which adds to their charm. Feathery plumes complement the ears of long-coated Chihuahuas. The ears become erect by about six months of age. If they don't stand up by eight months, they may never be erect. Floppy ears do not indicate deafness,

A Chihuahua puppy is hard to resist, but don't bring one home unless you understand the care and commitment it takes.

hearing impairments, or any other problem. They will, however, disqualify your dog from the show circuit.

DOES A CHIHUAHUA FIT YOUR LIFESTYLE?

Does your job require frequent travel, including trips to China, India, or Australia? Are you in and out of meetings twelve hours a day and take files home to review? Do you rent a summer getaway on the weekends during July and August or ski for a few weeks in winter? Is your relationship stable or are you single? If you are married, will there be a family soon, or did you recently give birth to twins? Is retirement in the offing? Do you plan to travel the country in an RV or settle into a 65+ community?

All dogs come with expenses, even little Chihuahuas. Expect to pay for veterinary bills, food, supplies, and, if you travel, boarding fees. Sometimes life throws the unexpected curve ball, so who will care for your Chihuahua if you become seriously impaired from an accident or illness?

Are you willing to scoop smelly poop on a daily basis? You either have to clean the waste in your back yard or pick up after your Chihuahua while walking in public. You may face a fine or the wrath of your neighbors or home owners' association if you do not.

Consider all of these issues and other issues before you bring home a Chihuahua puppy. If you are your dog's primary caregiver and you work as a sales rep and travel out of town three weeks out of the month, dog ownership is not for you. If you recently married and plan to start a family soon, put off getting a Chihuahua; other breeds are more suitable around toddlers. If you plan to retire and move into a community of seniors, a Chihuahua would be an ideal companion, but make

Male or Female?

Some Chihuahua owners say that it makes no difference whether you live with a male or female Chihuahua. Others say that females are more independent, moodier, and pickier. Males are said to tolerate children better than females and are easier to train. No hard data prove or disprove these theories. Every Chihuahua is different, but there is no question that unaltered males are challenging. Increased testosterone levels lead to aggressive behavior in unaltered dogs. A female in heat nearby will attract your Chihuahua, and he will do anything to escape. Furthermore, unaltered males exhibit the annoying behavior of marking with urine, including lifting his leg on the couch. Unless you plan to breed responsibly, surgically alter your male. It is better for his health and behavior. You'll be a contented pet owner as well.

sure that the building management allows pets. Never obtain a Chihuahua without proper landlord approval; building owners or managers do not like surprises. You may end up having to move.

Chihuahuas are hard to resist, especially when they are puppies. They are unquestionably adorable. But unless you are ready to commit to a lifetime of care of that dog(s), do not bring a puppy or an adult Chihuahua into your life. If your family is involved, the entire household should agree that it wants a Chihuahua. Impulse decisions often strand a Chihuahua in the backyard, at an animal shelter, or with a family member or friend who may not want a dog. That is not

Want to Know More?

For more information on grooming your Chihuahua puppy, see Chapter 3: Care of Your Puppy.

good for any Chihuahua. Owning a dog is a lifelong obligation.

Exercise

If you want a hardy canine companion who enjoys the great outdoors and hikes the Grand Canyon National Park lugging his own backpack filled with bottled water and a week's worth of kibble, look for another breed. Chihuahuas cannot endure that kind of vigorous exercise. Their small bodies have exercise limitations.

Chihuahuas are not suitable jogging companions either. Do not expect them to blaze around the track or run along city streets with their speedy owners. Their small hearts cannot endure the cardiac stress.

A Chihuahua may enjoy a casual stroll around the block or a quick sniff in the back yard. Although his exercise needs are minimal, short walks keep him fit and trim. He also benefits from fresh air and social interaction with other dogs and people.

Grooming

Chihuahuas, especially the smoothcoats, are fairly easy to care for. Get them used to the grooming process as puppies so that they do not squirm or fuss when taking a bath as adults. Bathe your puppy within the first few days. Use a gentle puppy shampoo. After he shakes off excess water, pat him dry with a soft towel. You might use a blow dryer on a long-coated Chihuahua, particularly if you live in a cold environment. Smooth-coated Chihuahuas dry off fairly quickly. Bath water should be

lukewarm, and the room temperature should be warm and toasty.

Remember to brush. Do not be fooled by the short-coated Chihuahuas. They still need regular combing and/or brushing. All dogs shed to some degree, even short-coated Chihuahuas.

Long-coated Chihuahuas require frequent brushing and/or combing so that their coats remain smooth, silky, and tangle-free. Always check a long-coated dog after he has been in a dog park or the back yard. Sometimes debris and dirt cling to their fur. Remove them right away.

Handling

Observe as your friends and family pick up and handle your puppy. Make sure that they are gentle. Let them feed him too. Treats always warm the welcome, especially if you have a shy, timid puppy. Your puppy should feel at

A long-haired Chihuahua will need more grooming than a short-haired Chihuahua.

ease around strangers, including children. His inner circle should be a source of comfort and calm, not distress or anxiety. Discourage loud or brusque people from picking up your puppy. Do not be discouraged from saying no to friends or family if they do not show respect for your puppy.

Health

Major health issues in Chihuahua puppies generally result from bad breeding or neglect. As a breed, they are not prone to the serious medical problems that are discussed further in Chapter 8.

Make an appointment for a health check within the first few days after you bring your Chihuahua puppy home. This is an ideal time to establish a relationship with a veterinarian, someone who plays a key role in your dog's health and well-being for years to come.

Initially your veterinarian will administer a series of inoculations until your puppy is four months old that protect him from a string of serious ailments such as canine parvovirus and distemper. Puppy diseases are discussed at length in Chapter 3.

The breeder or rescue group should provide you with a health agreement that details what vaccinations, if any, your puppy has already received. Take that with you on the puppy's first veterinary visit. If this is your first dog, it is particularly important to prepare a list of questions about your Chihuahua's health care and behavior to ask the veterinarian.

If you have other dogs in the home, they should be current on vaccinations prior to bringing a new puppy home. Other dogs at home should not be sick either. A new puppy lacks a fully formed immune system and can become ill.

Sociability

Chihuahuas are independent little dogs, with minds of their own. No one pushes them around, but underneath their thick skin they are lovable dogs. Even if you are a strapping 6-foot (2-m) man who watches football on Sunday afternoons, your Chihuahua will nuzzle next to you as you catch the latest action from the NFL. Chihuahuas can be nosy and inquisitive. They do not like being ignored, shut out, or cast aside. Bring them into the family action and your Chihuahua will be content.

Never buy a Chihuahua from a breeder or adopt one from a shelter to leave outside all the time or chained to a doghouse. Besides Chihuahuas' intolerance of extreme cold or heat, depriving them of human companionship is cruel. Chihuahuas should become part of the family. Dogs without socialization often become fear biters or develop problem behaviors. Plus they are lonely and sad outside all by themselves. Outdoor Chihuahuas are not as healthy as indoor dogs either.

Children and Chihuahuas

Children and dogs can be best friends under nearly all circumstances. They play together, sleep together, and eat together. Children sometimes read to dogs as a way to improve their reading skills. Small children, however, must be carefully supervised around all dogs, including Chihuahuas. Toy breeds like the Chihuahua are not playthings. They cannot be bobbled like beach balls or tossed around like flying discs. Unsupervised children may accidentally drop or squash a delicate Chihuahua, with fatal results. Toddlers learning to walk could slip and fall onto a Chihuahua, breaking the dog's back.

Some children display behavior that scares a Chihuahua. For example, misbehaved children may throw toys, scream, or play roughly, all of which may frighten a Chihuahua. The dog may growl as a sign that he feels threatened. If the child shrugs off the warning and no adult is present, the Chihuahua could lunge at the child and bite. Nearly all dog bites involve young children and are sometimes disfiguring. A few are even fatal. Chihuahuas do best around children over the age of ten.

Follow a few simple steps when introducing a Chihuahua puppy to children. Give each child time to bond with the puppy. For example, a parent should demonstrate proper handling techniques to children so that they learn that the puppy is a living sentient being and not a plaything that is tossed around. No dog should ever be left alone with an infant or small child, and that includes a puppy.

Children of any age should never be solely responsible for the Chihuahua's care. Older children, around nine and above, can help with the dog's feeding, grooming, and cleanup. For instance, parents can alert their children to watch for an empty water bowl

Older children should be partners in the Chihuahua's care but never assume the entire responsibility.

and show them how to fill it. Children can assist parents with feeding and complete simple grooming techniques such as brushing the dog's coat or holding the blow dryer. And they can pick up waste in the back yard and dispose of it properly. Parents should let children accompany them on daily dog walks, especially to meet the neighbors and their pets. That is a fun way for a family to meet and greet their neighbors. Older children should be partners in the Chihuahua's care but never assume the entire responsibility. That is inappropriate and places too much burden on young children.

Around Strangers
Slowly introduce your Chihuahua puppy to your social network, which includes your friends, neighbors, family, and coworkers. A Chihuahua who is surrounded by warm, friendly faces is less likely to become fearful and suspicious. Instead, he will grow up feeling confident, safe, and secure. He will see his world as kind and good.

Until he is fully vaccinated, shield him from dog parks, animal shelter fundraisers, and other public places where he might encounter unvaccinated dogs. That sets up the potential for disease transmission that could be harmful as well as costly. Contagious diseases like parvo and distemper are highly preventable with a simple vaccine but very hard to cure once a puppy is infected.

Check with your veterinarian about the timing for his first visit to the dog park. Dog parks are a good outlet for socialization. Owners network with other dog owners and dogs get to run and play in a safe setting.

Typically it is safe to visit after his third or fourth set of vaccinations. Many parks are built in two enclosed sections; one for small, inactive dogs and one for dogs that run and romp around. Your Chihuahua puppy is safer around smaller, less active dogs. The more active area is usually filled with raucous large dogs that could inadvertently trample on your Chihuahua.

Chihuahuas and Other Pets
Chihuahuas may act bossy and domineering around other dogs and cats, but once they get used to each other, a Chihuahua usually accepts other pets into the home, especially if it is another Chihuahua. Chihuahuas nearly always welcome other Chihuahuas. They seem to know their own kind and offer no resistance when a new Chihuahua puppy or adult is added to the family brood. Always supervise introductions, however, to make sure that they go smoothly.

Introducing another breed may be touchier. Chihuahuas throw their weight around in front of dogs three times their size. As long as the new dog or cat knows that the Chihuahua is top dog, then everything should be fine. Avoid situations where your Chihuahua confronts a larger dog who might assault him. Not all dogs accept the Chihuahua's bold, brash behavior. Add only a mellow and subservient non-Chihuahua to the household. Chihuahuas can go after cats too.

In a multi-pet household, there may be a battle over who sleeps on the bed or snuggles on the easy chair, but the Chihuahua and the other pets usually sort things out. Bringing home a cat or a dog of another breed may require more work, so be prepared. Every Chihuahua is different, so each situation should be evaluated separately.

Trainability
Rumors suggest that Chihuahuas are so stubborn that they are hard to train. That is simply not true. Every Chihuahua can be

A Chihuahua may try to boss around a much larger dog—things will go much smoother if your other dog is mellow in temperament.

obedience trained and housetrained. The key is having a committed and dedicated owner who is willing to devote sufficient time to the new puppy.

Start a training regimen shortly after you bring you puppy home. You will regret it later if you do not. A well-behaved Chihuahua gets invited to family picnics and holiday get-togethers. He is welcomed by friends, family, and neighbors and is a delight to be around.

Everyone shuns a bratty dog, and an untrained Chihuahua can jangle your nerves. Train your puppy while he is young. Eight-week-old puppies are not too young to start training. They can start to learn simple behavior techniques, although don't make them more intense until the puppy is 12 weeks old.

Training is a two-step process that involves housetraining as well as behavior training requiring your time and money. It is an investment that pays off handsomely, though. Your Chihuahua will know his limits, act accordingly, and you will be a satisfied pet owner.

Housetraining should be one of your first steps after the puppy comes home. Invest in a sturdy, reliable crate appropriately sized for your puppy. If you are not sure about the crate, ask your veterinarian or other dog owners for a recommendation. Not only does a crate aid in housetraining, but it is a key in behavior training too. Chihuahua puppies are cute, but they get into trouble if left alone. They might urinate on the new Persian rug or rip apart the iPod you left on the coffee table. Crate training spares you of headaches and keeps your Chihuahua out of trouble. This is a win-win situation.

Along with housetraining, introduce your puppy to a leash. All puppies should learn how to walk on a leash. If you stall too long, you may have an unruly little dog who will resist the leash. If you live in an apartment or a condo, a defiant dog can be a problem, even one the size of a Chihuahua. He has to go outside, and walking a dog without a leash is dangerous—he may wander and get hit by a car. In most communities, a dog at large is also illegal, a violation of leash laws. Condo or apartment managers usually do not allow dogs to run loose on the grounds either. Be persistent and firm—your dog can accomplish walking on a leash. Chapter 4 covers more aspects of leash training.

During training, keep in mind that Chihuahuas respond to praise and meat snacks. A few trainers use only praise, but most recommend a combination of praise and treats. Whatever training method you choose, always reinforce positive behavior. Never yell or use

force if your Chihuahua soils inside the home or misbehaves. Expect accidents to happen or something to be chewed. This is all part of owning a puppy.

Consider behavior classes for your Chihuahua. Animal shelters, behaviorists, and pet supply retailers offer them at reasonable prices. Training classes provide owners with valuable lessons about puppyhood and widen your network of dog owners. Behavior classes can help you bond with your puppy. Chapter 4 covers training aspects in more depth.

Multi-Dog Tip

Chihuahuas do not make good gifts. Do not buy a Chihuahua puppy as a gift for friends or relatives, even if they boast of loving the breed. They may have dogs, cats, or family members at home who do not want company. Someone may have allergies. The recipient may not have landlord approval either. Owners should obtain dogs on their own terms.

Start a training regimen shortly after you bring your puppy home.

CHAPTER 2

FINDING AND PREPPING FOR YOUR CHIHUAHUA PUPPY

As a potential dog owner, you researched different breeds and decided that a Chihuahua puppy fits your lifestyle. The next step is finding the right puppy, a dog who becomes part of your family. Chihuahua puppies are available from several sources. Not every source is reputable, however. This chapter will help you make an informed choice when picking out a Chihuahua puppy and tell you how to prepare your home for your newest family member.

ARE YOU READY FOR A CHIHUAHUA COMMITMENT?

Cute and cuddly, Chihuahuas beg to be loved. They require years of dedication, energy, and money. Are you ready for behavior training, housetraining, and socialization of your puppy? A Chihuahua's average life span is 12 to 17 years. Annual expenditures include the costs of food, veterinary care, licenses, and supplies such as leashes, collars, toys, and bedding. Add the expense of sweaters or coats if you live in a cold, blustery climate. (Frigid weather can be hard on some Chihuahuas). Remember to include boarding costs if you

take vacation or travel for your job. Those bills can pile up.

Although Chihuahuas are small, they still need exercise. A Chihuahua might even enjoy a romp around the dog park, albeit a short romp. All dogs, even the toy breeds, should be walked at least once a day and take several potty breaks, even in the rain, wind, or snow. Keep in mind that dog walking does not take a break during inclement weather or if you have a pounding headache. Your Chihuahua needs to go out at a few times every day, seven days a week and twelve months a year.

Show Quality Versus Pet Quality

Do you want a show-quality puppy? Not every puppy in the litter will meet the standards to be a show dog, but even a puppy of less than show quality will still be one heck of a family pet. If you think that dog shows are in your future, a puppy needs show potential. Ask an American Kennel Club (AKC) breeder about show-quality puppies.

Participating in the show circuit is both prestigious and grueling for the handler and the dog. Out of town travel is often required. Expenses include those for transportation, lodging, food, frequent

Raising two puppies is like having twins—the experience can be very rewarding, but it is twice as much work.

grooming, and show fees.

Showing dogs requires a serious commitment. It is not for everyone. Visit a local dog show and talk to participants to get an idea of what is involved. Alternatively, contact a local Chihuahua club to inquire about the show circuit. Then you can decide whether showing Chihuahuas is in your future.

More Than One?

Raising one puppy to be a good canine citizen requires dedication, hard work, and considerable expense over the dog's lifetime. Some people prefer that their Chihuahuas have company, so they will pick out two puppies, either from the same litter or from different ones. Some Chihuahua experts suggest

that if you want two puppies they come from different litters; others say that they can come from the same litter. Talk about your decision with the breeders or your veterinarian and then make an informed choice.

If you decide on two puppies, be prepared to spend sufficient time, money, and commitment with those puppies. Raising two puppies is like having twins. The experience can be very rewarding, but it is twice as much work. And you will spend twice as much money too. Your dog list doubles to include two of everything: beds, leashes, collars, and toys. Be ready to pay double veterinary and boarding bills. Further, one puppy may wake up at 2:00 a.m. to urinate. The other may wait until 3:30 a.m. to do his business.

Are you sure that you are prepared for those interruptions?

Puppies sometimes bond to each other and avoid their owners. Naturally, the owner feels left out. Chihuahuas often bond with just one person in the household out of loyalty. They exclude all others and do not hide their preference. With another puppy around, especially one from the same litter, the Chihuahua may be confused and pledge loyalty to his littermate. If that happens, the owner will have to gently work with both Chihuahuas to assure them that there is enough love to go around.

If you procure a male and female puppy and have no plans to breed responsibly, one puppy must be surgically altered or you will have unwanted litters and add to the pet overpopulation. Be responsible and do the right thing. Ideally, spay or neuter them both.

HOW TO FIND A CHIHUAHUA PUPPY

The Chihuahua Club of America (CCA), the AKC, and the local Chihuahua club maintains lists of breeders. Reputable Chihuahua breeders produce healthy and happy puppies in the comfort of their homes. Their goal is not to squeeze out money from each litter but rather to further the welfare of the Chihuahua breed. Only their best-quality dogs are bred. Dogs who are old, sickly, or known to carry inherited disorders such as hydrocephalus or cryptorchidism are not bred.

Responsible Breeders

Responsible breeders screen customers to weed out inappropriate owners. For example, they back off on sales of Chihuahuas as a plaything for a three-year-old or if the puppy will be chained outside. They deny sales to customers if the Chihuahua will be alone for 12 or 13 hours a day. They want their puppies placed into permanent, loving homes.

Furthermore, conscientious breeders rescue dogs from their litters if they end up in animal shelters or the owner no longer wants or can care for them. Some Chihuahua breeders rescue all unwanted Chihuahuas in their area and find them good homes.

People who breed responsibly usually belong to the aforementioned associations: the AKC, the CCA or to a Chihuahua club in their city. Membership alone does not make a breeder conscientious, but she should follow the principles of these organizations about breeding and Chihuahua care.

A breeder who advertises the sale of puppies on a light pole or in a corner market is not acting responsibly. The sign may say AKC puppies, but breeders affiliated with the AKC rarely operate in this manner. In fact, puppies so advertised may not even be purebred but rather Chihuahua mixes. Their health could be compromised. They may even be products of a puppy mill.

Reputable breeders do not sell their

Responsible Breeders

Most Chihuahua breeders adhere to strict standards, but some are sloppy and careless. Signs of a responsible breeder are:
- allows home visits
- screens for genetic diseases before breeding
- carefully vets potential owners
- provides quality care for the animals
- rescues dogs from shelters
- says no to unfit buyers

Good breeders are committed to their dogs and the betterment of the breed.

litters to people who intend to resell them. Breeders want their puppies placed into good homes. Dealing with sellers of dogs takes away the breeders' control because buyers are not screened in any way. A Chihuahua breeder, for instance, would ask a customer who rents an apartment if she had landlord approval before selling a puppy. Resellers are in many cases concerned only with profit, not with animal welfare.

Sources to Stay Away From

Never purchase a Chihuahua from retail establishments that use puppy mills as the source for their puppies, even though the cost may be less than a dog from a private breeder. Puppy mills are notorious large-scale operations in which purebred dogs are raised in filthy, disgusting conditions. Stuffed into metal or wire cages, they live outdoors and swelter in the summer or freeze in winter. Poorly socialized, adult dogs and

puppies receive little or no veterinary care. Dogs are often shoved around like livestock. Puppies can be sick or dead upon arrival. Supporting puppy mills perpetuates animal cruelty. We recommend against it.

Backyard breeders advertise Chihuahua puppies for sale in the newspaper, the local supermarket, or on street corners. Some try to sell the puppies in front of retail markets or on street corners. Those breeders often lack affiliation with the AKC or a Chihuahua club. One parent may not even be a purebred Chihuahua. Backyard breeders operate for extra income, to let their children experience birth, or simply out of ignorance. These owners may or may not provide adequate food, water, shelter or veterinary care for their Chihuahua. No genetic testing is done. Veterinary care is often scarce or nonexistent. Puppies are poorly socialized and may not make good house pets. Backyard breeders do not screen buyers. Anyone with enough cash leaves with a Chihuahua puppy. They have no commitment to their dogs, customers, or the betterment of the breed.

Visit the Breeder

Conscientious breeders have absolutely nothing to hide. They do not object when a potential owner wants to inspect their home or view the dogs' living space to see whether it is clean and sanitary. If a breeder hedges about a home visit, find someone else. She is hiding something. Sales with shady breeders often take place in grocery store parking lots. That indicates that something is amiss. Dealing with backyard breeders perpetuates animal misery and does not assure that your puppy is healthy.

Here's what to look for:

- Chihuahua puppies should be perky; they should feel soft and smell fresh.
- Nasal discharge, coughing, or external parasites should not be present.
- The puppies' eyes should be bright and clear.
- Examine the surrounding living area—water bowls should be full and free of debris; bedding should be clean and large enough to accommodate all of the dogs and puppies.
- All of the animals, even the family cat, should live indoors.
- The home should be odor free and orderly, without clutter.
- If it is summer, the environment should be appropriately cooled. In winter, expect ample heat.

All household members should inspect and visit with the litter before making a selection. Picking out a puppy is a family matter and a lifetime decision. If that is not possible, delay your choice until the entire family is available. Visit a few breeders before making a final selection.

Puppies from reputable breeders are nearly always the offspring of AKC champions. Even those who are not show quality still qualify for AKC registration. Ask the breeder for a show-quality puppy if you are interested in the show circuit. If there is a wait for a show-quality puppy, ask whether the breeder keeps a waiting list. Many usually do.

Talk to the breeder about Chihuahuas, especially if this will be your first. Breeders know their puppies' health and behavior issues. A breeder who balks about discussing them or does not know, may be breeding only for money. A responsible Chihuahua breeder has a wide range of knowledge about the breed and Chihuahuas' unique characteristics and is pleased to discuss those issues with potential customers.

Picking a Puppy

Once you have selected a breeder, call to make time to view the puppies. Carefully handle the puppies with both hands; make

Conscientious breeders do not object when a potential owner wants to inspect their home.

Online Sales

Internet puppy sales are another option, but it is risky to buy from an out-of-state breeder, especially if you do not know the person's background or reputation. Buying online prevents personal interaction with the puppy. There is no way to inspect the breeder's premises either. The breeder could indeed be reputable but might run a shabby puppy mill out of the back yard. An e-mail guarantee is no assurance of quality or solid health. Neither is a phone call. If you buy from an out-of-state breeder via the Internet, you incur all of the shipping costs. The puppy could be transported to the airport in an overheated dilapidated truck with bald tires or in an air-conditioned Audi. You have no way of knowing.

If you proceed with an Internet sale, ask the breeder to book a direct flight during the week. That lessens the chances of your puppy's being lost in transit or flown to the wrong destination. Expect the breeder to explain all of the travel information, such as date and time of arrival. Be at the airport on time, with a leash, crate, and towel. Airports are busy places with heavy security measures in place. Your puppy may be frightened from lots of handling and loud, unfamiliar noises. Calm and soothe him on the ride home.

sure that your hands are clean to avoid spreading germs. Choose a puppy because that is the one you or your family really wants, not because he is skinny or hiding in the back of the pen. Pity is not a good reason to choose a puppy. A timid puppy may be a sign of a dog who may have behavior problems later. Look for outgoing and friendly puppies, the ones ready to jump into your hands. Take time to bond with the puppy before selecting. Remember, this is a lifetime commitment, so do not rush. If a breeder pushes you into making a decision, shop around for someone else. Be like a Chihuahua and do not let anyone push you around. A conscientious breeder understands that you may not even pick out a puppy on the first visit. You may need time to think or discuss your choice as a family or couple.

What to Expect From a Breeder

What you should expect from a breeder includes:

1. a health guarantee, usually for one year.
2. papers certifying the pup's pedigree status.
3. AKC paperwork to transfer ownership from the breeder to customer (it is the new owner's responsibility to register a new Chihuahua with the AKC and to pay all of the applicable fees)
4. medical history to include inoculation schedule and whether the puppy has been de-wormed (most puppies are born with worms, even the offspring of show dogs; a puppy with worms is not unusual, but worms must be treated)
5. food history (what brand of food has the puppy been fed and what is the puppy's feeding schedule?)
6. contact information so that you can reach the breeder for any reason

Gift Pets—A Bad Idea

Buying a Chihuahua as a gift is not recommended. Although your friend or relative may boast how much he or she loves Chihuahuas, do you know whether that person is prepared to spend at least 15 years or perhaps longer with a Chihuahua? If the potential gift receiver lives in an apartment, does the landlord allow pets? Does the recipient have a job that requires constant travel? Can she afford the lifetime care of a dog? If you are not sure, do not buy a Chihuahua puppy. You have several options instead.

Present your friend or relative with a gift certificate to an animal shelter so that a Chihuahua can be adopted when a dog fits in with her lifestyle, or give a book about Chihuahuas or a subscription to a Chihuahua magazine. Lastly, make a donation in the gift receiver's name to a Chihuahua rescue group.

BEFORE YOUR CHIHUAHUA COMES HOME

Whether you live in a two-bedroom apartment or a multi-level house surrounded by a neatly clipped lawn, pick an area where the Chihuahua will stay when no one is home. This can be a fenced-in kitchen or a laundry room. Make sure that the Chihuahua is not exposed to excessive heat or cold. Puppies should not be kept outside under any circumstances.

Puppies are curious and will get into just about anything—make sure you puppy-proof before you bring him home.

Puppy-Proofing

Puppy-proofing a home is like child-proofing it. Items like household cleaners, perfumes, medications, plants, food (both human and pet), and health care products can be toxic to puppies and should be out of their reach. Secure all garbage and recycling cans. Hide even shoes, socks, and clothing. Quite a few dogs, including Chihuahuas, undergo emergency surgery after scarfing down clothing items.

Deny your puppy all access to expensive lamps, pottery, and vases. A curious pup can easily tip these household items over. Not only can the decorative article shatter, but your puppy may be harmed. Hide plastic bags or electrical cords so that your Chihuahua puppy does not choke or get electrocuted. Antifreeze is poisonous but tasty to puppies. Keep it safely stored away.

Do not leave a Chihuahua puppy unsupervised in your yard, because he can get hurt or cause damage. All gates and fences should be secured, especially if you live near a busy street. The yard should be free of clutter. If there are poisonous plants, it is time to get rid of them or safely secure them so they are beyond the reach of your puppy.

For outdoor activity, consider fencing off a small area for your Chihuahua where he can play, relieve himself, and relax if the weather is cool and sunny. But do not let your Chihuahua stay outside all the time. Chihuahuas are house pets. If you own a swimming pool, surround it with a secure gate so that your Chihuahua does not drown. A gate is also a good idea to keep children from drowning in your pool if they are outside playing with the Chihuahua.

Because your Chihuahua puppy may not be housetrained or behavior trained, consider a crate or confinement in an exercise pen (ex-pen) while you are at work or school. This will prevent him from soiling in your home or chewing on furniture. Remember, all puppies teethe. It is a natural process. They are curious and, if not supervised, can rip apart furniture, shoes, and other household items. Confining a puppy will make you a satisfied pet owner, and your Chihuahua will be a better-trained dog. Excessive confinement, however, is cruel. The crate is used as a training tool, not as a form of punishment.

SETTING UP A SCHEDULE

Set up a schedule as soon as your puppy becomes part of your household. Puppies

By the Numbers

Do a safety check before your puppy comes home. A curious two-month-old puppy will explore his new environment. Trouble awaits unless you do a home check before the puppy comes home. Take the following six steps:

1. Did you pick out a special place for the pup in your home, apartment, or condo?
2. Did you ask for time off to supervise the pup's transition?
3. Did you buy initial supplies, such as food, toys, and bedding?
4. Did you tidy up your house?
5. Did you put away household cleansers and prescription drugs?
6. Did you buy a puppy gate or crate?

Make sure your puppy's collar fits well.

must go out often. How often is debatable, but a puppy cannot hold his bladder much longer than two to three hours. If you or someone in your family cannot let your Chihuahua out at least every few hours, ask a trusted neighbor or family member. An alternative is to hire a pet sitter or take your puppy to doggy day care.

Puppies thrive on regularity. Fit your work and/or school schedule into your puppy's routine. Once you set a schedule, stick to it. For instance, if your Chihuahua goes out every morning around 6 a.m., asking him to wait until 8 a.m. throws off training.

Start leash training him quickly. He is too young for long walks or hikes but old enough to wear a collar. You may walk him around your living room or back yard on a leash. If he adjusts to a leash, he'll be less likely to resist as an older puppy or adult.

SUPPLIES

Your new puppy will need a variety of supplies, including bedding, collar and leash, crate or ex-pen, flea/tick control, food and treats, food and water bowls, identification, sweater and/or raincoat, and toys and chew bones.

Bedding

If you do not want your Chihuahua puppy to sleep on the furniture or share your bed, he needs bedding of his own. The bedding should be washable, soft, and cuddly. Blankets or pillows are also alternatives. Remember, Chihuahuas enjoy the utmost in comfort.

Collar and Leash

Invest in a good-quality collar and leash about 4 to 6 feet long (1.2 to 2 cm). Nylon is just fine and reasonably priced. Puppies may try to chew on the more expensive leather collars and leashes, so save money until they have passed through the teething stage. Get your puppy used to walking on a leash while he is young. He may resist at first by pulling or sitting down. Chihuahuas can be stubborn, so it is important that he knows that you are in charge. Gradually increase his time on the leash. Never use force or use a harsh voice. Gentle praise and tiny bits of food are rewards to which Chihuahuas will respond. As your puppy grows, you may have to replace the collar once or twice. Two fingers should fit comfortably underneath the collar. A too-tight collar can hurt the dog's neck, and he can escape from (or get hung up on) one that is too loose.

Training Tidbit

Is your Chihuahua a candidate for being a pet therapy dog? If so, most hospitals, nursing homes, and rehab centers require pet therapists be registered with either the Delta Society or Therapy Dogs International. Both organizations administer stringent behavior tests that involve loud noises, exposure to wheelchairs and walkers, introduction to other dogs, and handling by strangers. Your Chihuahua must pass this test to become a pet therapist and then be recertified every few years. Do not overlook behavior training while he's a puppy.

Crate

Invest in a good-quality crate. You will not feel like pulling your hair out, and your Chihuahua will become a well-trained, housetrained dog. Two popular types are available: wire and plastic. There are many sturdy plastic crates available. Wire crates allow more air circulation, but if you plan to take your Chihuahua on an airplane, only sturdy plastic crates are allowed.

Flea/Tick Control

Fleas and ticks nag a lot of dogs, including Chihuahuas. Fleas are most severe in warm, steamy climates like the Southeast. Ticks are most common in the desert Southwest but are found throughout the United States. Ask your veterinarian about the many forms of flea/tick prevention such as collars, monthly pills, and powders. Your puppy is not immune to fleas and ticks. External parasites can find their way indoors!

Grooming Supplies

Grooming is yet another aspect of a puppy's overall health plan. Besides inoculations and proper feeding, he must also be groomed regularly. Regular brushing, bathing, and nail clipping makes a Chihuahua look sharp and feel good. A properly groomed dog is a healthier dog.

Here are some supplies he will need:
- blow-dryer
- canine toothpaste and child's toothbrush
- cotton balls
- flea and tick control
- mat splitter (long coats)
- nail clipper
- shampoo and conditioner
- soft bristle brush and rubber comb (long coats)
- towels

Want to Know More?

For more information on fleas and ticks, see Chapter 8: Chihuahua Health and Wellness.

Introduce him to grooming and bathing while he is young so that he does not see the bath as traumatic. Most likely he will not flinch when you take out a comb or brush. Who wants to live with smelly dog odor? You do not want company entering your home scrunching up their noses. It is also cruel to ignore your dog's grooming needs.

Food and Water Bowls

Food and water bowls should not tip over easily because puppies sometimes run into them during play. Avoid the temptation to buy flimsy plastic bowls from discount stores. Stainless steel bowls are ideal. They last longer and can be attached to a dog crate for travel or dog shows.

Identification

Nearly every city and town requires puppies to be vaccinated against rabies and licensed at around three or four months of age. Check with your veterinarian or local animal shelter to be sure.

Always keep your dog's license on his collar. It serves as a valuable form of ID if he becomes lost. Puppies can get away from even the most responsible owners. A puppy can always be traced with his ID tag or dog license. Microchips are widely available at reasonable costs from veterinarians and animal shelters. Many responsible breeders implant microchips into their litters. Attach ID with your name, address, and phone number to the pup's collar.

Dogs who wear ID are more likely to go home. Dogs without often end up euthanized at shelters. If you move or change phone numbers, buy a new dog tag, license your dog at your new location, and contact the microchip company.

Toys

All puppies engage in play. Chihuahua puppies are no different. Buy them small toys appropriate for their size, like Nylabones. Puppies get bored quickly, so buy a bunch of toys and vary them so that your dog does not lose interest. Do not let him play with your old shoes, socks, or dolls. Dogs do not know the difference between a pair of beat-up sneakers and your new expensive Italian leather shoes. Stick to dog toys. Suitable chew toys are made out of fleece or rope. Balls and nylon bones, like Nylabones, are good too. Dozens of toys are available on the market. They all should be washable and nontoxic.

Sweater/Coat

Chihuahuas are chilled easily, even indoors. Outfit your Chihuahua with a cozy sweater or coat. Make sure that his outfits are

Your Chihuahua puppy won't know the difference between expensive shoes and a puppy-safe toy.

washable. Males sometimes soil their garments when they lift their legs to urinate. There are plenty of adorable sweaters, coats, and even sweatshirts on the market for toy breeds. Your Chihuahua can look quite stylish and be snug at the same time.

BRINGING PUPPY HOME

Excitement swirls. Your stomach tingles. Soon you will pick up your Chihuahua puppy from the breeder. Make a few plans before that special day. If this is your first puppy ever, you are probably nervous too.

Carry a Crate

Carry a crate with a soft, clean towel inside so your puppy feels safe and snug.

Remember, he is leaving the comfort and security of his family, both animal and human, where he spent the past seven or eight weeks. He may experience separation anxiety from his safety net.

A crate prevents your new pup from slipping off the front seat or getting loose in the car where he could get hurt or cause you to have a car accident. Some people may prefer holding their new puppy on the ride home. That is okay if you have company, but driving alone with a puppy, especially a brand-new one, in your lap or on the front seat can be unsafe. In some states, it may be illegal. Have your friend or family member bundle the puppy in a soft towel or blanket and hold him for the ride home.

Wait for Introductions

Your new Chihuahua does not need company for the first few days although your friends and family may be eager to see your new bundle of joy. Ask your social network to wait a few days before visiting or bringing him gifts. Let the pup adjust to his new environment, whether it is a house or apartment, and then invite people to meet him. He needs you to comfort and cuddle with him because he is in a strange new environment.

Introduce Him to Your Home

Place a bowl of fresh water down right away and let your dog take a drink. Take him outside in the yard for a quick potty break. As soon as he relieves himself, offer praise and come back inside. If it is blustery and cold outside, you might put a sweater on the pup, even for the indoors. Puppies do not tolerate the cold very well.

Let him sniff his way around your home so that he knows his surroundings. Keep an eye on him because you do not want accidents or chewing on furniture. Remember, he is only a pup, so there may be accidents in the beginning. That is par for the course of having a puppy.

The First Night

Your home may feel strange to your new puppy. The security of his littermates and mother are gone. He may wonder where she is and why he has been separated. Be calm and patient as you help him ease through the adjustment phase.

For safety, your Chihuahua should sleep in his own bed or crate. If you are comfortable, place your Chihuahua's bed inside your room so that he feels secure. If that's not an option, keep him in a warm, cozy place but never outdoors. He may wail or cry the first few nights because your home is new to him. Gradually he will realize that this is where he belongs. He will feel at home. Be patient, though; some Chihuahuas adapt right away but some need a little more time. All puppies react differently.

Your home may at first feel strange to your new puppy.

THE FIRST FEW DAYS

For at least two days after the puppy comes home, the family routine should be as close to normal, even if you live alone. That spring cleaning project or family barbecue you planned for months—let it slide a few more days. Ask your teenaged son to turn down the boisterous thumping rock music in his room. Be gentle and calm around the puppy. Avoid overstimulation, loud noises, and confusion. After several days, the household can return to its normal routine.

Multi-Dog Tip

Your new puppy should adapt to the resident dog's schedule. Of course a pup needs a third meal until he is about four months of age, but all dogs should eat at the same time. They should go out at the same time. They should become family at the same time. Shower love and affection on all of the dogs. Dogs thrive on regularity and companionship.

CHAPTER 3

CARE OF YOUR CHIHUAHUA PUPPY

Now that you have a Chihuahua puppy, you are thrilled. This could be your first experience with a puppy, or he could be your fifth Chihuahua. Even though he is a purebred Chihuahua, every puppy is different. He will eventually develop his own unique personality with endearing qualities and a few quirks. That is what makes him special.

He settles into your home, but what about his care? He deserves the very best, as of course all Chihuahuas do. If you already own a Chihuahua or another breed, you know about puppy needs—namely bathing, grooming, and feeding. But if this is your first puppy, learning with your puppy is fun and adventuresome. It can also be tricky at times. We will guide you through the process so that you can become an informed pet owner and make the most appropriate choices for your new puppy. A lot is involved. In some ways it is like having a newborn baby. You may start out nervous and unsure, but as each day passes, you will become more confident until you eventually become a Chihuahua expert.

Use care around the new puppy at home. A Chihuahua puppy is delicate and fragile. In the beginning, keep him confined to the kitchen or other area so that he is safe. Inadvertently stepping on your puppy could have disastrous results. Always make sure that you or the family knows where the puppy is. Some owners dust off old playpens stored in the garage and use them for the Chihuahua's first few days.

Chihuahuas are excellent teachers. Their communication skills and body language let you know how to meet their needs. Okay, humans help out too, but your Chihuahua does tell you a lot.

FEEDING A PUPPY

Let's start with the basics of puppyhood: food. Puppies all must eat at least three times a day until they are four months old, so picking out the right food is at the top of your list. For the new dog owner, this may seem like a dizzying choice. A multitude of dog food brands are available on the market. They are found in pet stores, retail chains, grocery stores, and local food markets. You can also order dog food on the Internet and have it delivered. Only you can decide where to shop, but we will discuss choosing the most suitable brand for your puppy.

Should you stick with familiar brand names that have been around for decades or pick a newer premium brand that costs more? There are little-known specialty labels and low-priced generic products available too. It is hard to know which brand to select. Many seem to offer a decent product for your puppy. In this section, a lengthy discussion follows about the various aspects of feeding, such as time of day, type of food, and amount.

Buy Small-Breed Kibble

Chihuahua puppies have itty bitty teeth and tiny mouths. Buy small-breed kibble because it is easiest for a puppy to eat and

Puppies need to be fed more often than adult dogs.

digest. If you have a bigger dog at home, the Chihuahua needs his own food. Adult food is not appropriate for puppies for several reasons. First, they cannot bite into the large chunks. Also, puppies need food that is formulated for their growth and has plenty of protein, fat, calcium, and phosphorus. Adult food contains a different blend of nutrients that would lead to a deficient diet for a puppy. The brand you select should say that it's for small-breed puppies.

Feed Puppies More Often

Feed puppies more often than adult dogs because they are in the growth and development phase. They should eat a minimum of three meals a day until they are at least four months old. An ideal feeding schedule for puppies under four months is a meal in the morning, midday and in the early evening. Cut down to twice daily when the puppy is four months old.

Brand Name or Premium?

Brand names of dog food are everywhere. So are inferior brands. Stick with a known premium brand because premium brands are easier to digest and are made with high-quality ingredients. They cost a bit more, but a 10-pound (4.5 kg) bag of kibble stretches far for a Chihuahua.

Stay away from bargain brands. You pay less, but the food is loaded with substandard ingredients, additives, colors, dyes, and synthetic preservatives that are not easily digestible. A good-quality food is crucial to your Chihuahua's overall health. Be leery of dog foods if the first ingredient says chicken or beef "flavor." Meat then is not a primary ingredient. Most likely it is broth or meat flavoring. If by-products are listed as the first ingredient, they can be chicken feet, lips,

Spaying and Neutering

Unless you plan to enter the show circuit or engage in responsible breeding, spay or neuter your Chihuahua. Animal shelters in the United States are overcrowded. Chihuahuas are among the breeds with an overpopulation problem. Reliable figures suggest that at least four to five million dogs are euthanized annually in our shelters because they are unwanted. Thousands of those dogs are Chihuahuas. Do not carelessly breed your Chihuahua and add to this staggering problem. Discuss the simple operation with your veterinarian and schedule the surgery while your dog is still a puppy.

Females
- Spay before the first heat and there will be a significant reduction in mammary gland cancer and pyometra.
- No unwanted heat cycles with discharges of blood and a scent that attracts every unaltered male dog in the vicinity.
- Reduces unwanted pregnancies.

Males
- Curbs aggression and dominance.
- Reduces the urge to lift his leg and mark with urine, even indoors.
- Lowers the risk of prostate cancer.
- Cuts down on the urge to roam and mate.

Males and Females

Nearly all cities and towns offer reduced rates on licenses if your dog is spayed or neutered. Some cities impose significantly higher fees for unaltered dogs as a way to cope with overloaded shelters and to pay for animal control.

or cow intestines—meat products not fit for human consumption. Wheat or corn as the first ingredient is mostly filler and not nutritious. Some dogs develop allergies to wheat, particularly if the dog food is loaded with fillers.

Scheduled Feedings

Set up a feeding schedule convenient to your daily routine, even if you are retired or work from home. Chihuahuas, like all other dogs, should be fed around the same time every day, preferably in the morning and evening. If you work at night, set up a schedule and stick to

it. Your Chihuahua will adjust as long as he is kept to a regular routine.

How Much to Feed

Puppies grow just a little bit every day. Some say that they should eat three times a day. Others say four times. Whether you feed your puppy three or four times a day, spread meal times out evenly. Serve a half cup at each meal. Cut out a meal when your puppy starts leaving food in his dish. And when he shows no interest in the third meal or eats only a partial serving, it is time for two daily meals of half a cup each. That is usually around four

Feed your Chihuahua puppy around the same times every day.

months of age. Keep him at two daily meals after that time.

Avoid overfeeding so that your Chihuahua stays within his weight range. If you notice that he is a little chunky, switch to a light or low-fat brand. There are plenty of decent healthy diet foods on the market.

If you ever have questions about your puppy's diet, consult your veterinarian.

GROOMING YOUR PUPPY

Grooming is the responsibility of every pet owner. Grooming does not have to be a chore. It can be fun, the chance to spend quality time with your new puppy. Invite older children to watch the process and learn how to contribute to the Chihuahua's care. And grooming lets you examine your

puppy for external parasites, such as ticks or ear mites or unusual lumps or growths that require veterinary attention. A puppy is unlikely to have parasites or cutaneous growths, but careful examination of his coat while grooming will help to keep him healthy.

HEALTH CARE

The patient/doctor relationship plays an important role in your dog's health care. Similarly, you want a veterinarian who is responsive to you and your dog's health care and behavioral needs throughout his lifetime. Establishing a relationship with a veterinarian is a top priority once you bring your puppy or adopted dog home. Do not wait until a crisis arises.

A licensed veterinarian who specializes in small animals with an experienced, caring, and concerned staff will provide your dog with the most up to date medical and/or surgical care. Some veterinarians operate alone, especially in rural areas and small cities, but a practice with at least two doctors can be more responsive to patient calls and concerns. Calls can be returned more quickly, for example, with a group practice. If your usual veterinarian is away on vacation or at a conference and your dog is ill, the associate can just as easily treat your dog.

The office staff is just as important as the competency of the veterinarians. Technicians should be capable, experienced, and caring because they work side by side with your veterinarian. They should be comfortable working with animals. Some dogs are hard to control, particularly when they are sick or injured. Staff members should be patient and concerned. Even the receptionist should be pleasant and thoughtful. Often she talks to pet owners in times of crisis, such as when a dog is hit by a car or has swallowed Uncle Jim's heart pills. She serves a vital role on the veterinary team. This is not a job for someone with a snippy attitude.

Ask the veterinarian how she deals with overnight or weekend emergencies. Does the clinic take after-hours calls or are patients referred to an all-night emergency hospital? If you are referred to a 24-hour animal hospital, that can be fine as long as the hospital meets basic standards for care. Are the veterinarians licensed? Is the staff capable, caring, and helpful? Is the hospital a member of the American Animal Hospital Association (AAHA)? These are important questions to ask, because you may use this animal hospital in case of an emergency. You want your dog to receive top-quality care if he is injured or critically ill.

How do you find a veterinarian? Ask the breeder, the local Chihuahua club, or other dog owners in your neighborhood or from the dog park. The state veterinary society and the American Animal Hospital Association maintain a list of licensed veterinarians. Do not wait until your Chihuahua becomes ill or is in a crisis to find a veterinarian. Then you lose control and lack choices. You may have to select the first veterinarian with an open appointment. That could work out just fine, but it is better to establish a relationship before a crisis occurs.

Select a veterinarian with a convenient location and hours. Some Chihuahuas

Multi-Dog Tip

Children adore dogs, including Chihuahuas. Whether you have one Chihuahua or six Chihuahuas, toy dogs and children are not always the best partners. To keep your children and your dogs safe and sound, teach your children how to respect animals by offering the following tips:

- Never disturb a sleeping puppy.
- Do not take food from a puppy.
- Do not grab a toy from a puppy's mouth.
- Do not put hands into a puppy's mouth.
- Never tease or mistreat a puppy.
- Handle the puppy gently.
- Children should contribute to the Chihuahua's care, but a child should never be the primary caretaker. That is the adult's responsibility.

Ask your veterinarian about a preventive care or wellness plan for your puppy.

do not handle car rides very well, so location can be critical when picking out a veterinarian. Most veterinarians have weekend appointments, particularly on Saturday mornings to accommodate working owners.

The First Checkup

Once you make your decision, call for an appointment right away, even if your puppy seems healthy. Take your puppy's health record from the breeder or shelter so that the veterinarian can set up a vaccination schedule. If the breeder or shelter administered a de-worming medication, bring a fresh stool sample on your first visit anyway. A microscopic examination looks for hookworms, roundworms, and tapeworms. Nearly all puppies are born with worms and usually respond to one or two de-worming treatments with no aftereffects. The veterinarian can make sure that the worms are gone. A new pet owner may bring up the inoculation schedule. How many vaccinations does the puppy need until he is fully protected? Does he need a bordetella vaccine? At what age can the Chihuahua puppy be spayed or neutered?

Ask questions you may have about your puppy's expected growth, feeding schedule, or training. The first visit is a great time to set up a preventive care or wellness plan for your puppy. Always ask about fees up front so that there are no surprises at the checkout counter. Expect to receive an itemized bill. Most veterinarians accept debit and credit cards.

As a dog owner, it is your responsibility to pay for service. Cancel an appointment rather than simply miss it. The office can schedule another pet owner in your place. Be timely. Do not show up one hour late unless you call in advance to see whether the veterinarian can accommodate your dog. Do not expect free care. If you are on a budget, ask for a special payment arrangement. Remember that your veterinarian has expenses for staff, insurance, supplies, rent, etc. Vets care about animals, but they also operate a business. Call first if you have an emergency. The veterinarian may have a packed office or be in the middle of a surgical procedure. You may be directed to an emergency hospital instead. Be understanding if that happens.

Vaccinations

Vaccinations protect against a range of infectious diseases, such as distemper and parvovirus, which are common in puppies. They can also be fatal. At two months of age, puppies receive the DHLPP vaccination (distemper, hepatitis, leptospirosis, parainfluenza, parvovirus) every four weeks until they are four months old. Not only is the low-cost DHLPP vaccination available through your veterinarian, but it can also be obtained at animal shelters and through special clinics held at giant pet retailers, pet resorts, or other pet-related outlets. A vaccinated Chihuahua will be a healthy Chihuahua.

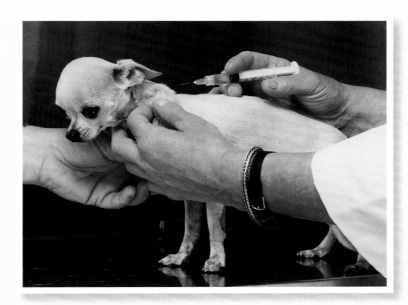

Vaccinations protect against a range of infectious diseases.

Let's find out what diseases vaccinations can protect your dog from.

Distemper

Airborne, distemper is highly contagious and attacks the respiratory and central nervous system. Distemper primarily affects unvaccinated puppies, although some older dogs contract it too, especially if they have a spotty vaccination history or are in poor health. Easily preventable, distemper is extremely difficult and expensive to cure. Symptoms include coughing, nasal discharge, lethargy, lack of appetite, fever, and even convulsions. Survival depends on early intervention. Even with treatment, however, not all adult dogs survive. Distemper is almost always fatal to puppies. The best way to prevent distemper is to vaccinate your dog regularly but especially as a puppy so that he can build up his immunity. Without vaccinations, he has no protection from distemper and other diseases.

Hepatitis

Canine hepatitis strikes the liver, as it does in humans. Infection occurs when dogs have direct contact with contaminated feces, saliva, or urine. Unquenchable thirst is a sign of hepatitis. Other symptoms, such as coughing and nasal discharge, mirror distemper. If your dog displays these symptoms, seek veterinary help immediately. Adult dogs often recover from hepatitis, but puppies usually do not.

Leptospirosis

Caused by a spirochete, this microorganism is carried by rodents. It is also found in livestock urine. Dogs who eat or drink something that is contaminated, such as stagnant water, can become sick, especially if they are not inoculated. The disease, more common in rainy areas, can damage a number of organs, especially the liver. Symptoms include vomiting, muscle or joint pain, blood in the feces, jaundice, fever, hemorrhage, and increased thirst. Seek veterinary attention right away if your Chihuahua has any of these symptoms. Dogs usually recover with antibiotics and diuretics, but the disease is almost always preventable with the standard DHLPP vaccination. Indoor dogs rarely contract leptospirosis, but it is common among unvaccinated farm dogs who drink water from stagnant cattle pens.

Lyme Disease

A deer tick carries a spirochete called *Boredella burgdorferi*. In 1975 the disease was first reported among a small group of people complaining of arthritis, fever, skin rash, and other symptoms in the town of Lyme, Connecticut. When a preferred host such as a

By the Numbers

Your puppy's first trip to the veterinarian can be exciting and informative. Bring the following five documents:
- paperwork from the breeder
- adoption agreement from animal shelter, or rescue because some veterinarians give a free first examination
- puppy or adult dog's vaccination history and health record
- list of questions about health and behavior
- stool sample to check for parasites

Parvovirus strikes unvaccinated puppies and adult dogs.

deer or human is not available, a tick jumps onto a dog's body or other warm-blooded animal. Symptoms of Lyme disease in dogs do not include the telltale bulleye's red circle around the tick bite. Infected dogs experience lameness, limping, pain, and fever, particularly after a tick bite or infestation. Blood tests only confirm exposure to Lyme disease. Treatment includes antibiotics and tick preventive medication for the rest of the dog's life. A preventive vaccine is available. If you live in an area prone to deer ticks, discuss the vaccine with your veterinarian.

Parainfluenza

Parainfluenza is also known as kennel cough because it usually occurs in crowded places like kennels or animal shelters. The disease is a contagious but treatable upper respiratory infection in adult dogs and puppies. Spread by direct contact, such as nose to nose, parainfluenza is spread through the air as well. Symptoms include a persistent dry cough with occasional nasal discharge or slightly elevated fever. Beyond the cough, the dog may seem fine. He will remain active, although some will be lethargic. The disease can run its course over several weeks, but treatment, especially for puppies, is often a short course of antibiotics to prevent complications. If your dog has parainfluenza, isolate him from your other pets to prevent infecting them.

Parvovirus

Often lethal and highly contagious, parvo strikes unvaccinated puppies and adult dogs. Spread through direct contact with contaminated feces, the dog may not show signs of illness until a few days after infection. The disease upsets the stomach and small intestine, resulting in bloody, loose stools. The puppy may also vomit and become lethargic and depressed. Infected puppies under four weeks of age face a daunting challenge. Their heart muscle has to fight off the disease too. Some adult dogs may pull through but at great expense to the owner. Treatment includes fluids, antibiotics, and a bland diet. Parvo is highly preventable with a simple, inexpensive vaccination. But the disease is tough to eliminate in the environment. If your puppy or adult dog dies of parvo, do not bring another dog home for at least five months. Thoroughly clean your home, washing down every area where the puppy lived with a bleach and water solution. Dispose of all the dog's toys and bedding. And the new puppy or adult dog must be vaccinated before coming home.

Rabies

Caused by a virus, rabies is one of the few diseases that dogs can spread to humans through bites or contact with an infected

> ## *Want to Know More?*
>
> For a more detailed listing of Chihuahua-specific illnesses, see chapter 8: Chihuahua Health and Wellness.

animal. The crippling disease has been around for thousands of years. Although it is nearly always fatal, there is good news, at least for Americans. Routine vaccinations officially wiped out canine rabies in the United States. Every municipality imposes different requirements for rabies vaccinations in dogs, but the standard age is about four months. No dog can be licensed in the United States without proof of a current rabies vaccination. If your Chihuahua bites someone and is not currently vaccinated, by law he will be quarantined, at your expense, either at the local animal shelter or a private kennel to observe for signs of rabies. You may pay a fine as well for failure to license and/or vaccinate and may face liability for the bite. Call your local animal shelter or your veterinarian to find out the licensing/rabies requirements for dogs in your community. Rabies is still present in wild animals like skunks, bats, and raccoons. On the slim chance an unvaccinated dog is bitten by a rabid animal, however, he must be euthanized. There are no current treatments available to treat infected animals.

HEALTH PROBLEMS IN CHIHUAHUAS

Even puppies from responsible breeders may occasionally become sick. Health issues are much more common, though, in puppies who come from backyard breeders or puppy mills. Listed below are some of the typical health problems found in Chihuahua puppies.

> ## *Multi-Dog Tip*
>
> The resident dog(s) must be current on vaccinations in the unlikely event the pup has a contagious disease. Alternatively, do not bring a puppy home if the resident dog is sick. Wait until he is recovered. Do not risk transmitting a contagious disease to the new puppy.

Cleft Palate

A cleft palate is an inherited condition sometimes seen in Chihuahua puppies. When two bony plates at the top of the mouth do not join in utero, the puppy will have a cleft, or hole, in the roof of the mouth between the nasal and oral cavities. Puppies with the condition may have trouble nursing because the mother's milk drips out of the puppy's mouth. Affected puppies may need additional bottle feeding to thrive. Small openings may close on their own or with surgery.

Like many other toy breeds, some Chihuahuas are born with hypoglycemia.

Hydrocephalus

Chihuahuas born with hydrocephalus, or water on the brain, have unusually large heads. They may stumble as they try to walk. Seizures are common. The eyes look in the opposite direction (east–west eyes.) Puppies born with hydrocephalus are often in pain. Treatment options are rare, and euthanasia is recommended to end their suffering.

Hypoglycemia

As with puppies of other toy breeds, some Chihuahuas are born with hypoglycemia, also known as low blood sugar. Most grow out of it when they are puppies and have no ill aftereffects. Untreated hypoglycemia can be life threatening for the few Chihuahuas that have it. If your Chihuahua staggers, becomes limp or rigid, or has glassy eyes, his blood sugar has dipped dangerously low. Administer a sugary treatment right away. Karo syrup or sugary water will do the trick. If he is conscious, lift up his gums and pour in the liquid. Then take him to your veterinarian right away. If your Chihuahua is prone to hypoglycemia, feed him smaller meals at least three to four times a day. Also, check the ingredients in his food. Avoid buying dog food and snacks with too much sugar. Regulate his sugar level because too much sugar is just as bad for him as too little.

Molera

A slight indentation on the head, a molera is like a soft spot on a baby's skull. In some Chihuahuas, the molera closes on its own by age three. Never press or hold down on the molera, but otherwise it poses no health concerns for a Chihuahua.

CHAPTER 4

TRAINING YOUR CHIHUAHUA PUPPY

Animal shelters in the United States are packed with healthy young dogs given up by frustrated owners who neglected behavior training out of either ignorance or laziness. As the puppy grew into an adult dog, he barked, dug up the backyard flowers, and jumped on Grandma. He did not know how to behave well.

Owners often expect too much from puppies because they do not understand how to communicate with them. Instead of researching proven behavior and training methods or consulting with a behaviorist or dog trainer, they yell, confine the dog outside, or surrender him to an animal shelter. Worse yet, some frustrated or angry owners abandon the pup in the desert, mountains, or in city parking lots. Puppies cannot learn to become good canine citizens unless owners show them the way.

Do not let your Chihuahua become an animal shelter statistic or a rowdy little dog that all the neighbors avoid when they see you walking him. With direction, praise, and reward nearly all puppies can become house trained and learn good manners.

THE IMPORTANCE OF TRAINING

No one wants a Chihuahua who yaps uncontrollably, refuses to walk on a leash, soils the carpet, nips at heels, or chews on the reclining chair. Any dog who displays this kind of unruly behavior is a nuisance. Neighbors often complain about the noise. You may be hit with an ordinance violation, pay a fine, or be asked to move.

Even the smart, curious, and cuddly Chihuahua can get out of control if his owner does not impose reasonable limits on his behavior. Not every Chihuahua will master the skills of the show ring, but they can all accomplish simple obedience commands.

Behavior training starts the day you bring your Chihuahua puppy home from the breeder or shelter. For the next few months, behavior training is a constant learning process for you and your puppy. He is young, so do not expect too much too soon, but have expectations. He is capable of learning. Be patient, firm, and determined and your puppy will slowly pick up the basics. With your help and guidance, he can advance to more complicated commands.

Puppies respond to positive training that includes praise and food.

He wants to please you, so show him the way. The two of you can go far as a team.

POSITIVE TRAINING

Puppies respond to positive training that includes praise and food. Some trainers use only praise. Most professionals, however, recommend a combination of praise and food. Use tiny pieces of meat snacks or cheese as rewards. There are plenty of training snacks available on the market ideal for training purposes.

Never use physical force or scream if your puppy has an accident or does not respond to a training command. Dogs do not mess up on purpose or to annoy you. They make mistakes because they are young and in the learning stage. Every single dog has a beating

heart. All animals feel pain just as we do. A smack to the head hurts a two-month-old puppy. Shoving a three-month-old puppy's nose into a pile of fecal matter on the living room floor does not speed up housetraining. It will only confuse and scare him. He might get the impression that going potty is somehow wrong. That is not the lesson you want to teach.

Chihuahuas are animals, not humans, and are incapable of thinking like humans. Canine behavior is best shaped by rewards and praise. The puppy's mind says *If I do this, then I get more food or more hugs*. Puppies like both. If they are hit, tossed around, or shouted at, they cower in fear. They might also be hurt. You become someone threatening, not fun or loving. And they will never learn the desired behavior that you have in mind. You may damage your puppy for life, both emotionally and physically.

SOCIALIZATION

Puppies are like children. Both flourish with socialization and suffer without it. Socialization is spending time around people or other household pets—making your Chihuahua a house dog and including your Chihuahua as part of the family. The dog goes on walks, sleeps in a cozy bed, and visits the dog park.

Responsible breeders interact with their puppies early and often. They are affectionate and loving with them. They spend quality time

How to Find a Trainer

A state or federal license is not required to work as a dog trainer, so anyone can hang a shingle outside their front door and call themselves a dog trainer. They may or may not be capable or experienced. Some may not even like dogs. How do you find the right trainer for you and your dog?

The following sources can help you locate a qualified trainer who can work with you and your Chihuahua:

- responsible breeders
- veterinarians
- animal shelter managers
- dog groomers
- Yellow Pages
- Internet (Association of Professional Dog Trainers: www.apdt.com)
- dog or breed-specific magazines
- other dog owners
- friends, relatives, or coworkers

The ADPT has a certification process for their members. To learn more about this organization, visit their website at www.apdt.com.

Pick out at least three trainers. Contact each trainer and ask about his or her qualifications For instance, how long has the trainer worked with dogs? Where did he or she acquire experience? What training methods does the trainer use? If a trainer employs corporal punishment, find someone else—work only with trainers who use positive reinforcement. Are obedience classes taught individually or in groups? And how available is the trainer? Does he or she take calls or respond to e-mails? Make house visits? Ask for references or the names of satisfied customers. Before signing a contract, find out about fees and terms of service. Ask for a contract in writing.

Go and visit the trainer during a class. Training classes should be fun and relaxing. The trainer should display an upbeat attitude and enjoy the job. Above all, you should sense a love for animals. If you do not feel at ease with the person or the person's methods, look for another trainer. There are usually plenty available, even in smaller cities and towns.

Socialize your puppy to different people and places so he becomes a confident adult.

with them. Their dams, sires, and puppies are part of their family.

Puppies acquired from unethical sources are often treated as commodities and kept outside in decrepit wire crates with little or no human contact. They are exposed to excessive heat in summer and frigid cold in winter. An undersocialized puppy may grow up into a nervous, timid, and shy dog. He may become a fear biter. He may or may not become a good household pet.

Dogs are social creatures who thrive on human companionship. Do not obtain a Chihuahua puppy or adult if you plan to isolate him in the back yard, chain him to a tree, or confine him to the basement. Separating a dog from his family, both human and animal, is cruel and inhumane.

Chihuahuas, like all other dogs, descend from wolves. They maintain a pack mentality and crave company.

How to Socialize

Socialization is an important part of your Chihuahua's puppyhood. Introduce your new puppy to your circle of friends, family, and neighbors. He is now part of your family. Walk him regularly. Once he has been vaccinated, visit a dog park so that he is around other dogs. Consider doggy day care if you work long hours. Take your dog to community events, such as animal shelter fundraisers. Keep him social and active. He will benefit from your social network and so will you. Dogs break down barriers among people. Neighbors may not know each other's name, but they usually know the dog's name.

Make socialization a family affair. Everyone in the household should always socialize your Chihuahua. If one person dislikes the puppy or never wanted him to begin with, the Chihuahua is smart enough to sense the unease. When company comes over, the Chihuahua should be part of the gathering, not locked away. Part of having a Chihuahua is sharing him with family and friends.

CRATE TRAINING

Crate training serves a dual purpose. First, it is a valuable housetraining aid. Puppies normally do not eliminate in the space that surrounds them. They learn to hold their bladder and bowels so that they do not have to lie in filth. That is part of the reasoning behind crate training. Secondly, confinement prevents your puppy from chewing on furniture or knocking over plants while you are out. Puppies get bored quickly. If left unsupervised, they get into mischief. Nearly all puppies do. Chihuahuas are no different, and sometimes they get hurt. For example, they might bite into an electrical cord and get electrocuted or severely injured. They might inadvertently start fires. Crates stop bad behavior before it starts.

How to Crate Train

Coax your puppy into the crate after he has been outside, but never force him inside or he'll see the crate as punishment. Do not feed your puppy, then put him into the crate, because he will probably have an urge to eliminate after eating. As a rule, exercise stimulates a puppy's bowels. Allow your puppy time to relieve himself after vigorous exercise before going in the crate or he will have to go potty inside. He will be uncomfortable and dirty sitting in his own excrement. Crates are not meant as punishment. The time inside a crate should not be excessive either. No puppy should spend all day inside his crate. Puppies should be crated only a few hours at a time. Anything longer is punitive and harsh. If you cannot let your puppy out during the day at least once for a break, give someone you trust access to your home or hire a reputable pet sitter.

Place the crate in a shaded area of your home where your puppy will be relaxed and comfortable. Keep the crate away from stairwells, where it could be accidentally knocked down. Avoid leaving the crate near heaters or boilers. The noise and vibrations can be unsettling to a Chihuahua puppy. Never leave a crated puppy outdoors, especially in the summer or winter.

Training Tidbit

Socialize your puppy while he is young. By introducing him to as many people as possible, he is likely to grow into a confident, self-assured dog and less likely to fear strangers. Let him meet people such as:

- friends or family who wear glasses
- men with beards and mustaches
- wheelchair or cane users
- men and women in uniforms
- joggers, bikers, and skateboarders
- tall, husky men
- senior citizens
- delivery people

Select a crate that is the appropriate size for your Chihuahua. Ask a salesperson if you are not sure. Take your Chihuahua along to be sure that the crate is the proper size. He should have room to move around and roll over but not walk and play.

Encourage your puppy to view the crate as a comfy den or refuge by feeding him in it or placing a snack inside. At first, let the puppy check the crate out. Leave the door open so that he can inspect his new quarters for himself. Make the crate snug and cozy by lining it with a fluffy towel, pillow, or blanket. Leave a toy or chew bone inside. Until training is complete, some owners put their puppies inside the crate at night. This will prevent the puppy from wandering around the house alone, soiling on the floor, or tearing up shoes or eating houseplants.

Want to Know More?

To learn more about ex-pens, see Chapter 2: Finding and Prepping for Your Chihuahua Puppy.

Some puppies resist crate training for any number of reasons. If your puppy shows fear or screams and howls while inside, try another method. Buy a baby gate. Section off a small space inside the kitchen or laundry room for your puppy. Leave him with soft bedding, a bowl of water, and toys. Do not put out food. Exercise pens, also called ex-pens, are another option. An exercise pen is kind of like a crib for puppies.

HOUSETRAINING

Is it a myth or the truth that Chihuahua puppies are hard to housetrain? Housetraining any dog can be prickly, but it can be done without even thinking of giving up your dog to an animal shelter. Owners must be committed to the process or there will be failure. Puppies cannot pick up lessons without reliable teachers. Indeed, some puppies are smarter than others, but even the slowest puppy has potential. Housetraining is a dual process, both for puppies and for owners.

Housetraining teaches your puppy to eliminate outdoors, on newspapers or puppy pads in a certain part of the house, or in a litter box. It also trains you, the owner, to respond to signs when a puppy says *I have to go out*. Housetraining encourages communication between owner

If you live in a high-rise apartment in the city, you may want to train your puppy to use Wee-Wee Pads.

and puppy and puts them both on a schedule to be followed daily. A responsive owner is the key to a successfully housetrained puppy. A puppy may stand by the door and whine, but his owner is so wrapped up in a telephone call that he or she ignores the pup's urgent plea. The owner seeing a puddle by the door should understand that the owner caused the problem, not the puppy.

Most people prefer that their dogs relieve themselves outdoors. Some, however, are okay if their Chihuahua goes on puppy pads or in a litter box filled with shredded newspapers. The issue is control. Teach your Chihuahua not to eliminate where he wants and when he wants. Control over his bladder and his bowels are the key to successful housetraining. Small messes around the house or on the furniture will reek of urine and feces and become unsanitary. If you ignore housetraining while he's a puppy, your dog may never learn how to eliminate outside. Think of the repercussions if you become ill or have to leave your dog with someone else in an emergency. Your friends or the dog sitter may not be happy with a Chihuahua who

poops or pees wherever he feels like it. The mess is small but it is still a mess.

How to Housetrain

Begin housetraining as soon as you bring your puppy home. Chihuahuas are bright, intelligent dogs. With steady guidance they can easily master housetraining, but only if shown proper direction. All dogs, including Chihuahuas, want to please their owners. Keep that in mind as you train your pup.

If you live on the 55th floor of a big city high rise and do not want to walk your Chihuahua puppy at 2:00 a.m. in the rain, train him to eliminate on puppy pads (like the ones Four Paws makes) or inside a litter box with shredded newspapers. Leave either the pads or the box in the same place. Remember, dogs like consistency. As soon as you observe signs that your Chihuahua is about to relieve himself, such as circling or sniffing at the ground, pick him up and take him to the puppy pad or the litter box. Tell him to go. Wait for him to eliminate and then pick up the pads or clean the box. Shower praise on him when he is done. A snack might also reinforce the positive

In the cold make sure your Chihuahua has on a sweater or coat.

behavior that you want him to achieve.

If your Chihuahua will take care of business in the back yard, the grass must be kept short. Otherwise, it will be over his head or so thick that he will not be able to walk around. Then he cannot eliminate.

For the Chihuahua who goes outside, be careful about spraying pesticides in the yard for weed control. The Chihuahua is low to the ground, so inhaling or ingesting toxic chemicals may sicken him. Consider eco-friendly products instead. Ask your veterinarian for suggestions.

Stick to a Routine

Stick to a routine, regardless of your work, volunteer, or school schedule. Dogs are creatures of habit. They do not like it when their routine is upset or suddenly changed. Feed, water, and exercise them at the same time every day. Once a dog develops daily habits, he becomes more self-assured and confident. A secure dog learns at a steady, even pace. He copes with going outside in the pouring rain, the biting cold, and the searing heat. For those rainy days, keep a towel or two by the door to dry him off. On scorching days, limit walks to the early morning or after dark when it is more comfortable for the two of you. And in the cold make sure your Chihuahua has on a sweater or coat. Some owners even outfit their Chihuahuas with tiny booties to keep their feet warm and dry while outdoors in the harsh winter months.

Walking your Chihuahua, however, is part of responsible dog ownership. Do not stay out during inclement weather any longer than you have to. So once your Chihuahua takes care of business, you will both be happy to rush back inside where it is warm and cozy.

Clean Up After Your Dog

Always carry a plastic bag to clean up after your dog. Be a responsible owner and pick up feces on the street. Further, if you live in a condo development, owners or managers sometimes decline to rent to people with pets if current occupants do not clean up after their dogs. Your actions often have consequences for others.

Example of a Training Routine

The following is an example of a housetraining routine for you and your family.

Morning

Take your puppy outside as soon as he wakens. After he eliminates, bring him inside. Feed him a bowl of kibble and give him water. Of course, give him a lavish display of affection. Within half an hour it will be time for another potty break. Then it is playtime with your Chihuahua. Let him drink afterward because he will be thirsty. Take him out to potty one more time and then pick up any uneaten food. Into his crate or pen he goes while you are gone. Playtime tuckers a puppy out, so he should sleep soundly for a while.

Afternoon

Someone must let the puppy out. He cannot hold his bladder and bowels all day long. Young puppies need more frequent feeding. Either you or someone else has to feed him that extra bowl of kibble in mid-afternoon. He should go outside as soon as he finishes eating and then go back to the crate if you are pressed for time. If you are home, let him stay out of the crate. Watch over him, though, to look for

Doggy Doors

Doggy doors are clever inventions. They allow dogs to come and go as they please. Owners stuck in rush hour traffic do not have to fret about getting home on time to let their dogs out. With doggy doors, you can stop on the way home for groceries and your dog's bladder will not be ready to burst. Puppies can easily be taught to use a doggy door, but there is a safety issue. Puppies left alone in a yard may start digging. The curious pup may sneak under the pool gate and drown. Or they may nibble on plants and become sick. If you teach your puppy to use a doggy door, limit the size of his outdoor area. Perhaps surround it with a pen so he will be safe until you come home. Note: watch for large flying birds, which can fly off with a very small Chihuahua.)

A puppy should never have unsupervised access to a back yard or open space, because the possibility of theft exists. Thieves sometimes patrol neighborhoods looking for solitary dogs, especially purebreds, to steal. These pets are often sold to unscrupulous animal dealers who bypass the government rules and regulations about lab animals. Do not let your puppy become a victim. Protect him while you are not at home.

Don't punish your puppy for making housetraining mistakes.

signs he has to eliminate. If need be, keep him close to you to prevent accidents, even if that means holding him on a leash. Remember to love and adore him while you are home. All dogs enjoy praise from their owners.

Evening

Once you come home, take off your coat, put down your keys, and let your Chihuahua out of his crate or pen. Give him a big hug and tell him what a wonderful dog he is. Either take him outside for a walk or let him into the back yard. Once he takes care of business, it is time for his evening meal. Afterward, he gets to play and snuggle with you as you read, listen to music, or watch television. Take him out one more time before bedtime. If you feel that he is sufficiently trained, let him sleep in his own bed. If not, he should sleep inside the crate for the evening. Listen for whining in the middle of the night. Sometimes puppies wake up and have to go outside.

Dealing With Accidents

Expect your puppy to have accidents. Nearly all of them do. If you leave at 9 a.m. and do not return until 5 p.m., your puppy cannot hold his bladder or bowels that long and will eliminate in the house. Shoving his nose in the feces, swatting him with a rolled-up newspaper, or shouting does absolutely no good. Locking him in a closet or the crate teaches him nothing either. If he relieved himself at 10 a.m. and it is now 5 p.m., he has no memory of what happened earlier that morning. If you continue this pattern of leaving him all day and then hitting him for soiling in the house, he will eventually starts to fear you. He will grow into a timid adult dog.

If your puppy has an accident, take him outside anyway and see whether he relieves himself again. He may or may not have to go. Wait a few minutes and see what happens. If he relieves himself again, come inside right away.

Clean up the mess with an odor neutralizer or vinegar. Eliminate the smell because dogs have keen noses. They will be tempted to return to that particular spot and do their business again. Vinegar and the odor neutralizers mask the smell of urine. Ammonia is not as effective, but many fine odor neutralizers are available. Any one of them covers the urine scent. Soak up urine from the carpet thoroughly. Make sure that the area is dried, then use an odor neutralizer or cleanser to disguise the scent of urine.

If you catch your puppy about to squat, firmly tell him "No." Some trainers suggest making a loud noise, such as shaking a can full of coins, to catch the pup's attention. Then quickly get him outside so that he can relieve himself. Once he eliminates, take him inside. Do not allow him playtime outside right away until he masters potty training. Gently impress upon him that going outside means using the bathroom. When your puppy goes outside, reward him. Puppies learn through positive reinforcement. Negative attention never works.

Housetraining can be frustrating, but be patient; your puppy will eventually master it. Some puppies catch on quickly, while others need more time. If you are tense, your puppy will sense your frustration. You may have to leash your puppy and keep him with you at all times while you are home. Doing so will allow you to catch him in the act and to appropriately correct it.

BASIC OBEDIENCE COMMANDS

Why teach your puppy obedience? Unless a puppy knows simple commands such as *sit*, *stay*, and *come*, you will have an uncontrollable little dog who will be the neighborhood menace. When called, he will turn up his nose and ignore you. If he is caught off the leash, you may receive a hefty fine. He could run off and get hit by a car. Guests leaving your home may find a Chihuahua scratching at their new leather shoes, sandals, or boots. His rowdy behavior will unsettle you and may even embarrass you and your family.

Puppies love your company and want to please their owners. Give yours a task that keeps him busy and for which he gets rewarded. Practicing obedience is also a chance for the two of you or the entire family to bond and grow together.

A well-behaved dog lives longer too. Neighbors, friends, and family look forward to

Multi-Dog Tip

Your adult dog is already housetrained, but now you have a puppy to train. Keep an eye on your puppy and recognize signs when he has to go out:
- circles or sniffs at the floor
- walks into another room
- pants
- whines
- sits by the door
- gets ready to squat

If your puppy displays any of these behaviors, take him outside. He most likely has to eliminate.

To teach the *sit*, hold a treat above your Chihuahua's head and move it backward.

seeing the polite friendly dog. There will be no temptation to surrender him to a shelter that probably cannot place him. Take time to teach your puppy a set of simple obedience skills. He depends on you to teach him to grow into a good canine citizen. Be creative and resourceful so that obedience training can be a joyful and pleasant experience if you follow the few simple lesson plans outlined below.

Come

Why should a puppy respond to this command? If he runs up to a child who is fearful, your dog should return to you quickly. If he gets away from you on a walk and runs toward the curb of a busy street; you want him back at your side as soon as possible to avoid a calamity. You open the front door to pick up the newspaper and your Chihuahua takes a hike. You do not want your dog to become lost or disoriented.

These are just a few examples of why it is important that all dogs come when their name is called. At some point, we see skinny stray dogs wandering in city streets, along rural highways, or lost in the mountains. It is reasonable to suggest that some lacked behavior training and failed to respond when frantic owners called them. The dogs turned up their noses and ran the other way. They may suffer miserably as a result.

Let us review a few steps that you can use to teach your Chihuahua puppy to come when called.

How to Teach It

First, always use a reward, such as praise or a meat snack. You might also hold up your pup's dinner dish. Call his name, but don't put down the bowl until he responds.

1. Practice the *come* command using praise and food rewards. Remember that puppies thrive on repetition and rewards.
2. Always use his name when calling him.
3. Make sure that you speak clearly and never use a harsh tone, which frightens dogs.
4. Vary the exercise by asking a friend or family member to hold your Chihuahua. Call his name and, when he runs to you, offer a reward.

It's important not to give your puppy the *come* command to punish him if he has had an accident or knocked over your rolodex. He will then associate the command with negative consequences and may not obey the next time. Also, refrain from teaching your dog to come for a nail trim or to have his ears cleaned. Chihuahuas are clever enough to know what they like and do not like. Nail trimming does not rank up there with belly rubs. Most likely he will ignore you.

Sit

An obedient Chihuahua should sit when told. Not everyone wants to be greeted by a tail-wagging dog when they enter your home or apartment. You love your Chihuahua, but the repair person may not. Children who accompany adult visitors may be frightened by exuberant dogs, even a little Chihuahua, at the front door.

How to Teach It

If you notice that a door is inadvertently open, your Chihuahua should obey the *sit* command and not chase after a neighbor's dog or run in front of a truck. Obeying the *sit* command can often save a Chihuahua's life. So spend time when with your puppy and teach him how to obey this command.

Realize that since Chihuahuas are so small, they are almost always looking up. They may teach themselves how to sit because they get tired of always looking up. But you as the owner must teach them to sit on command. The desire to have them sit is your choice, not theirs.

Some Chihuahuas may be averse to handling. To teach the sit:

1. Hold a treat above your dog's head and move it backwards.
2. He will lean back and end up on his hocks in a sitting position.
3. Again, offer praise and a reward.
4. Repeat the command several times a day until he gets it.

Down

Asking your Chihuahua to stay down is another aspect of good canine behavior.

How to Teach It

1. Once he sits, bring your right hand to the ground while saying "Down." He should be moving into the down position.
2. Show him a treat as a reward.
3. Let him stay down for a few seconds before saying "Release."
4. Repeat a few times until he catches on. If it seems like he grasps the command, you

are able to use a hand gesture for down and he'll obey.

Repetition helps reinforce the good behavior. Do not repeat the command so many times, however, that the exercise becomes tiresome or boring. Remember that puppies have shorter attention spans than adults do.

Walk Nicely on Leash

How many times have you seen an out-of-control dog pulling his beleaguered owner down the block? The frantic owner seems ready to stumble while the dog is about to lunge at just about anyone. Okay, Chihuahuas lack enough power to knock anyone down, but still, who wants to walk even a small dog who is out of control?

How to Teach It

Accustom your Chihuahua to a leash while he is a puppy. Fit him with an adjustable collar that expands as he grows. Even if you plan to train your Chihuahua to eliminate on puppy pads, get him used to a leash when he is young. If you wait until he is an adult, he may resist. Leash training is part of responsible dog ownership.

Don't yank on his leash if he refuses to budge. You may frighten him and physically damage his neck or trachea.

1. Gently coax him to follow you, offering generous amounts of praise. Show him the way. A treat helps too.
2. Repeat this practice twice daily until your Chihuahua looks forward to going for a walk.

Most dogs go out twice a day. Do not, however, take him on long, exhaustive walks. You may enjoy lengthy brisk outings, but your Chihuahua has his limits.

PUPPY KINDERGARTEN

Socializing your puppy is crucial for his well-being and yours too. Puppy kindergarten may be a good option if you live alone or have a small social network. It is ideal if you have a shy, timid pup.

Puppy kindergarten is similar to children's kindergarten. Puppies attend small classes taught by behaviorists, trainers, veterinarians, or shelter managers so that they develop into good canine citizens. Whoever teaches the class must have ample experience working with dogs.

In kindergarten, puppies learn the value of play. They share games and have fun. The leader supervises playtime to tamp down if a puppy becomes too aggressive. At the same time, he or she will gently encourage a quiet pup to join the fun. Owners pick up handling skills as well. They learn the latest behavior training methods from professionals and network with other dog owners. That may result in dog-sitting opportunities and new friends. Puppy kindergarten classes can be especially helpful to new owners. They build confidence in puppies and their owners.

How to Prepare for Puppy Class

Whether you enroll in puppy kindergarten at an animal shelter, veterinary school, or with a dog trainer, your puppy should have at least one set of DHLPP vaccinations. Many trainers will ask that your puppy be inoculated against kennel cough too. No one wants to send their puppy to class if there is a chance he might become ill. Inoculations protect all participants. Puppy kindergarten operators have to provide a safe, clean environment for all participants.

Dog parks may be temporarily off limits while your pup is in kindergarten. Although dog parks are terrific settings for people and pets to mingle and have fun, not every dog is up to date on shots. Puppies' immune systems are still developing, and they are susceptible to diseases that can be spread at dog parks.

To enroll, puppies usually have to be at least two months of age. They may be separated by age with younger puppies in the same group. Puppies older than six months are in another group. Older puppies have often mastered some training steps that young pups still grapple with.

Prices and length of sessions vary, so check around for a puppy kindergarten class that you feel comfortable with. To find a reputable class, check with your veterinarian, animal shelter, or breeder. Ask about the qualifications of the person teaching the class. How long are sessions, and how many puppies are in each class? What is the price? Where does the class meet? Is the teacher available for a private consultation? Ask to sit in on a puppy kindergarten class or visit the facility. Request a brochure or talk to the trainer before making a decision.

Puppy kindergarten classes can be a valuable way to start your puppy on a happy, healthy life. Owners benefit because they pick up tips about puppy behavior and training and learn that every pup is unique. The experience builds trust between owner and dog that will last a lifetime.

By the Numbers

Start housetraining a puppy the same day he comes home. The puppy is usually about two months old and old enough to start learning. Decide what method you will use—puppy pads, going for walks, or using the backyard. Then stick to a routine. Puppies thrive on regularity. Consider crate training, a proven reliable method of housetraining. Remember that puppies cannot hold their bladders and bowels more than a few hours. Expect accidents. All puppies have them. Be patient. Your Chihuahua puppy can master housetraining, and the key is a steady, consistent owner.

PART II

ADULTHOOD

CHAPTER 5

FINDING YOUR CHIHUAHUA ADULT

What if a puppy does not fit your lifestyle because you work full time or just do not want to deal with puppy stuff like housetraining, but you still want a Chihuahua? Plenty of healthy and often young Chihuahuas are available from animal shelters and breed and pet rescues.

WHY ADOPT A CHIHUAHUA?

Chihuahuas are left homeless for a variety of reasons, such as:

- The owner died and the family could not or would not assume responsibility for the Chihuahua.
- The family fell on hard times and could not care for their Chihuahua.
- The Chihuahua was an impulse purchase at a mall pet store and the owner wasn't prepared to assume responsibility for the dog's care.
- The Chihuahua came to the shelter as a stray and was never reclaimed.

There are many reasons why Chihuahuas end up without homes. Chihuahua rescue groups and shelters across the country work tirelessly to save them from unsafe situations and to place them into permanent loving homes.

Training Tidbit

Your adult dog may be housetrained and behavior trained, but spending time in a shelter may set his skills back, so help him refresh his potty and good boy behavior. Consider the following:

- Take your Chihuahua out right away if you live in a house or condo with a patio. Remind him where the door is located.
- If you plan to let him eliminate on potty pads, place one out right away. Show him where the pad will be kept. To prevent confusion, keep the pads in the same location.
- Walk him on a leash. Even if you own a house or a condo, your adult dog must keep up his leash manners.
- Advanced behavior training may be in order with a private trainer or an animal shelter.

Chihuahuas typically get along with other Chihuahuas or Chihuahua mixes.

By adopting, you save a Chihuahua's life and free up space in a shelter or rescue for another unwanted Chihuahua. Pet overpopulation is a nagging problem in the United States, so every adoption counts.

Once you decide to adopt, visit an animal shelter or research rescue groups in your area. Some rescue groups work strictly with Chihuahuas and others save dogs regardless of the breed. They may rescue just dogs; some save both dogs and cats.

SHELTERS AND RESCUES

If you already have a Chihuahua at home, introductions to another Chihuahua usually go well. Chihuahuas typically get along with other Chihuahuas or Chihuahua mixes. If you have a different breed, let all of the dogs meet in a neutral setting before bringing the new Chihuahua home. Ask whether the Chihuahua is feline friendly if you have a cat. If the shelter or rescue does not know the Chihuahua's dealing-with-felines history, arrange a dog/cat meeting before finalizing the adoption.

Everyone in the household should decide on the adoption. The Chihuahua should become part of the family. Each member, including the children, should interact with the Chihuahua before finalizing the adoption.

Costs for rescued Chihuahuas are considerably less than for American Kennel Club (AKC) puppies and usually include the spay/neuter surgery, vaccinations, and a microchip. A license is often part of the adoption package at municipal shelters.

Depending on the availability of donations, shelters and/or rescues may give you a leash and collar or a bag of dog food with your new Chihuahua.

Each shelter/rescue adoption agreement maintains different standards. Nearly all ask that owners promise to provide the Chihuahua with a good home that includes regular food, veterinary care, and proper shelter. They ask that the Chihuahua be returned if the owner can no longer care for him. Some have a health guarantee for the first 30 days. Some offer longer terms, while some have no assurances at all. Still others offer one free medical exam with a licensed private veterinarian.

Remember, you will incur expenses for a Chihuahua whether you buy from a breeder or adopt. That is part of responsible dog ownership.

Animal Shelters

Animal shelters are either municipal or private. They accept unwanted animals, generally dogs and cats, although some take small pets such as birds, rodents, and rabbits. A drop-off fee is is often mandatory. Municipal shelters are obligated by local or state law to take every dog or cat surrendered to them. Private shelters, however, can be more selective, especially if they are a limited-intake facility. However, most private shelters will not turn down an animal in need, even if they later transfer the animal to a municipal shelter.

Municipal shelters try their best to restrict euthanasia to older, injured, or ill-tempered animals, but healthy adoptable animals are still humanely destroyed due to lack of space. Because private shelters can be more selective about the animals they accept, they generally have lower euthanasia rates.

Private shelters operate on donations, fundraising activities, and private grants. Municipal shelters are maintained by taxes, dog licenses, and fees for services such as adoptions or vaccinations. Naturally, they accept donations. Some private shelters in small cities and towns perform animal control and are paid only for these services.

By the Numbers

If you cannot adopt a slightly used Chihuahua, there's still plenty you can do to help unwanted Chihuahuas. Here's five ways in which you can do so:

- Foster for a shelter or rescue group. Temporary homes are one of their biggest needs besides money. Needy Chihuahuas may need only a few days or a few weeks to recover from emergency surgery or to settle down after rescue from an abusive situation. By fostering, you save a Chihuahua but don't yet make a permanent commitment.
- Donate used towels, sheets, or blankets to a Chihuahua rescue or shelter.
- Organize a pet food drive at your job, church, or community center for a Chihuahua rescue or shelter.
- Volunteer if your local Chihuahua rescue holds a special fundraiser. Extra help is always appreciated.
- Collect aluminum cans and donate proceeds from their sale for Chihuahuas.

By adopting, you save a Chihuahua's life and free up space in a shelter or rescue for another unwanted Chihuahua.

They retain their private status and must raise funds for all other activities.

Stray dogs are held for a certain time, depending on state law, to give the owner a chance to reclaim a pet. That confinement period can last from as little as two days to as long as a week. When the holding period ends, animals are evaluated. Healthy, well-behaved dogs are placed for adoption or transferred to a rescue group for placement. Sick, injured dogs or dogs with temperament problems are euthanized. If the shelter has enough resources, dogs receive a veterinary examination. Almost all shelters administer at least one DHLPP vaccination and rabies shot prior to the dog's adoption. Many, though not all, spay/neuter dogs they place for adoption. Again, the surgery depends on their resources. Some shelters give customers a certificate they can redeem at a local veterinarian to defray the cost of spay/neuter surgery.

Shelters screen potential adopters. The adoption application may ask such questions as source of income, whether the landlord allows pets, personal pet history, and if everyone in the household wants a pet. You may be asked to provide a lease proving that pets are allowed. Shelters try to match dogs and cats with the best possible homes. They reserve the right to turn down applicants they do not think are good fits. For example, if someone wants to adopt a Chihuahua but is away for 12 to 13 hours a day, a responsible shelter (or rescue group) would say no.

Rescue Groups

Rescue groups, including Chihuahua rescues, are privately funded groups of volunteers that operate with meager budgets. Because of their love for Chihuahuas, they take them out of animal shelters or from owners who no longer want them. They function similarly to shelters. Dogs are spayed/neutered before adoption and receive at least one inoculation. Sick dogs are treated before adoption. Anyone interested in adopting must meet their criteria and pay a fee to adopt. Some rescue groups even require

home visits and check your personal and veterinary references.

Rescued Chihuahuas can be as young as a few months to as old as 15. A few may have minor health problems, while some may have separation issues, but all need good homes. They want to cuddle on someone's lap and be loved.

WHAT TO LOOK FOR IN A SHELTER OR RESCUE

Nearly all dogs in a rescue live with foster families in their homes or apartments. Adopting from a rescue involves visiting the dog at the foster home. If you are not comfortable with the rescue, then look for another unwanted Chihuahua. There's probably a reason for your discomfort.

Some animal shelters are old, but the cages should still be clean. The kennels should not reek of urine and feces. Water bowls should be full. On the other hand, due to generous donations and creative fundraising, other animal shelters are state-of-the-art facilities

Will Your Adopted Dog Need Training?

Every rescued Chihuahua has his own needs, depending on his background. If the Chihuahua was neglected as a puppy, he may need brushing up on his housetraining and obedience skills. A short course of behavior training may be in order. He could have lived in an abusive situation where he was whacked around, ignored, or yelled at. He may act timid and need lots of TLC to adjust to a normal household without violence.

An older Chihuahuas may fit right in; reassure him that he is loved and cared for. He may have lived with an owner who passed away but who doted on him for years. Ask the rescue group/shelter what, if anything, they know about the Chihuahua's history. It will help you and your new dog adjust.

Many shelters offer low-cost obedience training on their premises for their adopted dogs. Some retain behaviorists either on staff or on call to assist owners with their adopted dog's transition to his new home. Take advantage of this wonderful benefit if your adopted dog exhibits any issues once he is home.

with eco-friendly features, such as vegetative roofing, solar power, and drought-resistant landscaping.

Some shelters only have staff and resources to feed dogs once a day. Volunteers help plug the gap. Information about a dog's history, if it is available, is usually disclosed to potential adopters by staff members and/or volunteers. Alternatively, ask questions that you may have about a dog you are considering for adoption. Staff or volunteers should be pleased to provide it. Also, interact with the dog outside his cage. Dogs often behave differently when they are not confined or surrounded by loud barking. Most shelters set aside fenced-in areas for customers

Want to Know More?

If you'd prefer a puppy to an adult Chihuahua, see Chapter 2: Finding and Prepping for Your Chihuahua Puppy for more information.

to interact with dogs they consider for adoption. Bonding with a dog is an important part of the adoption process. Some shelters insist on dog meets if you already have a dog(s) at home. It is better to find out at the animal shelter that the dogs do not like each other. This will prevent the heartbreak of returning the Chihuahua or breaking up an ugly dog fight.

Some shelters insist on dog meets if you already have a dog at home.

Dogs with nasal discharge and a dry cough are probably sick and should not be available for adoption. If you pass such a dog while passing through a kennel, mention it to the staff.

BRINGING HOME AN ADOPTED DOG

Your adopted Chihuahua may have lived with one person. He may have bounced around ten homes in five years. He may have lived on schedule but his routine was interrupted by a stay in a shelter. With rescued dogs, their past is not always known.

Dogs thrive on consistency, so introduce him to a new schedule right away. If you have

Multi-Dog Tip

You are considering adding a second Chihuahua to your home. This time, however, you want to rescue. Shelters and rescue groups are flooded with Chihuahuas. How do you choose? Fostering a Chihuahua is an option. See how the new dog fits in with your lifestyle. Does the new Chihuahua get along with your resident dog(s) or cat? By fostering, you provide a valuable service to the shelter and/or rescue without making a permanent commitment. At the same time, you give temporary refuge to a needy Chihuahua. If the arrangement works out, adopt the Chihuahua. If not, keep the dog until he finds a good home. Foster homes are always valued by shelters and rescues.

a doggy door, show him where it is. Make sure that he knows how to use it. If he does not get how it works, use meat snacks or cheese as an incentive to get him used to it. Food works nearly all the time. Praise also helps.

Alternatively, show him the back door if you have a yard. Let your Chihuahua out soon after you get home. Watch him until he knows his way around. Until he feels at home, train your new Chihuahua to stand by the same door when he has to eliminate. Remember, your home is new to him. You want his transition to be smooth and easy.

If you plan to walk your Chihuahua, make sure that he has a proper leash and collar. The collar should always carry current identification in case he becomes lost. If it is cold outside, buy him a sweater or coat. Chihuahuas do not tolerate the winter very well.

Start with a quick walk after you arrive home. It is possible that he is housetrained; he just may need brushing up. Chihuahuas do not require much exercise, so a walk around the block will probably be enough, especially on those first few days.

Keep his food and water bowls in the same place and feed him at the same time every day, which is usually morning and evening. Consistency will help him adjust to your home and put him on a schedule.

CHAPTER 6

CHIHUAHUA GROOMING NEEDS

Feel grungy if a few weeks pass without taking bath, brushing your teeth, or combing your hair? Your body odor would probably send people running the other way. Chihuahuas look, smell, and feel good when they are properly groomed. Stinky matted dogs with long nails are a sign of indifferent owners. If grooming is neglected altogether, owners can be cited for animal cruelty and hauled into court in some communities. Regular grooming is another part of responsible pet ownership.

Grooming a Chihuahua is usually a cinch, especially if you introduce your puppy to the bath, toothbrush, comb, and nail clippers while he is in his formative weeks. But do not fret if you adopt an older Chihuahua who spent years in the backyard without a bath or teeth cleaning. He too will get used to grooming. A neglected Chihuahua may require more time and work to warm up to grooming, but sprucing up a small dog generally presents little or no challenge. All Chihuahua owners should be prepared to groom their dogs on a routine basis. Look at grooming as an opportunity for bonding.

This chapter will take you through the various aspects of grooming, including brushing, bathing, nail clipping, dental care, and eye and ear care. I will also present you with suggestions on how to find a conscientious groomer near you in the event that home grooming is not possible.

WHY GROOMING IS IMPORTANT

All dogs, including the smooth-coated Chihuahua, can pick up dirt, debris, or external parasites from backyard potty trips, playing in the dog park, or walking around the block. The debris usually becomes trapped on their underbellies. If ignored, long-haired Chihuahuas get matted, tangled coats that not only look unkempt but must feel uncomfortable to the dog. Foreign matter clogged in a dog's coat can start to smell too. External parasites can cause disease or fall off inside your home.

Incorporate grooming into your Chihuahua's routine care for a healthy, happy dog. A properly groomed dog is a sign of a dedicated, loving owner. When a Chihuahua looks good, he feels good. You as the owner can feel pride and dignity walking a well-groomed dog through the neighborhood. Besides, who wants to be seen with a matted, messy, and stinky dog?

Grooming supplies were discussed on a limited basis in Chapter 2, so let us now go over the supplies every Chihuahua owner should have for home grooming. They include but are not limited to:

- quality shampoo
- conditioner (optional)
- blow dryer
- terrycloth towels (small)
- cotton balls
- nail clippers
- flea comb
- slicker brush (for long-coated Chihuahuas)
- mat splitter (for long-coated Chihuahuas)
- natural bristle brush
- hard rubber comb
- canine toothpaste and toothbrush
- grooming table

BRUSHING

Regular brushing removes dirt, debris, and excess fur on all dogs, including Chihuahuas. Yes, even the short-coated Chihuahuas shed. All dogs shed to some degree. Some shed more than others. Frequent brushing means less fur to collect on furniture, throw rugs and carpets or to build up in corners or nooks. Owners who neglect brushing frequently find dog fur clinging to their clothing. So will their family, housemates, or guests. Dog fur is especially noticeable on dark-colored clothing. Imagine trying to impress important clients or your new boss in a navy blue wool suit or dress that is covered with Chihuahua hair!

Brushing has other purposes. It invigorates your dog's skin by removing dead skin so that his fur will shine with a healthy glow. New fur growth is stimulated by brushing too. A well brushed Chihuahua does not need as many trips to the bathtub either, because his coat has less dirt and debris.

Chihuahuas shed in cycles, as do most other dogs. They retain thick coats in winter and start shedding them at the onset of warmer weather. Because they are house pets, Chihuahuas have coats that are not as thick as those of dogs who live outdoors. No dog needs extra fur in the summer, but Mother Nature sees that he keeps it during the winter, even if he lives inside. The growth process can take up to 135 days, but it varies depending on where you live. Chihuahuas in the arid desert sections of Arizona or Nevada, for example, shed more often than dogs in more temperate climates, such as in Vermont or New Hampshire. A Chihuahua can shed anytime, but in lesser amounts than the larger breeds like the Husky or Malamute. Brushing a dog routinely

Multi-Dog Tip

Does your Chihuahua need a bath and you do not feel like giving it? Animal charities often sponsor dog washes for a worthy cause. An Ohio dog groomer supplied stylists to groom and wash dogs, including Chihuahuas, at a benefit to help homeless animals on September 13, 2009, for the Humane Society of Greater Dayton. The dog wash was part of a mega fundraiser called Wine, Washes, and Wet Noses that raised more than $2,000 for the shelter. More than 100 dirty dogs were treated to a special day at the spa. (Courtesy of the Humane Society of Greater Dayton.)

Long-coated Chihuahuas should be brushed at least every other day.

controls his shedding.

As you comb or brush your dog, take the time to examine his body for bumps, lumps, or any suspicious lesions that may require veterinary attention. Malignant lesions, as an example, are slightly elevated, asymmetrical, dark in color, and have irregular borders. A simple grooming session could end up saving your dog's life. If you see anything out of the ordinary, make an appointment with your veterinarian.

Owners with allergies can live with dogs, especially those with short coats like a Chihuahua, but the dogs must be brushed often to control fur loss. Daily vacuuming also helps owners with allergies to live with short-coated dogs.

Smooth-coated Chihuahuas should be brushed several times weekly. Long-coated Chihuahuas require more frequent brushing so that their coats are free from mats, clumps of fur, and tangles. At the very least, brushing should be every other day. More, though, is always better than nothing at all.

How to Brush

Wear casual clothing and be comfortable. You might brush while you watch television or listen to music. Never brush your dog if you are rushed, preoccupied, or in a cranky mood. Engage in casual talk with your dog as you groom him. He will feel calmed by your soothing voice. Gently hold your dog on your lap or on a nonslip surface such as a grooming table. He should wear his collar so that if he attempts to escape you have something to hold onto. If you have a patio, shut the door so that he cannot get out.

Your Chihuahua's head should face away from you with his rear snug against your body.

Use a natural bristle brush or a hard rubber comb. If he is a long-coated dog, brush first and then finish with the comb. You can either brush or comb a short-coated Chihuahua. Stroke his fur a few times from his rump toward his head. Repeat in the opposite direction. Stroking in the opposite direction efficiently removes dead hair and skin. Then run the brush or comb along his neck and the side of his body. Next turn him on his back. Take the brush or comb to his neck, chest and underbelly.

Long-coated Chihuahuas are most likely to tangle along the ears, tail, and elbows. Take more time to comb through these areas and fluff them out so that he looks pretty. If he resists, try a soft brush. He may not like the steel comb or wire brush. It could also be a sign that you are using too much force. Although Chihuahuas often act fierce, they are

Want to Know More?

Some owners use a flea comb in combination with other flea control products if they live in areas prone to infestation. Follow the same methods for combing as indicated in this chapter. Chapter 8: Chihuahua Health and Wellness discusses external parasites in further detail.

actually quite dainty.

As a last resort, send the extra-fussy long-coated Chihuahua to a groomer for a crew cut. If you have no plans to enter him in the show circuit, your Chihuahua can live without his long coat, especially if he resists all efforts to groom him. A Chihuahua with a clipped coat

Run the brush or comb along the side of your Chihuahua's body.

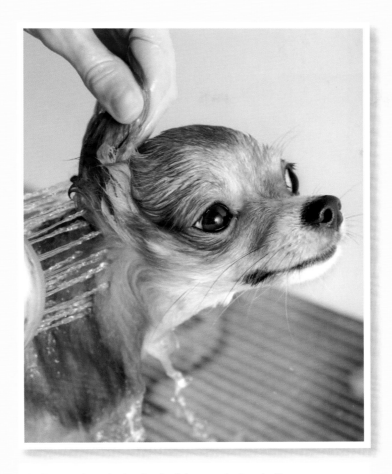

Make sure that absolutely all of the soap is rinsed off or your Chihuahua will itch.

should wear appropriate clothing to keep him warm in winter, but otherwise he will lead a normal life.

At the end of a brushing session, praise your Chihuahua. Tell him that he is a wonderful dog. Let him know how spiffy he looks. You might reward him with a treat. Definitely give him a kiss. Grooming should be viewed as fun, not with dread.

Mats

If you find a mat, there are several ways to remove it. Apply detangling spray, then gently comb through the clump of fur with a slicker brush. Mat splitters separate the individual hairs, but that takes time. Your Chihuahua may not have the patience for this process. You may not either. If all of your efforts fail, you may have to snip off the mat with a pair of scissors. Fur will grow back in the bald area. Long-coated Chihuahuas, as mentioned previously, need more frequent brushing than short-coated Chihuahuas to remain smooth, silky, and tangle-free.

Keep an eye on your dog's anal area if you have a long-coated Chihuahua. Fecal matter sometimes collects there, and you may have to trim it from time to time so that he is fresh and nice. You may not be pleased if your dog plops into your lap with a dried piece of poop hanging from his behind. Neither will your guests.

BATHING

A frequently brushed Chihuahua needs fewer baths, unless of course he rolls in something that smells like bad egg salad. Some groomers suggest monthly baths; others say every other month is just fine. You should decide what works best in your household, but your Chihuahua does need regular bathing, even if he is a house dog.

Excessive bathing, such as weekly, is

Use Warm Water

By mid July, it is so hot that the pavement feels as if you can fry eggs on it. You may be tempted to wash your Chihuahua in the back yard with a garden hose. That is probably not a good idea, despite the sizzling heat. Immersion into cold water may likely shock your little dog. Wash him inside using the warm water routine.

detrimental to your dog's healthy skin and coat. Too much shampoo, especially if it is of poor quality, washes away his natural oils that protect his skin and fur. Keep that in mind when setting up a bath schedule. Humans need daily bathing. Dogs do not.

On bath day, you need the following:
- comfy old clothes for the owner
- terrycloth towel
- good-quality shampoo with optional conditioner
- unbreakable cup and/or spray hose attachment
- cotton balls
- wash tub or sink
- washcloth
- mineral oil, ear wipes, or ear cleanser

How to Bathe

First things first. Brush your dog before bathing. If your long-coated Chihuahua is already matted, water will make his coat resistant to untangling. Make sure that your Chihuahua eliminates before starting his bath. If he has to relieve himself during or after a bath, this poses a problem. You cannot let a wet dog outside if you live in a cold, blustery climate. The room should be warm and toasty for both of you. Owners often get soaked too during dog baths, because a Chihuahua will sometime slosh around the water.

When bathing your Chihuahua, first insert a cotton ball in each ear to prevent water from entering. Wet your dog with warm water, sparing his face and head. Test the water first to see whether it is warm. Either gently pour water over him with a plastic cup or gently spray him with a nozzle.

Add a few drops of shampoo on his back and massage it into a lather. Then spread it around his body. Remember his underbelly and legs. Add a few drops of shampoo to those areas too and work that into a lather. Once you are sure that he is soapy and washed, rinse him off. Make sure that absolutely all of the soap is off or he will itch. His coat may lose its shine because of flaking and dryness. Conditioner is optional. If you add conditioner, follow the instructions on the label. Make sure to rinse him thoroughly. Many good-quality shampoos come with conditioner already added. Next, dampen a washcloth to pat down his face and head. Remove the wet cotton balls. Apply a dab of mineral oil or ear cleaner (available at pet stores) to fresh cotton balls to clean out any debris in his ears. Finally, let your Chihuahua shake off excess water and then dry him off with a soft towel. If it is winter, be sure that he is dry.

Some owners blow-dry their long-coated Chihuahuas, particularly if the climate is frigid. Set the dryer on a warm setting. A high setting held too close to a Chihuahua could burn his skin. Once his coat is dry and fluffy, take out your brush, preferably one that has natural bristles. Pay attention to the fringes along his legs, ears, and the plume. He should look beautiful! Praise him for being a good dog and give him a dog biscuit.

If you have older children, consider letting them help with grooming. An 11-year-old, for instance, could hold the blow-dryer or towel dry your dog. Grooming can become a family affair.

At least once a month, check your dog for ticks or other external parasites because they transmit illnesses such as Rocky Mountain spotted fever and Lyme disease by injecting toxins via their saliva into your dog. If you remove a tick and your dog exhibits signs of illness such as vomiting, loss of appetite, pain upon walking, or fever call your veterinarian immediately. Your dog probably needs medication.

Chihuahuas' erect ears help to make them less subject to the ear infections commonly suffered by other breeds.

Dogs with more than one tick may benefit from a professional tick bath given by a groomer. Tick baths are less toxic than in the past but are still effective at removing the offending ticks.

EAR CARE

Remember the ears. Air flows easily into a Chihuahua's erect ears, so infections are minimal. Dogs with floppy ears, such as Basset Hounds, Bloodhounds, and Dachshunds, are more prone to ear infections.

How to Care for the Ears

Healthy ears on any dog, including a Chihuahua, should be firm and pink. Check them regularly for debris, which can accumulate over time. Clean only the visible ear parts with a cotton ball. Some owners use mineral oil, ear wipes, vinegar/water solution, or commercially available ear cleansers on the cotton ball when cleaning ears. Do not poke the cotton ball down into the ear canal, as that may cause permanent damage. Your dog will resist if you jab him too hard.

Cleaning ears can be a two-person job if you have a persnickety Chihuahua.

If the debris in your dog's ears is dark and has a rank smell or your dog constantly shakes his head, take him to a veterinarian. He most likely has an ear infection or mites that require medical attention, including medication. Untreated infections and parasites can cause a grossly painful swollen ear and make your dog very uncomfortable. His behavior and appetite may change. Permanent damage may result, such as loss of hearing.

Canine ears are a favorite resting spot for ticks. Always examine the ears for ticks if you live in an area prone to these tiny invaders. Be vigilant but avoid the urge to clean healthy ears excessively. You may irritate the ear lining, especially if no infection is present.

Oddly enough, hair may grow inside the ear canal. If that happens, do not pull or tug on it.

You can clean the area around your Chihuahua's eyes with a damp cloth.

Your veterinarian is the one to professionally remove the hair, because it is located in a narrow, delicate place. A mistake made while plucking hairs in the ear canal can damage your dog's hearing.

EYE CARE

Healthy Chihuahua eyes should be large, bright, and clear. There should be no discharge, redness, swelling, or inflammation. In some cases, toy breeds like Chihuahuas develop tearstains below their eyes, the result of ducts that are too small to allow drainage. Wipe away the tears daily with a soft cloth. Consult your veterinarian for the best treatment, but tearstains pose no significant health

Chihuahua nails grow quickly and need frequent trimming.

problems for a Chihuahua. As a rule, healthy Chihuahuas, even those with narrow tear ducts, require little eye care.

How to Care for the Eyes

There is no agreement on how often to clean a healthy Chihuahua's eyes. Some groomers suggest weekly, while others say monthly is satisfactory. You may include eye care for the healthy Chihuahua with his regular bath. As long as his eyes are healthy, simply dampen a washcloth or tissue and wipe the small area that surrounds his eyes.

However, if you notice redness, swelling, or change in pupil size, that is cause for concern. Take your Chihuahua to the veterinarian right away to determine the cause.

NAIL CARE

Chihuahua nails grow quickly and need frequent trimming.

How to Care for the Nails

Not long after your puppy is home, practice by setting up his paws for a trim. Get him used to nail trimming because it needs to be done often. Hold each paw and gently spread his delicate toes with your fingers. Talk to him calmly during the process. If your Chihuahua seems jumpy, have someone assist you. A fidgety puppy can cause you to cut too deeply into the quick, the blood vessel inside the nail, and cause him to bleed. Make sure that you invest in a good-quality pair of trimmers, available at most pet stores. Avoid flimsy trimmers from discount stores. They can harm your Chihuahua.

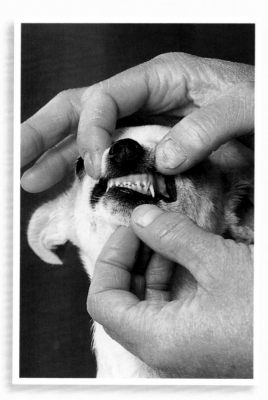

Periodontal disease is common in toy breeds like the Chihuahua.

The lighting should be sufficient in the room where you will trim his nails. Snip off only the tiny hook at the end or tip of the nail. The quick of the nail is more visible in lighter Chihuahua nails than in darker ones. With the darker Chihuahuas, use more caution. If you get too close to the quick, you have cut too far. Your dog may squeal as he bleeds. Apply a styptic pencil to stem the blood. Cornstarch works too. But if you make him bleed, he may resist nail trimming in the future.

DENTAL CARE

Pay careful attention to your Chihuahua's teeth. Your puppy will develop 28 teeth by the time he is three to four weeks old. Around four months, he loses his needle-like puppy teeth and 42 permanent teeth emerge. That is it for the rest of his life.

Dogs need dental care just as humans do. Periodontal disease such as gingivitis is common in dogs, especially toy breeds like the Chihuahua. A dog with gingivitis has red, inflamed, and swollen gums. If ignored, gingivitis attacks the root, causing pain, discomfort, and eventual tooth loss. The American Veterinary Dental Society (AVDS) says that 80 percent of dogs exhibit signs of oral disease by age three. That covers a lot of dogs.

A dog with a sore mouth has trouble eating. Not only does his mouth ache, but it smells too. Rotting teeth emit a foul odor. Teeth darken and eventually turn black. Untreated dental disease can cause life-threatening infections of the heart and mouth. Eventually, teeth will either fall out or need to be surgically extracted.

Bacteria from food and saliva form the plaque that builds up on a dog's teeth. That is why it is important to discuss tooth care for your new puppy or your adopted dog.

How to Care for the Teeth

Start your Chihuahua on a brushing regimen not long after you bring him home, even though his teeth are clean and bright. Plaque buildup begins right away.

Tenderly rub your Chihuahua's teeth and gums with a soft cloth dipped in a mixture of warm water and baking soda. You can also use your index finger. Get him used to gentle manipulation of his mouth before you clean with toothpaste and a brush. Use only canine toothpaste, which is usually beef or chicken flavored. Human toothpaste has sodium and other ingredients that dogs do not tolerate. It can sicken some dogs. Canine dental products are available from your veterinarian and in pet stores. Some animal shelters with retail shops may sell doggy dental products too. Buy an appropriately sized brush for your Chihuahua. Baby or children's brushes are good sizes for small dogs.

Moisten the toothbrush with warm water and apply a small amount of toothpaste. Then casually brush his front and back teeth. Do not forget the inside. Most dogs resist the toothbrush inside their mouths. Chihuahuas are no different. They may try to chew, bite, or spit out the toothbrush.

Chihuahuas are smart, intuitive dogs and may even run away when you break out the toothbrush and toothpaste. Be patient, because dental care is important for your Chihuahua's health. Never force the brush into your dog's mouth—he will ultimately get used to dental care.

There seems to be disagreement on how often you should brush your Chihuahua's teeth. Some veterinarians say three times a week; others say daily. As a responsible owner, you can decide how often is best for you and your dog. Just do not neglect his teeth.

The AVDS recommends that your dog have at least one professional dental cleaning every year. Besides brushing, other steps to prevent dental disease include:

By the Numbers

Grooming begins when you bring your Chihuahua puppy home from the breeder. Get him used to nail trimming, brushing, dental care, and bathing while he is young so that when he is older you will not have to fuss with him every time you take out the nail clippers or run the bathwater. A Chihuahua who is unaccustomed to grooming will give the dog groomer a hard time. Even though Chihuahuas are compact, they are easier to groom if they cooperate.

If you are having trouble grooming your Chihuahua yourself, consider going to a professional groomer.

- Feed a diet mostly of dried premium kibble. A diet of only soft, semi-moist or human food leads to early dental decay, bad breath, and plaque buildup.
- Give your dog chew toys, such as Nylabones, and hard dog biscuits. They will help remove plaque and keep his teeth healthy.
- Keep your dog indoors. Outside dogs tend to have more health issues, including dental disease. Out of boredom they will chew on rocks or other hard surfaces that can crack teeth. An indoor dog fed a proper diet and current on his vaccinations is less inclined to develop dental disease.

FINDING A DOG GROOMER

If your Chihuahua squirms too much when you trim his nails or brush his teeth, or he ducks under the bed when you run his bathwater, there is an alternative. Call a dog groomer. There are many professionally trained and skilled dog groomers around who love their jobs and can handle touchy dogs. To find a reputable groomer, consult your breeder, veterinarian, Yellow Pages,

Internet, animal shelter, or other dog owners. The National Dog Groomers Association of America (NDGAA) is another source. No government agency regulates or licenses dog groomers, however. Ask for references from satisfied customers or call the Better Business Bureau (BBB) to see whether any complaints have been lodged. Some groomers, because of privacy considerations, may not share names of customers but may have testimonials available from customers who have authorized use of their names.

Some groomers work out of mobile vans and will even come to your home. You can locate such a groomer on the Internet. Call a groomer first for his or her price list and see whether you need an appointment. Most groomers ask that your dog have a valid rabies certificate. Be ready to present the certificate if asked. Prices to groom a Chihuahua are generally reasonable.

You may settle on a groomer from word of mouth or the groomer's website or advertisement. Or you may visit a few salons before making an appointment. If you visit in person, look around to see whether the premises are clean. Of course, expect there to be dog hair scattered on the floor. But the lobby area should be neat and orderly. The salon should smell fresh. There should be plenty of lighting. In winter the heat should be on and in summer the facility should be adequately cooled. Employees should be friendly to customers and gentle with the dogs and cats. (Yes, there are occasional cat clients at dog grooming salons.) Record keeping is important. Staff should maintain records on each client. That is a sign of a

reputable groomer.

You as a dog owner have responsibilities too. If you neglect your Chihuahua and his coat is severely tangled or filthy, a groomer can do only so much. Do not expect miracles, but the groomer will do his or her best to clean up your Chihuahua and make him look presentable.

When making an appointment, tell the groomer whether your dog has special needs—for example, is your dog epileptic or on heart medication? Be on time for your appointment. If you cannot keep the appointment, call in enough time to cancel. That opens up the time for another client. Your dog may be at the salon for a few hours, so leave your contact information so that the groomer can reach you when your dog is ready to go home.

Groomers obviously care for animals, but they are in business to earn a living. Ask what forms of payment they accept, such as checks or credit cards, and be prepared to pay for service.

CHAPTER 7

CHIHUAHUA
NUTRITIONAL NEEDS

Most people enjoy eating scrumptious nutritious meals. Good food makes you feel good and look healthy. Your Chihuahua deserves the same: balanced, nutritious, tasty food. A dog should wag his tail while eating, not turn up his nose at what is served and walk away. Certainly the food should not make him sick.

Chihuahuas don't need a lot to eat, so you should invest in a high-quality dog food. Nutritious food adds to a shiny coat, adds years to your dog's life, and prevents dental disease. A premium bag of kibble may cost a few pennies more than a bargain brand, but in the long run your dog's health is worth the investment.

Good nutrition is essential because it:
• aids digestion
• builds strong bones
• is crucial for normal growth and development
• is essential for responsible reproduction
• is useful in producing healthful skin oils
• maintains health and well-being
• tones muscles

The pet food industry is a huge multi-billion industry with a slew of manufacturers. A handful of well-known companies garnered significant market share, but as pet owners began to demand more nutritious, additive-free dog food, many smaller companies squeezed their way in. Now the thriving industry offers dog owners a large variety of healthy foods and treats from which to choose. This chapter will guide you when picking out a quality brand for your Chihuahua.

BUILDING BLOCKS OF NUTRITION

Dog foods may look alike, but they are not equal. Feed your Chihuahua food that has a scientifically formulated combination of fats, vitamins, proteins, carbohydrates, and other vital components. That's best for his health. Food deficient in building blocks is detrimental to your dog's health.

Fats

All dogs, including Chihuahuas, need fat as part of their daily diet. Fat is one source of energy that most dogs easily digest. Kibble would be dry and tasteless without added fat, and most dogs probably would not eat it. Fat promotes healthy skin and coat. Reproductive

Active dogs require more protein than couch potatoes.

organs and kidneys depend on adequate fat intake. Fats also aid the absorption of fat-soluble nutrients such as Vitamins A and E.

The fat content of most commercial dog food averages 5 to 10 percent, an amount the pet food industry considers sufficient. Too much fat, especially in a Chihuahua, can lead to obesity or pancreatic problems. If the label has more than 10 percent fat, look at another brand. It is not a quality dog food. The average amount should be 4 to 5 percent fat.

Fat can be derived from either animal or plant sources, but the most likely source is animal.

Protein

All dogs need protein, an essential nutrient for muscle growth, immune function, energy, and transporting vital oxygen to the blood. A series of amino acids, protein is the most important component of dog food. Protein sources are both plant and animal, but animal protein is more digestible. Neither meat nor vegetable protein offers a dog an adequate amount of protein. Combined, however, chicken and cornmeal are an excellent protein source, a fact known by reliable pet food makers.

Dogs on a diet with insufficient protein often have dull coats and lower immune function, do not maintain proper weight, and are depressed. Nursing females may produce less milk, so the puppies may be malnourished.

Puppies and active older dogs require more protein than couch potatoes. Too much protein, however, can lead to renal malfunction. A good-quality dog food should have a minimum of 25 percent protein from meat, not from grains, meat broth, or meat byproducts.

Keep a dog food manufacturer's reputation in mind when buying dog food. Overcooked food can diminish protein levels, but such information is not required to be on the label. So research a dog food manufacturer, especially if it is one you are not familiar with. Make sure that they employ quality-control measures. Not sure? Call the number on the package and ask or check its website for more information.

Carbohydrates

Carbohydrates provide your dog with energy too. Without sufficient energy, your dog will be lethargic and eventually become ill. Cereal grains, a common source of complex carbohydrates, make up about half of the ingredients in dried dog food. Fiber, another carbohydrate, fights canine obesity. A dog food properly formulated with bran makes the dog feel satisfied after each meal. Bran prevents constipation by keeping him regular.

Read the label, however, when making your selection. Although grains are an important ingredient, they should not be listed first. That is the sign of a low-quality dog food. Further, dog foods loaded with grains, such as soy or corn, can cause allergies in some breeds. Excess intake of carbohydrates can cause canine obesity.

Minerals & Vitamins

Vitamins and minerals play different roles in your dog's body. They can boost his immune system, aid the absorption of fats and carbohydrates, and keep him healthy and

Does Your Dog Need a Daily Vitamin?

If a dog food says it is 100 percent nutritionally complete, it is supposed to have all of the vitamins your dog needs. Some owners like to give their dogs, especially puppies or seniors, a daily vitamin anyway. If humans eat a nutritionally balanced diet, they do not need to take a multiple vitamin every day. But if they take one, no harm is done. The same is true for dogs. A good-quality multiple vitamin will not harm your dog. Simply follow the instructions on the container. Vitamins are not treats, however. Dispense only one per day, and check with your vet first.

Minerals such as zinc, iron, and calcium are important for your Chihuahua's health. Calcium builds strong bones and teeth. Iron prevents anemia. Zinc maintains a shiny coat. Again, good-quality dog food has all of the minerals your dog needs to be healthy and fit. Rather than pay for vitamin and mineral supplements, buy a premium dog food that is nutritionally complete.

Glucosamine, a supplement, improves mobility and eases the pain in some dogs with arthritis or broken bones. Unless your dog has a deficiency or disorder, however, do not add minerals or supplements without consulting your veterinarian; this is especially important in the case of a Chihuahua. His small body may not be able to shed the excess minerals, vitamins, or supplements, and he might experience a toxic buildup.

It's up to you to make sure your Chihuahua is getting nutritionally balanced meals.

fit. Good-quality dog food is made with a sufficient blend of vitamins and minerals to keep your dog healthy. Unless your dog has a known vitamin or mineral deficiency, avoid supplementing his diet unless you consult with your veterinarian first.

There are two types of vitamins: water soluble and fat soluble. Water-soluble vitamins (such as B, C, and E) not used by the dog's body pass in his urine. Excess amounts of fat-soluble vitamins (such as A, D, and K) build up in the fatty tissues and can cause problems.

Water

No dog survives without water. Your dog's water bowl should be filled with fresh cool water at all times. Water regulates body temperature and lubricates body tissues. Every major organ depends on an adequate water supply. A dog's body naturally stores water, and deprivation can be harmful.

Dogs naturally lose water through defecation, respiration, nasal secretions, and, to a lesser degree, when dry skin flakes off. A dog with prolonged diarrhea or severe dehydration from too much exercise or exposure to the heat may need fluid replacements to restore his body functions.

Besides lapping from their bowls, dogs obtain water from canned and semi-moist foods. Metabolic processes that take place inside their bodies also generate water, but there's no replacement for a bowl of cool fresh water.

A Chihuahua, especially one who is sedentary, drinks little water. Seniors do not drink much either. Lactating females need more water for milk production. A standard requirement is that dogs require 1 milliliter of water for each kcal of energy expended.

Keep the water bowl filled and in the same place so that your dog can drink when he is thirsty. Water intake increases after exercise, eating salty foods, and during the sizzling heat of summer.

Too much water intake could be a sign of illness, such as diabetes, or that the food your dog eats is too salty. If that occurs, take him to your veterinarian to rule out disease. Alternatively, you may have to switch his diet to a brand with lower salt content. Table scraps loaded with salt increase a dog's water consumption.

COMMERCIAL DIETS

Stroll down the aisles in any supermarket, pet food retailer, or pet store and you can be bombarded with dozens of dog food brands from which to choose. Familiar names that have been around for years compete with lesser-known names. Some brands boast of all natural ingredients made without additives, colors, or dyes. Still others say that they are ideal for dogs with digestive, kidney, or skin problems. Foods are specially blended for dogs of all ages: puppies, adult dogs, and seniors. No matter what kind of dog you have, it seems that there is a brand for you. Your Chihuahua cannot pick his food, so as his guardian make sure that he eats nutritionally balanced complete meals. He deserves to live a long, healthy life. Good food will help him achieve that.

Dried Food (Kibble)

Dried foods come in sturdy multilayered bags with a long shelf life. Storage is fairly easy. The bag fits into a closet or pantry. For owners on a budget, dried food makes sense because it is economical. Kibble is available almost everywhere, such as grocery food chains, pet food retailers, and pet stores. Bags start as small as 5 pounds (2.5 kg) and go up to as large as 40 pounds (18 kg). Unless you have other dogs at home, buy a small bag for a Chihuahua. By the time one 6-pound (2.5 kg) Chihuahua eats halfway through a 40-pound (18-kg) bag, it will be stale and unappetizing.

Kibble comes with other advantages. A nutritionally complete quality-brand kibble has all of the vitamins and minerals your Chihuahua needs. Eating kibble helps prevent plaque buildup on his teeth, especially the back ones. Dogs use their back teeth more than the front to chew the kibble.

Be sure to check out the size of the kibble. Really big-sized kibble will turn off most Chihuahuas from eating it. Buy the small-sized kibble or kibble made for small breeds.

For variety, some owners supplement kibble with fresh vegetables or tiny bits of meat. Others add a small scoop of canned food or drizzle dog food sauce or broth on the kibble. These special touches offer variety, but make sure the dog's meal remains mostly kibble. Too much human food or wet dog food can be harmful.

Always store dried food in a cool, dry place. Keep it away from drafty doors and windows. If it is exposed to moisture, mold can form. Excessive heat will make it stale.

The bag, whether it is opened or closed, should be out of the dog's reach. A mischievous Chihuahua may try to rip apart the bag while you are out and help himself to an afternoon snack. If there are other pets at home, they may join in the fun but make themselves sick from eating too much food. Worse yet, they could all fight over the food and one of them could get hurt.

Some owners prefer to empty the bags into large sealable plastic bins or containers. Storage bins of all sizes are sold in pet stores and other retail establishments. Owners have the options of automatic feeding systems that dispense a certain amount of food at each meal. Colorful ceramic jars with cute and clever designs can also hold dog food. These decorative containers are usually more expensive than standard plastic bins, so make sure that they are free of toxins. If the label says the product is safe for human consumption and you have extra money to spend, then go ahead and perk up your kitchen.

Regardless of the storage method you pick, close the bag or container tightly after each use.

Specially made plastic clips are available for this purpose. Too much air reduces shelf life, so the food will taste dull, bland, and unappetizing. A tight lid or sealed container keeps out unwanted critters such as ants and other insects, which sometimes crawl their way into open pet food bags or opened containers. Infestation will ruin your supply of kibble. Your dog will not eat it and neither will anyone else's dog.

Whether you store kibble in a plastic storage bin or a ceramic jar, wash the container out regularly with warm soapy water. Crumbs can build up inside and need washing out from time to time.

Keep your dog on a dried-food diet. Semi-moist foods are like canned foods. Too much leads to digestive problems and tooth decay. You get more bang for your buck with a bag of kibble, and your Chihuahua will stay fit and trim.

By the Numbers

Does your dog tip the scales? Canine obesity borders on a national epidemic. Here are eight ways to keep your Chihuahua fit and trim.

- Buy good-quality food.
- Limit intake of wet food.
- Feed only the daily recommended amount.
- Avoid table scraps.
- Go easy on treats.
- Walk him at least once a day.
- Keep his water bowl full.
- Take him for an annual veterinary checkup.

Wet or Canned Food

All dogs, including Chihuahuas, savor the taste of canned food. Soft and juicy, it is made mostly from liquid (water, broth, and blood). In some cases moisture content is as high as 75 to 80 percent. That is not sound nutrition. Although a dog rarely turns his nose up to a bowl of canned food, such a diet eventually leads to digestive problems and dental decay.

Canned food is also more expensive than kibble and takes up more shelf space in your pantry. Nearly all pet food cans have a lift-off lid, but in many places you still have to dispose of the cans in your recycling bin. A shopping bag full of canned food is heavier to lift than a 5-pound (2.5-kg) bag of kibble.

Restrict a finicky eater to one scoop of canned food at either the morning or evening meal, not both. Your Chihuahua's health will benefit from eating mostly dried food. He may develop the habit of eating only the canned portion and leaving the rest. Weak-willed owners cave into the Chihuahua and start feeding him canned food. Be wary of Chihuahua games. They know how to get what they want. There may be times, however, when your Chihuahua has to eat canned, but keep it to a minimum unless, of course, he has few or no teeth.

If your Chihuahua is limited to canned food, the same American Association of Feed Control Officials (AAFCO) regulations apply. Food should be 100 percent nutritionally complete. For a top-quality canned food, water will be the first ingredient (for processing), but meat— chicken, beef, or lamb—should follow as the next ingredient, not meat byproducts. Be cautious of too many additives, food dyes, preservatives, fillers, or colors.

All dogs, including Chihuahuas, savor the taste of canned food.

Semi-Moist

Semi-moist foods contain less water than canned (about 25 percent). So it is softer than kibble but not as mushy as canned. It is often loaded with corn syrup, preservatives, additives, beet pulp, and sucrose. Dogs enjoy the taste of semi-most foods, but they can live without all of the extra ingredients. So much all at once is not good for them, especially a Chihuahua with such a small digestive system.

Leftover semi-moist food should be carefully stored to preserve freshness and to keep away bugs. The label should say whether the food needs refrigeration, which some do. Most do not. Cabinet storage is fine.

AAFCO regulations nonetheless apply to semi-moist dog foods just as they do to dried and canned foods, so read the labels to see whether the one you're considering is 100 percent nutritionally complete. Avoid foods that are not.

NONCOMMERCIAL DIETS

Not every dog owner trusts the ingredients in pet food, despite safety advances in the pet food industry over the past few years. Some prefer to make their dog's food. Below is a discussion of the pros and cons of home-cooked meals for dogs.

Homemade Diets

Who does not appreciate sitting down to a home-cooked meal? It is mouthwatering and delicious. Good taste lingers on the palate. Your Chihuahua will enjoy a home-cooked meal too.

Before starting him on a homemade diet, consider the dietary ramifications. A dog who eats home-cooked meals will resist eating dog food. Why settle for a bowl of dried kibble after eating broiled chicken and steamed rice with carrots? Home-cooked diets require special storage, unlike kibble or canned food. You can easily toss a plastic container of kibble in the car for a long road trip, but you will need a cooler with ice to store the dog's home-cooked meal. Ingredients for home-made diets cost more too, depending on the vagaries of the agriculture market. If you are comfortable with these precautions, then put on your apron and start cooking. Canine cookbooks with an assortment of recipes are available for the novice chef.

Multi-Dog Tip

In a multi-pet household, all dogs should eat and get snacks at the same time. Pick up uneaten food after a few minutes. Restrict free feeding if there is an overweight dog in the house. Supervision may be needed if one dog hogs another dog's food. Keep cat food out of the dog's reach.

As with commercial dog foods, homemade diets should be nutritionally complete, so check with your vet before you begin. Ingredients should include quality meat, rice, and vegetables. Be careful to adjust the right balance of vitamins and mineral supplements so that your dog does not have too much of one and not enough of the other. Fried food is barely digestible for your Chihuahua's system, so bake or broil the meals instead.

Raw Diets

Raw food diets, also known as bones and raw food (BARF), are just like human raw food diets—a concoction of uncooked foods that supposedly retain the nutrients lost by cooking. In a dog's case, ingredients are uncooked meat, including muscle and other organs, eggs, yogurt, vegetables, fruits, cottage cheese with added supplements and vitamins, topped off with uncooked meat bones. Owners pick and choose from a variety of ingredients, such as chicken, beef, carrots, green beans, and eggs but never pork. Always check with your vet before embarking on a BARF diet.

BARF diets have supporters and dissenters. Some veterinarians say that there is a risk of feeding bones to dogs. They can splinter and lodge in the dog's throat, causing bleeding and choking. Is it safe to feed raw meat and eggs? The potential to transmit dangerous toxins that are killed by heat from cooking, such as *E. coli*, exists. As it happens, there is not enough evidence yet about the BARF diet and its long-term impact on dogs.

Defenders say that the BARF diet mimics what dogs ate in the wild thousands of years ago. But most dogs no longer live in the wild. They are domesticated. BARF supporters, however, claim that dogs on a raw diet have

Prescription diets are available for dogs with certain health problems.

higher energy, cleaner teeth, and healthier skin. Supposedly the raw diet is easier to digest, so there is less poop to scoop.

As with the homemade diets, BARF diets impose the same limitations. Refrigeration restricts travel. The diet is more costly and time consuming to prepare. Once a dog starts to eat human food, it will be nearly impossible to switch him to kibble.

There are many healthful premium brands of dog food on the market that are scientifically formulated and tested by professionals. Unless you have a strong aversion to dog food, stick with kibble. It is a simpler choice for dog and owner.

SPECIALTY DIETS

Advances in veterinary medicine have produced an assortment of specialty foods and prescription diets available for dogs with chronic or acute gastrointestinal disorders, allergies, dry skin, renal failure, pancreatitis, heart disease, and other ailments. Until recently, these foods were available only from your veterinarian, but now they can be purchased at pet food stores too. Prescription diets, available as kibble or canned, supplement professional treatment from your veterinarian and can ease symptoms of a serious ailment. They are not a substitute for medical treatment; rather, they complement it.

Some prescription foods are lower in salt, have more protein, or contain less fat. They are made specifically for dogs with certain disorders so that they can live more comfortably. Do not feed your Chihuahua a prescription diet unless recommended by

Dogs do better with two daily meals—feed your adult Chihuahua twice a day, preferably in the morning and evening.

your veterinarian. Prescription diets cost more, but they will generally improve your dog's condition. A Chihuahua with digestive problems will likely improve by eating a prescription diet.

Holistic Food

Part of a holistic lifestyle is an all-natural diet free from processed foods. Such owners want the same healthful food for their dogs, kibble that is free from preservatives, additives, colors, fillers, and by-products. Pet food companies, both start-ups and established manufacturers, cater to this small but growing segment of dog owners. Holistic dog food contains such healthful ingredients as venison, vegetables, brown rice, alfalfa, sunflower oil, oatmeal, blueberries, and omega-3 fatty acids balanced by just the right amount of vitamins and minerals. Holistic dog foods (canned and kibble) must comply with AAFCO standards and provide a list of ingredients on the packaging. Humans who practice holistic living are said to reduce illness and stress. Dogs that eat holistic food supposedly have higher immunity, fewer diseases and longer lives. Holistic foods are pricier, but if the testimonials are true—that they keep your pet healthier—they may be worth the extra cost. Only you and your veterinarian can decide whether a holistic diet is right for your Chihuahua.

TREATS AND BONES

Dog treats and bones often occupy nearly an entire aisle in some pet food stores. Snacks come in different flavors, such as chicken, beef, or peanut butter. Some have less salt for the older dog or are smaller for puppies. Bones are made of rawhide, cloth, or nylon in a variety of shapes and sizes. And the best part of having a Chihuahua is seeing their tails wag with treats or bones.

Treats

Who does not enjoy an occasional mid-afternoon crunchy cookie or a piece of homemade pumpkin pie after Thanksgiving dinner? Your Chihuahua will enjoy a tasty treat too, such as a Nylabone. Treats serve an additional purpose as well. They are wonderful rewards used during training to shape good behavior, so feed them sparingly. Do not dish them out like candy or popcorn. Make your Chihuahua earn his treats through good behavior. Otherwise the treat will lose its effectiveness as a training tool.

If your Chihuahua sits down when told, that deserves a treat. If he comes on command, that too earns a reward. During

housetraining, give out treats to praise elimination outside or on puppy pads.

Dogs will spin around, yap, or do almost anything for a treat. Buy small, thumbnail-sized commercially available treats. There are many healthful brands on the market with all of the ingredients listed. Dog bakeries sell fresh, appetizing dog cookies. Some even sell doggy cupcakes, cream puffs, and other baked goods. Just as with humans, limit bakery goods. They are appealing to your dog but probably contain a lot of calories.

Regardless of the selections you make for your Chihuahua, treats should not be his main meal but only a small part of his diet. Too many treats lead to canine obesity. Treats are available for puppies and seniors, and some have a lowered fat content.

Bones

Refrain from feeding your Chihuahua raw, uncooked bones. As mentioned in the earlier

A feeding schedule is healthier for a dog.

raw food section of this chapter, bones can splinter and become clogged in any dog's throat. If your Chihuahua swallows a sharp piece, it could slice through part of his insides, causing major damage to his vital organs. He might even bleed to death.

For the Chihuahua that likes to chomp and chew, buy him small nylon or cloth bones that are sold in pet stores and other retail outlets. Make sure that they are small enough for his size but not so tiny so that he could choke. Bones should be washable and nontoxic.

FEEDING SCHEDULE

Imagine eating just one meal a day. Which one would it be? Breakfast, lunch, or dinner? Dogs do better with two daily meals. Puppies or dogs with hypoglycemia of course must

eat more often. Feed your adult Chihuahua twice a day, preferably in the morning and evening. When you first awaken, let your dog outside to tend to his business or take him for a walk. After he is done, feed him a bowl of kibble. At the end of the day, either walk him again or let him in from the yard. Then feed him the second meal. If you work odd hours, such as the overnight shift, you may have to alter his feeding schedule, but stick to two daily meals. He should eat at the same time every day. Remember that dogs thrive on a regular schedule.

Some owners free-feed their dogs by leaving out a bowl of kibble all day so that dogs eat at their leisure. That works better with healthy adult dogs. Eating generally stimulates a puppy to eliminate. If no one is home, that poses a problem. Expecting a puppy to hold it for more than a few hours is unreasonable and cruel, especially if he is crated.

Free feeding may also be an issue in a multiple-pet household because dogs sometimes bicker over food and cats have been known to munch on dog food. You must weigh the pros and cons if free feeding is something you want to consider.

OBESITY

The average Chihuahuas do not compete on the show circuit or in agility trials, so they might tip the scales past the recommended weight. Most Chihuahuas weigh between 3 and 6 pounds (1.5 and 2.5 kg). Much more than 6 pounds (2.5 kg), though, is risky to their health.

Obesity threatens American public health, causing a surge of such chronic illnesses as diabetes, heart attacks, and strokes. The cost to treat obesity soars into the billions for health care and lost wages. The obesity epidemic hits our canine companions too.

A number of factors contribute to an increase in canine girth. As owners spend more time at the office or on the road, they exercise less. The dog's daily walk is cut short just to

allow elimination. As the population becomes heavier and less active, the dogs do as well. There may be fewer weekend hikes or trips to the dog park. Cheap, low-quality dog food contributes to obesity. Too many table scraps adds pounds too.

Your Chihuahua should remain as close to the suggested weight as possible. A chunky Chihuahua faces the same health threats that humans do, namely diabetes, heart disease, and stroke. Too much weight is stressful on a dog's heart, forcing it to pump harder and harder. His breathing will become labored, which is exacerbated by summer heat. Extra padding can harm his back. A Chihuahua's tiny frame was not meant to carry around so much weight. Obesity shortens a dog's life span. A fat Chihuahua is not a happy Chihuahua.

Several disorders cause weight gain in dogs, such as hypothyroidism and Cushing's disease. Hypothyroidism is more common than Cushing's in Chihuahuas. Still, even if your dog has a thyroid disorder, medication can ease the symptoms. A low-calorie diet plus modest exercise can mitigate weight gain.

If your Chihuahua is overweight, consult with your veterinarian before embarking on a weight-reduction plan. Disease must be ruled out first before reducing his food intake and increasing his exercise.

Want to Know More?

Spaying does not cause weight gain. Not a shred of scientific evidence supports this conclusion. The belief traces back to an old wives' tale that is based on pure fallacy, not fact. A dog faces no ill effects from the spay/neuter surgery. The health benefits of the surgery were discussed earlier in Chapter 3: Care of Your Chihuahua Puppy.

CHAPTER 8

CHIHUAHUA HEALTH AND WELLNESS

Chihuahuas are incredibly resilient little dogs. Unless they are the result of careless breeding or years of neglect, Chihuahuas generally have few health issues. Toy breeds, including the Chihuahua, can live a long time, up to 20 years. To ensure that your dog stays in shape and free from illness, start him on a health and wellness program right away. Maintain that wellness program throughout his lifetime.

THE ANNUAL EXAMINATION

A veterinarian is crucial to your dog's health and well-being. Your Chihuahua's veterinarian provides routine care to keep your dog healthy and gets him through a crisis when he is sick or injured. Establish a relationship with a veterinarian, either when you bring the puppy home or when you adopt. Do not wait until an emergency such as illness or injury strikes before you find a veterinarian. Then you don't have the time to shop around for a veterinarian of your choice. Visits to emergency clinics or overnight hospitals cost more than routine veterinary care. Show your Chihuahua that you love him by taking him for annual veterinary visits. Begin when he is still a puppy.

If abnormalities turn up as a result of the exam, your veterinarian will discuss them with you and list your options, such as medication, a change in diet, blood work, x-rays, or surgery. If your dog faces expensive surgery, you may want a second opinion. Serious illness or injury should never be ignored. Your dog's health only worsens.

The support staff should be friendly, making you feel comfortable and at ease, as suggested in Chapter 3. Remember, the office itself should be tidy and orderly. Exam rooms should smell fresh and be clean. Medical licenses or certificates should be properly displayed.

Mouth

The veterinarian should greet you warmly and welcome you to the office. Let the vet examine your dog first; ask your questions later. The doctor should concentrate on your dog.

Want to Know More?

For information on puppy health and wellness, see Chapter 3: Care of Your Chihuahua Puppy.

To start, he or she will open the puppy's mouth to check for a cleft palate. Most puppies born with a cleft palate do not survive. Then the jaws will be checked to see whether there is an underbite. A cosmetic issue, the underbite does not harm the dog—he can eat normally and does not require a special diet.

Eyes

The eyes are next. The veterinarian will look for discharge and how far apart they are spaced. Negligent breeders sometimes produce puppies with the eyes spaced abnormally far apart, giving the puppy an unusual appearance.

Ears

Then the vet will examine the ears. Healthy ears are pink and pain-free when touched. Mites and other smelly discharge should not be present. If the veterinarian suspects an ear abnormality, he or she will examine the ears further with an otoscope, and a tiny sample of the material will be removed for examination under a microscope. Once the nature of the parasite or infection has been determined, the vet will prescribe medication.

Heart and Lungs

Then out will come the stethoscope to listen to the heart and lungs. Some Chihuahuas are born with heart murmurs, which are usually asymptomatic, just as they are in humans. In rare cases the murmur, which sounds like the whoosh whoosh of a washing machine, is more severe and requires surgery.

Testicles

For male dogs, the veterinarian will look closely at the testicles. Neutering is strongly recommended for puppies with an

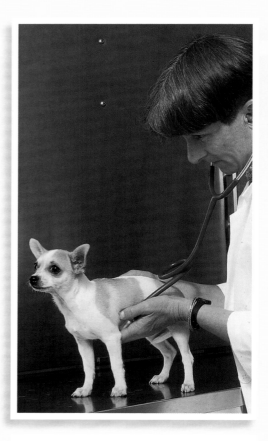

Show your Chihuahua that you love him by taking him for annual veterinary visits.

undescended testicle(s). A conscientious breeder will not breed a male puppy with an undescended testiscle. As a congenital defect, the condition can be passed along to offspring.

Abdominal Area

The veterinarian will also palpate the abdominal area for abnormalities. Tumors or enlarged organs are rare in puppies but occasionally occur. The veterinarian will then check for a luxating patella, a common knee problem in Chihuahuas.

Hernias

Hernias sometimes develop around the umbilical cord, so the veterinarian will examine that area too. Hernias can be open or closed. An unusually large or open hernia should be repaired surgically so that loops of the pup's intestines do not fall out. Surgical repair can be done when the puppy is spayed or neutered. Small hernias often heal on their own. Surgical repair of closed hernias is usually done to prevent the hernia from enlarging.

Temperature, Weight, and Vaccinations

A technician will take your dog's temperature, put him on the scale, and then update his vaccinations. Most rabies shots last three years except on adopted dogs with an unknown vaccination history or on puppies. Then they get a one-year booster. Thereafter, a three-year booster is acceptable in most localities. Always check with local authorities to find out what rabies vaccination they accept.

PARASITES

Even the most pampered Chihuahua who lives indoors can contract internal (heartworm and other worms) or external (fleas, mites, ticks) parasites. Parasites carry diseases, some of which are serious, and they are largely preventable through medication, proper sanitation, and routine hygiene.

Internal Parasites

Parasites cause a number of diseases in dogs, some relatively severe. These disorders are largely avoidable through preventive

Exercise will keep your Chihuahua looking and feeling good.

medication, proper sanitation, balanced meals, and routine veterinary care. The more common canine parasites are discussed in this section.

Heartworm

Infected mosquitoes transmit heartworm (*Dirofilaria immitis*). If a dog is bitten (it takes just one bite) the parasite travels through the bloodstream to the heart, where it causes major damage. Untreated heartworm disease is fatal. Symptoms take time to appear and include coughing, a swollen abdomen, and fatigue. There are abnormal lung sounds on physical examination. Only a blood test confirms heartworm infestation. Depending on the severity of the infection, treatment, usually with medication, can be expensive. Both the adult and immature worms must be killed.

The larvae that develop into heartworms can start at 57°F (14°C), so some veterinarians suggest year-round heartworm preventive medication. Others only recommend it during the steamy summer weather. Dogs who live in hot, humid climates where mosquitoes flourish should absolutely be on preventive medication. Mosquitoes can slip through holes in screens or open doors. Bites can occur during the short time your dog is outside taking care of business, on his daily walk, or visiting the dog park. Prevention is much less costly than the cure.

Before your dog begins preventive medication, he must have a blood test to rule out infection unless he is under six months of age. After that age, a blood test is mandatory. Preventive medications available in chewable forms are nearly 100 percent effective. Owners must be vigilant and administer the dosage as suggested by the manufacturer. A lapse of even one month can leave a dog susceptible to infection. Preventive heartworm medication is not a cure for the disease.

Hookworm

Hookworms (*Ancylostoma caninum* and *Ancylostoma braziliense*) are more often found in puppies, but adult dogs are not without risk. Most cases are found in the South, where the climate is hotter and more humid, but dogs in cooler climates are not immune to infestation. Transmission from several kinds of hookworms can occur in the following ways:
- from the infected mother to the puppy through the placenta or from her milk
- smelling or ingesting infected feces
- through the skin

Symptoms include bloody diarrhea, weight loss, anemia, and a dull coat. The hookworms live on the wall of the dog's intestines and hatch inside the blood. Infested puppies cannot thrive; their immune systems are not strong enough.

A fecal examination performed under a microscope at a veterinarian's office or animal hospital is the only way to diagnose hookworms. Treatment includes de-worming medication that is given orally or through injection. Two weeks later, another de-worming treatment is administered. For a severe infestation that leaves a dog with a bad case of anemia, a blood transfusion may be required.

Once your dog is diagnosed with hookworms, it is imperative to clean the environment. As soon as the dog defecates, remove the feces. Place it in a bag and dispose of it in the trash or flush it down the toilet. Rinse down metal or concrete surfaces the infected dog used with a 10 percent bleach solution. Wash the dog's bedding too. Vacuum the carpets thoroughly. If other pets are in the home, do not let them come into contact with the feces of the infected dog.

Human contamination by canine

hookworms is rare, but to be safe, use universal precautions such as rubber gloves when handling the feces or washing down infected areas. Do not allow a dog with hookworms to enter a child's play area, especially a sandbox. Contamination is hard to remove from sandboxes.

Roundworm

The two most common types of roundworms are *Toxascaris leonina* and *Toxocara canis*, and both have an incredible ability to reproduce. One female *T. canis* worm can churn out 200,000 eggs in one day.

Many puppies, regardless of breed, are born with *T. canis*. A pregnant dog can pass the parasite to her puppies in utero. After birth, puppies heave out worms and then ingest them. That explains the high infection rate among puppies. Infected mothers can also pass roundworms through the mammary tissues when nursing. The puppies swallow the infected milk. Ingestion of infected feces or water is the most common form of transmission with adult dogs.

Roundworms largely infect the intestines, so puppies or adult dogs will vomit, cough, or be lethargic. Sometimes it looks as if there is spaghetti or strings mixed into the stool. The infection can prevent nutrient absorption, so it is imperative that the condition be treated.

A stool sample is examined microscopically to determine which type of roundworm is present. Anti-parasitic drugs eliminate roundworms, although other medications are available. Treatment is usually repeated two to four weeks after the initial dose to kill any migrating larvae. Recheck a fecal sample at least six months after treatment to make sure that the medication was effective.

Female eggs primarily cause infection, so

as with other parasitic infections, treat the environment. Clean the dog's bedding and toys with a solution of water and bleach. Mop around the area where the dog sleeps, again with bleach, at least once a week. Promptly remove feces from the back yard. If the soil is contaminated with worms, either turn it over to a depth of 8 to 12 inches (20.5 to 30.5 cm) or cover it up with fresh soil. Check with your veterinarian for length of treatment, but you should expect to clean weekly for at least a month.

Tapeworm

Five types of tapeworms can infect dogs, but the most common is *Dipylidium caninum*. Flat and white, tapeworms can grow as long

Clean your Chihuahua's bedding regularly.

as 20 inches (51 cm). Initially they look like tiny pieces of rice squirming around in the dog's feces. With a hook-like mouth, they grab onto part of the dog's intestine. Dogs acquire tapeworms from worm-hosting parasites such as fleas. Symptoms include licking the anal area or scooting the butt along the ground. Worms are also visible in the dog's feces. Dried worms sometimes collect in the fur around the dog's anal area.

Diagnosis is made through a microscopic examination of the feces. Your veterinarian will prescribe an effective medication to kill the tapeworms. Consider flea control methods, especially the monthly pill. Dogs on flea control prevention usually do not develop tapeworms.

Whipworm

Known scientifically as *Trichuris vulpis*, whipworms are another parasite that infects dogs. Contamination occurs when dogs eat or drink tainted food and water. Whipworms live in the large intestine and cecum, the junction where the small and large intestine meet. Symptoms include weight loss, diarrhea, and the presence of excess mucus. Diagnosis is made through a microscopic examination of the feces. Several effective de-worming treatments are available. The environment, however, is harder to treat. Wear rubber gloves when washing the dog's bedding, toys, or living spaces. There is a slight but unlikely chance for transmission. Use a solution with bleach to rinse down the space where the dog sleeps or spends most of his time. Have the carpets professionally cleaned. Remove feces from the back yard right away.

Whipworm eggs can live in the soil for years, often resistant to freezing temperatures. Restrict all pets from known contaminated areas. No known methods exist to remove whipworm eggs from the soil. The only alternative is to replace the soil in the contaminated area.

External Parasites

Fleas

Insects, fleas are the most common external parasite to strike dogs. Fleas can be found in all parts of the United States but are most common during the summer when it is hot and humid. Infected animals or a compromised environment can transmit fleas. Interestingly, fleas do not have wings, so they jump from one host to another; they do not fly.

There are more than 2,000 species of fleas; *Ctenocephalides canis* is the one most commonly affecting dogs in this country. Fleas bite dogs and then feed on their blood. A single flea can deposit from 30 to 50 eggs per day, so infestation in untreated dogs can be severe. Fleas usually gather around the head or hindquarters, but they can be found anywhere on the dog's body.

Symptoms include itching, red lesions, and hair loss. Physical reactions are exacerbated when the dog is allergic to the flea's saliva. Puppies with widespread infestation can become anemic. Flea-infested dogs are quite miserable.

Diagnosis is fairly simple. Run a flea comb along your dog's fur. If the comb picks up flea dirt, or fecal material, your dog is infected. Start with an effective anti-flea medication. A lot of treatments are available. Once the fleas are controlled, put your dog on a preventive program that includes medication and a

controlled environment. Medication comes in chewable or topical form that is administered monthly. There are also collars, powders, sprays, foams, and shampoos to combat fleas.

Treating the environment is absolutely mandatory if your dog has fleas. Sprinkle flea powder on the carpets and vacuum the area where the pet sleeps or spends most of his time. Regular vacuuming is a huge help. Insect foggers or sprays also kill fleas in open areas of your home. Ask your veterinarian for advice about which product to use. Use caution if someone in the household is pregnant, has allergies or pulmonary disease, or is under 12 years old. Follow instructions on the fogger carefully.

Clean your pet's bedding regularly, including any beds restricted to outdoor use. Treat the immediate area with an insect growth regulator. Remember to include the car, garage, basement, or any other place where your dog spends time.

Fleas thrive in warm, moist areas. If your dog hangs out on the patio, apply insecticide out there as well. In cases of widespread infestation, treat the back yard. Fleas can live in the grass, straw, shrubbery, and leaves. For outdoor treatment, select an environmentally safe product. Remember that your dog takes care of business outside. Family members probably use the yard too. Refrain from using highly toxic products. There are safe effective products on the market.

Fleas can be kept in check, but the owner must be persistent and diligent. The best flea treatment is prevention. There are many effective ways to prevent fleas. Ask your veterinarian about the best one for you and your dog.

Ringworm

Ringworm is a misnomer; it is not a worm but a fungus called *Dermatophytes*, which means plants that live on the skin. Scientists originally thought the circular lesions were caused by worms, thus the name ringworm. The fungi live and grow on the dog's skin, causing patches of hair loss in circular lesions. Most commonly affected sites are the face, ears, tails, and paws. Symptomatic is red (inflamed) scaly skin in the infected areas. Your dog may or may not itch. Dogs infect each other through direct contact. Ringworm can be passed along to humans, so be careful and wear rubber gloves when handling an infected dog.

Fungal spores can live in your home. If your dog is infected with ringworm, completely sanitize the dog's bedding, brushes and combs, and toys. If possible, replace the dog's bedding. If not, wash the bedding in hot water. Wipe down surfaces where the dog stays with a solution of 30 percent bleach and water. Bleach easily kills the spores. Have your carpeting professionally steam cleaned.

Ringworm is diagnosed by looking at hair or skin samples under a Wood's lamp, also known as an ultraviolet lamp, or under a microscope.

Check your dog for fleas and ticks after he's been outside.

Antifungal drugs such as itraconazole are usually prescribed to treat ringworm. Your veterinarian can tell you about any side effects. Lime sulfur dips may help. Dips can be given at home or at your veterinarian's office. Follow instructions for mixing the dip, because it can stain clothing or furniture. Wear old clothes when treating your dog. The mixture can also leave your dog's coat temporarily discolored. It also reeks of old socks.

Mites

Ear mites (*Otodectes cynotis*) are tiny crab-like pests that live in a dog's ear canals, feeding on the healthy tissue. Highly contagious, they spread easily to other pets either at home or in a shelter. If left untreated, they find their way into the head and tail areas. Symptoms include shaking the head, itchy ears, and black crust inside the ear canal.

Diagnosis is made by looking into the dog's ears with an otoscope, then by examining a sample of the black crusty material under a microscope. Your veterinarian will carefully clean your dog's ears before dispensing anti-parasitic medication. In most cases, you'll go home with a solution to clean your dog's ears as prescribed by your veterinarian. Too much cleansing, however, may wash away the medication. Follow the instructions on the medication or from your veterinarian.

Check your dog's ears now and then for foreign matter. If he exhibits any of the symptoms listed here, take him to your veterinarian.

Ticks

One tiny tick causes most owners to panic. The tick, a parasitic arthropod, can be a dog's worst enemy. Ticks do not fly or jump; they crawl onto the dog instead, usually around the ears, between the toes, and within skin folds. Ticks feed on the dog's blood for periods as long as several days.

Not all ticks transmit disease, although many do. Ticks should be removed immediately because the disorders they can spread are serious, such as Lyme disease, ehrlichiosis, Rocky Mountain spotted fever, and canine anaplasmosis (commonly known as dog tick fever).

Symptoms vary with each tick disease but generally include fever, loss of appetite, weight loss, swollen lymph glands, swollen limbs, and nosebleeds. Diagnosis is made through a blood test. Your veterinarian will then prescribe medication, usually antibiotics, depending on the species that caused the infection.

To keep your dog tick free, follow the same approach used with fleas. Administer a preventive medication, which can be in chewable or topical form, and then control your environment. Shampoos, dips, collars, powders, and sprays are also available to prevent ticks. Wash your dog's bedding and the areas where he sleeps regularly. Vacuum the carpets often. If you find ticks inside the home, strongly consider using a fogger. Clear brush and leaves from around the house and yard areas, ideal tick habitats.

Remember that ticks live in all 50 states and are not deterred by frigid weather. Consult your veterinarian about the most efficient tick prevention method for your dog. Always follow the manufacturer's instructions for whatever tick prevention product you select.

Ticks can be harmful to humans too. Avoid walking with your dog in heavily wooded areas. Deer and other wild animals carry ticks. Lyme disease is a harmful disorder to both humans and dogs. Be careful when removing ticks from your dog that you dispose of them properly. Wear protective clothing. The Center for Disease Control offers guidelines about tick-related diseases among humans.

BREED-SPECIFIC DISORDERS

Most breeds have specific genetic problems, so potential Chihuahua owners should do background checks before buying a puppy. That does not mean that all Chihuahuas are born with genetic problems. On the contrary, most are born healthy. Conscientious breeders screen for inherited disorders. However, the following conditions are sometimes found in the Chihuahua.

Collapsing Trachea

Every dog, including the Chihuahua, has a small breathing tube also known as the windpipe that extends down the throat to the lungs. The trachea carries air into the dog's lungs. The most common symptom includes a persistent deep cough that sounds somewhat like a goose honk. If the dog gets too excited, he may collapse or faint from lack of oxygen. Genetically caused, a collapsed trachea ranges from mild to severe. Collapsed trachea is common in toy breeds.

Tugging too hard on the leash and rough handling exacerbate tracheal collapse. Diagnosis is made by x-ray or endoscope. Dogs with mild to moderate cases are managed by controlling stress and excitement. Cough suppressants may help. Severe cases require surgical replacement of the trachea with a prosthesis to keep the airway open. An obese dog with a collapsed trachea must lose weight to live a somewhat normal life.

Entropion

A common eye problem, entropion can manifest itself right after birth or later in the dog's life. The lower eyelids roll inward.

Want to Know More?

To learn more about ticks, see Chapter 6: Chihuahua Grooming Needs.

Tiny ulcers cause corneal abrasions because they face in the wrong direction. Symptoms include squinting, tearing, pawing at the eyes, discharge, or rolling of the eyelids.

A careful ocular examination by your veterinarian will confirm this disorder. Fluorescent dye can pick up tiny corneal tears. If lubricant eye drops do not work, surgery is needed. Your veterinarian can lay out the dog's treatment options depending on the severity of the disorder. The most common surgical procedure is removing skin around the affected eyelid. Entropion is an inherited condition in purebred dogs. Allowing affected dogs to reproduce is careless and thoughtless.

Mitral Valve Disease

As with human mitral valve disease, one or more of the dog's heart valves thicken and become deformed. Sometimes there is a heart murmur that a veterinarian easily picks up on a routine examination. Older male dogs are the most likely to be affected, although it can strike younger dogs, including females. A dog may have mitral valve disease for a few years without any symptoms. But when it progresses, symptoms include exercise intolerance, general weakness, fatigue, and shortness of breath. Diagnosis is made from X-rays, a complete blood panel or an electrocardiogram. There is no cure, and long-term prognosis is poor. Treatment options are limited to low-sodium diets, reduced exercise, and stress relief. The veterinarian may prescribe medication, but canine valve replacement is not available.

Retained Baby Teeth

All Chihuahuas are born with 28 deciduous teeth. By adulthood they have 42 teeth. Baby teeth in some Chihuahuas do not fall out naturally. That leads to malocclusion, also known as a bad bite. Adult teeth do not have enough room to grow in properly, so the dog has too many teeth. A mouth with too many teeth makes for an irritable and cranky Chihuahua. Chewing on food can be painful, and chomping on nylon bones or playing tug of war with rope toys may force the reluctant teeth to fall out. Stubborn cases may require veterinary intervention.

Patellar Luxation

Also known as a slipped knee, this common hereditary problem is seen in many toy breeds, including Chihuahuas. The kneecap, or patella, fits inside a groove or pocket in the femur, the largest thigh bone. If a Chihuahua is born with an abnormally small groove, the patella cannot glide smoothly against the groove and pops out towards the inner portion of the leg. Sometimes the condition can impact one or both legs. Luxating patella can be mild, causing little or no pain, or it can be serious enough to warrant surgical repair.

Pulmonary Stenosis

Pulmonary stenosis is a valvular disease that results in blockage of the right ventricle. The normal flow of blood is impeded. Consequently the right ventricle atrophies or thickens. Pulmonic stenosis can be mild, moderate, or severe. Mild and moderate symptoms need no treatment. Your Chihuahua will lead a normal life. Severe symptoms, such as trouble in walking, constant fatigue, or breathing difficulties, usually require surgical repair of the heart called vavluloplasty.

Seizures

Canine seizures are abnormal electrical impulses or misfires in certain parts of the brain. The cause is largely idiopathic—unknown—although genetics, allergies, and brain tumors also play a role. However, the disease is not widely understood in dogs. Young dogs, both male and female, between one and five years old are most commonly affected. A Chihuahua who experiences a mild or petit mal seizure loses some motor control or may simply collapse. Grand mal seizures are worrisome. The dog falls down, shakes uncontrollably, or involuntarily urinates. Disease is usually present when an older dog develops seizures, usually a malignant brain tumor.

If your dog starts to seize, keep him as calm as possible. Shield him from other household pets, who will probably be curious as to the thrashing. Seek veterinary attention right away. Anticonvulsive medication is available for grand mal seizures, but it must

Multi-Dog Tip

Fleas and ticks spread easily among dogs and cats. If you have a multi-pet household and live in an area prone to external parasites, all dogs and cats should take flea and tick preventive medication, at least during the hot and humid summer months. A dog with just one flea or tick can infect all of the other household pets. And your environment as well then becomes infested. Prevention is the best treatment all around.

Skin allergies will cause your Chihuahua to itch.

be administered daily. Never leave an epileptic dog outdoors or punish him if he soils the carpet during a seizure.

GENERAL HEALTH ISSUES

Conscientious owners feed their Chihuahuas premium dog food, exercise them regularly and take them for veterinary exams at least annually. Despite efforts to keep up their dogs' health, disorders may still appear. Below is a discussion of common canine ailments that your Chihuahua may experience in his lifetime.

Allergies

Allergies cause problems for dogs, just as with humans. Chihuahuas are not prone to allergies, but that does not mean that they will not ever get them. Ingredients in dog food such as corn or wheat are usually the culprits, although something else could trigger an allergic reaction. The most common symptom is itchy skin. No easy way exists to pinpoint the food allergy. Consult with your veterinarian first, but most likely you will have to experiment with different foods to see which one your dog can tolerate. Specific brands are made for dogs with sensitive stomachs.

Allergies can erupt on the skin too. Dogs will itch, lose fur, and be uncomfortable. They may be allergic to flea bites, food, dust mites, mold spores, pollen, or too much shampooing. Again, if your dog scratches too much, consult your veterinarian for a specific treatment for the particular allergy involved. Long-term treatment is available, usually with a change of food, medication, vitamins, and avoidance of the allergen.

Some dogs develop skin allergies as a result of stress. Dogs thrive on routine, and when their regular habits are disrupted, their immune system takes a hit. Sometimes the result is skin allergies. Examples are dogs moved to the back yard when a couple brings home a baby, constant squabbles at home, or surrender to a shelter. These dogs lose their routines, and some cannot cope with the change. As a result, their immune systems break down, which manifests as skin allergies.

Cancer

Cancer usually strikes older dogs, although younger dogs are sometimes affected. Chihuahuas live long lives, so it is possible that they may develop a cancerous tumor. There is good news, however. Cancer is not found often among Chihuahuas. Even when it does, the cancer diagnosis is not as fearful as it once was. Treatment can include surgery, chemotherapy, radiation, homeopathy, or a combination of these modalities, depending on the type of tumor and how far advanced the disease may be.

Always check your dog for suspicious lumps or bumps, especially if the bump has irregular borders or is darkened. Most are benign, but an alert owner can save a dog's life. Prompt intervention with cancer is imperative.

Ear Infections

The shape of the Chihuahua's ears protects them from most ear infections. Floppy-eared dogs like the Bloodhound and Cocker Spaniel are more prone to ear infections than the Chihuahua. Dogs who shake their heads or paw at their ears almost always have ear infections, which may be caused by ear mite, yeast, or bacteria. Healthy ears are pink. Infected ears will be swollen, discolored, painful, and malodorous. If your dog has an ear infection, he must see a veterinarian right away. The infection will not go away without anti-parasitic or antibiotic treatment that includes ear drops. The veterinarian will also thoroughly cleanse your dog's ears.

Prevention of hip dysplasia is possible only through careful, conscientious breeding.

If your Chihuahua goes swimming in the family pool, supervised of course, dry his ears thoroughly after he takes a dip. Dry ears are unlikely to become infected.

Eye Infections

Chihuahuas, like other small dogs, can experience eye infections, although they are rare. (Note: Tearstaining is very common in Chihuahuas, usually due to a lack of zinc.) But they can occasionally occur. Symptoms include redness, discharge, swelling, bloodshot eyes, squinting, and pawing at the eyes. Eye injuries and food allergies can cause some of the same symptoms, so it is important to have your dog examined by your veterinarian right away. Untreated eye infections or injuries caused by foreign objects can lead to permanent vision loss or blindness. Treatment usually includes antibiotic eye drops. Severe infections may require oral antibiotics. Eye infections can be contagious, so if you have other pets in the home, you may have to isolate your Chihuahua for the duration of his illness.

Hip Dysplasia

Hip dysplasia does not discriminate; all breeds, sexes, and ages are affected. Pain and inflammation are caused when the femur, also known as the thigh bone, does not fit into the hip socket. Hip dysplasia can be debilitating. Symptoms include lameness in the back legs, hesitance to walk, stiffness in the morning, and trouble climbing stairs.

The disease most commonly strikes the larger breeds such as German Shepherds, Labrador Retrievers, Great Danes, and Saint Bernards, but now and then it occurs in mutts and small breeds like the Chihuahua.

Researchers agree that hip dysplasia is inherited, so a reputable breeder should spay/neuter a dog with the disease because it can be passed along to the offspring. There is no cure. Prevention is possible only through careful, conscientious breeding.

Treatment options vary. Through a combination of diet, exercise, nutritional supplements, and pain and anti-inflammatory medication, some dogs can avoid costly surgery. Weight control is also crucial. Dogs with hip dysplasia should not be plump. They must be kept indoors and sleep on orthopedic bedding. Ramps should be available so that they can avoid climbing stairs, which exacerbates the condition.

Surgical intervention is expensive but sometimes the only alternative for severe crippling cases. There are several surgical options, including total hip replacement.

If your dog has hip dysplasia, discuss the various medical and surgical options with your veterinarian.

Training Tidbit

If you live in a region subject to earthquakes, tornadoes, wildfires, or hurricanes, make your Chihuahua part of your family's evacuation plan. Do not leave him behind, as he may not survive a natural disaster on his own. Practice the evacuation plan so that if an emergency arises, everyone in the household will be ready and know what to do. Check your emergency supply kit several times a year to make sure that it is up to date.

A healthy Chihuahua may result from alternative treatments.

ALTERNATIVE THERAPIES

Alternative therapies such as acupuncture, chiropractic care, herbal remedies, and homeopathy are widely popular among humans. Now those therapies compete as viable treatments for common canine ailments such as hip dysplasia, arthritis, cancer, digestive disorders, and allergies. Alternative treatments complement veterinary medicine; they are not a substitute for many standard forms of care or vaccinations. Traditional medicine still has its place. If your dog is seriously ill or injured, he still needs to see a veterinarian.

Acupuncture

Acupuncture is a traditional holistic or alternative approach to pain. For centuries, Chinese practitioners inserted thin needles into certain parts of the body known as meridians to relieve the discomfort of arthritis, rheumatism, headaches, and other painful conditions. Now it is used on animals, including dogs.

Acupuncture is based on the ancient yin/yang theory. Yin is negative, while yang is positive; yin is dark, while yang is light. A healthy state depends on blending the qualities of yin and yang, which acupuncture helps achieve.

Acupuncture is another option for dogs with chronic illness or pain. It also relieves stress in abused or neglected dogs. The procedure used is similar to the one used for humans. A skilled acupuncturist inserts thin needles along the dog's meridians, or pressure points, to give the dog balance and get rid of negative energy. Among the disorders treated include hip dysplasia, skin diseases, gastrointestinal problems, respiratory diseases, chronic pain, and neurological illnesses.

Redirecting negative energy brings about healing. Experienced veterinarians recommend at least six to eight treatments to produce results. Most dogs tolerate the painless procedure.

Only recently has Western medicine given the go-ahead for acupuncture on human ailments. Few follow-up studies exist to determine its effectiveness among dogs, but anecdotal evidence suggests that it now has a permanent role in veterinary medicine.

If you choose acupuncture, however, your veterinarian will examine your dog, determine the nature of the illness, and then discuss all options. Your veterinarian should have experience with acupuncture if you choose this treatment for your dog.

Chiropractic

Veterinary chiropractic deals with the dog's spine and joints, similar to human chiropractic. A trained technician or veterinarian will perform subluxations, or adjustments, around the spine to relieve pain caused by injury or disease, such as degenerative arthritis. Manual manipulation helps the dog to heal himself and restores impaired mobility. Chiropractic is deemed a safe, drug-free alternative method to treat pain and suffering in animals, including dogs.

Veterinary chiropractors are certified by the American Veterinary Chiropractic Association (AVCA). When selecting a chiropractic veterinary practitioner, look for someone with adequate qualifications and experience.

Herbal Treatment

Herbal medicines offer an alternative to conventional treatments for canine diseases. Holistic medicine looks at the whole dog. If the immune system breaks down, what is the cause? Is it the result of improper nutrition? Stress at home? Prior history of abuse? A holistic veterinarian would not just treat the symptoms of a deficient immune system but would look for the underlying cause.

Herbal treatments can include aroma therapy with eucalyptus, which helps unclog a dog with lung disease. Glucosamine and chondroitin supplements might improve an arthritic dog's gait. Or Bach Flower remedies, such as Aspen, could benefit a dog fearful of thunder.

Consult your veterinarian, however, before administering herbal remedies to a dog that takes traditional medicine. Doses need to be tapered for a Chihuahua to avoid toxicity.

Homeopathy

Homeopathy for human beings is based on the ancient belief that disease is caused when the flow of energy is disrupted, usually by an excess amount of stress. Introducing natural remedies restores well-being. The same is true for canine homeopathy. Homeopathy believes that good canine health and well-being can be maintained through proper diet, exercise, and removal of stress. It is a system whereby the whole dog is treated so that health is restored and maintained naturally.

Herbs and vitamins made from natural substances treat disorders instead of chemically made pharmaceuticals. Do not self-diagnose your pet's illness. Always confer with your veterinarian before starting a homeopathic treatment plan for your dog.

Veterinarians who share holistic beliefs say that it is a safe, effective way to cure animal diseases. In fact, the Academy of Veterinary Homeopathy (AVH), founded in 1995, is a

Dogs with pain from fractured hips, arthritis, or ruptured discs can benefit from physical therapy.

national organization dedicated to treating animals through natural care.

If you chose homeopathy for your dog, be selective about the practitioner. He or she should be adequately trained and skilled in this young but growing field.

Physical Therapy

Physical therapy is not just for humans; it has gone to the dogs along with other noninvasive treatments mentioned in this section. Dogs with pain from fractured hips, arthritis, or ruptured discs can benefit from physical therapy.

Canine rehab includes whirlpool baths, massage, treadmill exercises, and the Tellington TTtouch. As with humans, physical therapy reduces the need for surgery and pain medication and restores lost or impaired mobility. It also conditions dogs who work for a living, such as police dogs, guide dogs, and bomb-sniffing dogs.

Canine physical therapists can train owners to perform some exercises at home. Other exercises need supervision in the veterinarian's office or a veterinary rehab center.

A form of physical therapy, the Tellington TTouch was developed by Linda Tellington-Jones, a former horse trainer. TT can be performed by owners, veterinarians, dog trainers, groomers, or shelter workers. Adapted to reduce pain and improve overall health, TT begins by placing your thumb on the dog's neck, face, or somewhere else on his body. With your other four fingers, apply gentle pressure in a circular pattern that moves only the outer layer of the skin. Repeat the circular motions for at least five minutes. Sessions should be short so that the dog tolerates the procedure. By improving the flow of energy so that the dog's body can heal itself, TT curbs aggression, perks up shy dogs, and calms hyperactive ones.

Bites from insects, arachnids, or other animals are serious and can be life threatening.

Physical therapy comes with a cost, but some owners want their dogs to have the best. Costs depend on the nature of illness or injury and the type of physical therapy. Discuss physical therapy with your veterinarian to lay out a plan for your Chihuahua.

EMERGENCY CARE

A bee stings your Chihuahua or he slices his paw on a sliver of broken glass while in the yard taking care of business. He screeches in pain and his cries make your eyes water. What should you do? Remain calm and steady. An injured Chihuahua will sense your anxiety and nervous apprehension, so do not yell or scream. Rush him to your veterinarian or to an emergency veterinary clinic. Do not self-medicate your dog. Remember, dogs' bodies are different from humans' bodies. Wait for the veterinarian— the professional trained to handle medical emergencies.

If time permits, call a close friend or relative to join you for the ride or to meet you at the office. Coping with an emergency goes smoother with a trusted friend or close relative at your side. Remember that time is of the essence with any emergency. Leave right away. For afterhours crises, post the name, address, and telephone number of the nearest reputable emergency clinic on your refrigerator. If an emergency arises, that information will be readily available.

Bites

Bites from insects, arachnids, or other animals are serious and can be life threatening. Scorpions, snakes, and tarantulas, for example, can be lethal, especially to a tiny Chihuahua. Your dog must be treated right away with anti-venom medication.

If you live in a rural area and a wild animal such as a skunk, raccoon, or even a bat takes a nip out of your Chihuahua, he is at risk for rabies or other viral diseases. Canine rabies is virtually wiped out among domestic animals in the United States, but the disease is still found in wild animals. Take him to your veterinarian at once. If he is current on his rabies vaccine, he is very unlikely to contract rabies. The bite wound, however, will need care. If the rabies vaccination is outdated, a rabies vaccine will not prevent the disease if he was recently exposed. No known treatments exist for dogs infected with the rabies virus. If a rabid animal bites an unvaccinated dog, the dog must be euthanized.

Stings are equally troublesome. Bee and wasp stings are not only painful but also productive of allergic reactions. A swollen muzzle swells suggests an allergy. Ice will reduce the swelling, but your Chihuahua needs immediate veterinary care because the swelling may interfere with his breathing. For Chihuahuas with known allergies to bee or wasp stings, ask your veterinarian for a supply of antihistamine that you can administer.

If a bee or wasp stings your dog but he has no allergic reaction, thoroughly wash the area with alcohol or warm water. The bite area will probably be tender, so treat it with care. The stinger sometimes remains embedded in the dog's skin. Carefully remove it with tweezers. Apply ice to the bite area to prevent or reduce swelling.

Fights sometimes break out among dogs and cats. Be careful about stepping in the middle, or you may be bitten in the process. Turn on the garden hose or aim a fire extinguisher directly at the animals. That usually safely separates them.

If your dog ends up with deep puncture wounds, he needs emergency care. Quite a few dogs have had to be stitched up because of fighting.

Bleeding

Your dog may cut his paw on a broken bottle, or he may step on a nail on his daily walk. Bleeding can be mild, moderate, or life threatening. Excessive blood loss from a toy dog like a Chihuahua is worrisome. Get him to an emergency veterinary clinic right away. His life depends on your ability to act swiftly but calmly.

Use care when handling a bleeding or bloodied Chihuahua. If possible, ask a family member or friend to help. Wrap the dog in a towel or blanket. If an appendage is bleeding profusely, a light tourniquet may be used for a short period to control the blood loss until you reach the vet's office. If the bleeding is mild, don't use a tourniquet. Instead, apply a pressure bandage. Keep the dog warm, calm and secure. Staff at some clinics will transfer your dog onto a gurney then roll him inside for emergency care.

Broken Bones

On your morning walk, the leash inadvertently slips out of your hand. Your Chihuahua sees a cat and dashes into the street. A car driver slams on the brakes but it is too late. The front wheel hits your dog's back leg. What now? You feel like crying but remain calm because your dog is injured and in pain. Loss of blood may cause shock.

Dogs in pain sometimes try to bite when you attempt to move them. They are scared and hurt. When dealing with broken or fractured

Do not leave a Chihuahua outside in high temperatures for an extended time.

limbs, slowly shift the dog onto a hard surface, such as a piece of thick cardboard or wood. If two people are available, lift the dog in a blanket or sheet. Keep him quiet and warm as you drive to your veterinarian or emergency clinic without delay. Call ahead to let the staff know that you have an emergency. If for some reason your veterinarian is unavailable, the office will direct you to the nearest emergency clinic or animal hospital.

Frostbite

In the case of frostbite, a dog's extremities will either partially or completely freeze. Most commonly affected body parts are the ears, toes, tail, and scrotum on intact male dogs. Frostbite can be mild, moderate, or severe. In mild cases, the affected area turns white or pale because extreme cold cuts off the blood circulation. When the dog is brought inside and warms up, the area will redden because the blood will circulate again. Swelling may occur. Body parts may have to be amputated when frostbite is severe, because circulation never comes back. The limb is essentially dead.

The first step to help a dog with mild frostbite includes soaking washcloths with warm water and then applying them to the affected areas for 15 to 20 minutes. Then get the dog to a veterinarian or emergency clinic immediately. On the drive to the veterinarian, wrap the dog in a warm blanket. Your veterinarian will determine the extent of the damage and decide whether surgery or medication is needed. A warm environment will improve mild cases.

Heatstroke

Heatstroke is easily avoided by never locking a dog inside a parked car during the summer. Even with open windows or shade from a tree, temperatures can rise to over 120°F (49°C) in just minutes. If he is not rescued, a dog will perish or experience a life-threatening stroke locked inside a hot car.

Dogs kept too long outdoors are miserable during sizzling summers because dog houses usually fail to provide ample cooling. Water, especially if it sits inside a metal bowl, heats up rapidly as well. The dog sheds fur, but not enough to keep cool under a blazing sun.

Symptoms of heatstroke are high fever, vomiting, collapse, and gray tone to the lips and mouth. If your dog displays any of these symptoms, bring him indoors immediately to a cool house. Soak towels with cold water and wrap them around the dog's body. Administer cool water to the dog. If he refuses to drink, wipe the insides of his mouth with water. Place him in front of a fan. Call your veterinarian to say that your dog has experienced a heatstroke and that you are on the way.

Do not leave a Chihuahua or any other dog outside in high temperatures for an extended time. It is cruel and inhumane. Chihuahuas are companion animals who are meant to live as house dogs.

Poisoning

Simple household items like aspirin or scouring powder can be toxic to a Chihuahua. So can rat poison, chewing gum, and azalea plants. If your Chihuahua ingests any toxic substance, he needs immediate care. He also needs emergency care if that toxin comes from another animal, such as a snake. Call the National Animal Poison Control Center (NAPCC) at 1-888-426-4435 to speak with a veterinarian. Your credit card will be charged. Alternatively, get your dog in for emergency treatment as quickly as possible. Do not delay, and never self-medicate when you suspect poisoning.

CHAPTER 9

CHIHUAHUA TRAINING

Chapter 4 discussed basic obedience commands and how to teach your Chihuahua to obey those commands. The importance of obedience was also raised. A Chihuahua who is obedient to your instructions on command is a pleasure to be around. He is welcomed at dog parks, nursing homes, or at Aunt Maggie's country cabin. He is unlikely to pick fights with other dogs or cats or exhibit aggression while in the vet's lobby waiting to be seen for his annual checkup.

WHY INTERMEDIATE TRAIN?

Landlords and co-op boards may be particular about renting to tenants who own dogs. Owners must often show that their dogs have passed a canine good citizenship test before moving in. Eviction proceedings ensue when dogs, including Chihuahuas, behave badly. Housing issues are another reason why dogs should be properly trained. No pet owner should lose a home because of a misbehaved dog.

This chapter delves into intermediate obedience training and why these commands are part of responsible dog ownership. If a Chihuahua does not sit when told or scurries

away when ordered to heel, it is not his fault—he never learned how. The owner neglected obedience training when the dog was a puppy. Bad behavior is just one of the many reasons why dogs, including Chihuahuas, end up at animal shelters. Ill-behaved dogs are often young, social, healthy, and loving, just out of control. A naughty Great Dane is harder to handle than a Chihuahua without manners, but both dogs can become good canine citizens through proper behavior training methods.

Training begins at home with a responsible, dedicated owner. Practice with your adult dog every day for at least 15 minutes. Puppies, as I have mentioned, have shorter attention spans and lose focus after five minutes or so. It is best not to overwhelm your dog, so if you see he is tiring, call it quits. Try again later or resume the next day.

The key to solid training is consistency. If your schedule heats up and you miss a day of practice, your dog will not suffer. However, do not skip more than a few days unless a true emergency arises. Your dog may lose some skills after such a long lapse and require brushing up so that he does not lose ground.

Now your six-month old Chihuahua puppy or adopted adult dog has mastered basic commands. He sits or stays when told. He comes when you call his name. Be proud of these terrific accomplishments. Your dog has come a long way, but he still has the potential to learn more. What comes next? Remember that Chihuahuas are smart and clever, even though they can have a stubborn streak. Be patient, because Chihuahuas eventually emerge victorious from behavior lessons. Your dog may still cop an attitude, but he is a Chihuahua after all. That will not stop him from excelling in obedience; in fact, he may surprise you at all the skills he can accomplish.

WHEN TO MOVE TO INTERMEDIATE TRAINING

If your Chihuahua learned the commands from Chapter 4, he is ready to move up to the next level, especially if you plan to enter the highly competitive show ring or agility circuit. Therapy dogs also need advanced

Is Your Chihuahua a Well-Behaved Dog?

- Does get along with other dogs?
- Does he obey you?
- Does he like your family, friends, and neighbors?
- Does he walk nicely on a leash?

If the answer is yes to any of the questions, be proud that you live with a well-behaved dog. A "no" reply suggests that your Chihuahua would benefit from either a round of home obedience training or a class with a trainer or at an animal shelter. Classes are a great way to meet other dog owners and to learn the latest in behavior techniques from the professionals.

behavior training to pass the certification test that allows them to visit patients in hospitals, nursing homes, assisted living facilities, and rehab centers. Most groups require recertification every two years, so your therapy dog has to pass that same behavior test again.

Training sessions should be short and focused so that your Chihuahua does not lose attention. Have a purpose for each session, such as teaching him a particular command like *heel* or *sit-stay*. Older puppies and adult dogs can sometimes get distracted if family members are around. Work with your dog alone in a separate room. Each session should be pleasurable for both owner and dog, not a form of drudgery. For example, if you have houseguests, let your dog show off his commands. Alternatively, ask your dog to sit before you put down his dinner or give him a snack.

Again, if he fails to obey a command or has trouble grasping your instructions, never punish him. He may resist training because a whack is on the way. Take time to reflect. Either he needs more time to master a command or he does not understand your instructions. Perhaps your voice is too harsh or too garbled. Some men have naturally gruff voices, while other people do not speak clearly. Maybe there are distractions in the house such as loud music, another pet, or children playing. Or there is a remote chance that your dog has a hearing problem that should be evaluated by a veterinarian. Training your dog goes along more smoothly in a quiet, peaceful environment. Concentrate on his good behaviors and try to overcome what he has not accomplished.

Refrain from starting a lesson if you are tired, ill, or in a bad mood. Put off training until you are rested or feel better. At the same

When training something new, start in a distraction-free environment.

time, if your Chihuahua is napping, let him enjoy the rest. Wait until he wakes up before you start.

INTERMEDIATE COMMANDS

Working with toy breeds like the Chihuahua can sometimes require more patience because they are small and stubborn. You may have to get down to their level to effectively teach an obedience lesson. But you will be pleased to live with a well-trained dog.

Heel

The *heel* command is more common in dog shows but is nonetheless a good command to add to your Chihuahua's behavioral skills. Before teaching *heel*, he must already respond

to the *come* command. Otherwise, he will not learn to heel.

Basically, the heel involves having a dog who walks calmly on the leash and when told will sit by the owner's left heel. He will stay there until given a release command. A dog who heels does not spring at a passing dog, nor will he scramble after a cat in the neighbor's yard. Instead, he will stay by your heel once you give the command.

How to Teach It

To teach the heel, your Chihuahua must be leashed. Nearly all dog trainers and previously published behavior manuals recommend that the dog be on your left side during sessions. This does not mean that you cannot teach this command holding your Chihuahua with your

The *heel* involves a dog who walks calmly on the leash.

right hand. For consistency purposes, stick with the recommended left side.

1. Hold a treat in your right hand and encourage your dog to stay close to your left side.
2. Gently persuade him to walk as you grasp the leash. If he stays still, use the treat to lure him. Never yank or pull on the leash. That will hurt his neck or even his trachea. In training, the leash should be used only to keep the dog in place.
3. Because Chihuahuas are so small, you may have to bend over to reward him with a treat. Do not reinforce the bad behavior of jumping up for a snack. He will end up jumping up on others too. Discourage jumping behavior.
4. As you take a few steps with your dog, stop and say "Heel." Speak with calm encouragement.
5. If he responds correctly, praise him when he is in the *heel* position. Hold the leash to gently keep him from meandering off to the side. Repeat this a few times.
6. Every time he heels (only in training) offer him a tiny treat, such as a meat snack, piece of cooked hot dog, or bit of chopped carrot. After he has accomplished the *heel*, start skipping the treats or he'll expect one every time he heels.

Do not force a heel on every single walk when he has mastered the command. Let him sniff and take care of business on his daily outings. Use the *heel* command when it is needed. Say you run into a neighbor on your morning walk around the block and you start to chat. Then ask your Chihuahua to heel. He should sit nicely by your heels and not dart off. Dogs score points in shows for heeling.

Stay

The *stay* command sounds basic and uncomplicated. Really, it is. *Stay* serves several purposes for the dog and owner. If a guest arrives who is antsy around dogs, your Chihuahua should obey your *stay* order and not dash toward the door. Even a Chihuahua can be intimidating to someone who is fearful of dogs. On the other hand, say for instance a family member or friend inadvertently leaves the front door ajar. Your heart pounds when your curious Chihuahua scampers towards the curb and a car is speeding down the block. The *stay* command can save him from a fatal car accident. It can also prevent him from wandering off and becoming lost.

How to Teach It

Before he's ready to tackle the *stay* command, a Chihuahua must first know how to sit. If he is not fully trained to sit, then both of you need more practice before moving on to the *stay*. This is how it works:

1. With your Chihuahua in the sit position, raise your flattened palm like a stop sign and say "Stay." Speak calmly and gently.
2. Inch back a few steps, then return to your original position in front with your dog.
3. If he moves, offer no praise or snack but absolutely no punishment. Repeat that step again.
4. While your Chihuahua sits, raise your hand and say "Stay." Step back and return. If he has not moved, reward him with praise and a snack so that he understands the good behavior to repeat.
5. When you are confident that he can stay in the same position without moving for a

few seconds, gradually increase the space between you and your dog. Add a little time too before offering praise.

6. Release your dog with an "Okay.".

The eventual goal is to lengthen his stay for a full minute while you move at least 10 feet (3 m) away. A Chihuahua who can accomplish an extended *stay* is a well-behaved dog.

Training Tidbit

Chihuahuas sometimes have Napoleonic complexes, so training may send you into a hissy fit. But he needs you to help him become a good canine citizen. Let the following tips guide you during training:

1. Be patient at all times.
2. Show consistency.
3. Do not train when you are tired.
4. Offer treats and praise to reward good behavior.
5. Never punish the dog for mistakes.
6. Ask for help from other dog owners, veterinarians or trainers.
7. Vary sessions so he is not bored. Training takes time.

Your Chihuahua puppy or adult may not learn each behavior command on the first try. Each dog picks up skills at a different pace. Practice sessions should be fun, not exhaustive or punitive. A dog gets more out of pleasurable sessions. You will too.

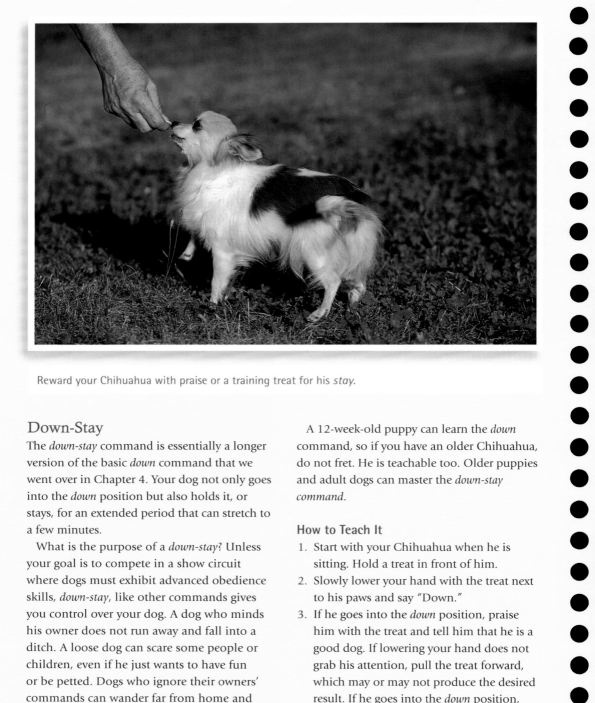

Reward your Chihuahua with praise or a training treat for his *stay*.

Down-Stay

The *down-stay* command is essentially a longer version of the basic *down* command that we went over in Chapter 4. Your dog not only goes into the *down* position but also holds it, or stays, for an extended period that can stretch to a few minutes.

What is the purpose of a *down-stay*? Unless your goal is to compete in a show circuit where dogs must exhibit advanced obedience skills, *down-stay*, like other commands gives you control over your dog. A dog who minds his owner does not run away and fall into a ditch. A loose dog can scare some people or children, even if he just wants to have fun or be petted. Dogs who ignore their owners' commands can wander far from home and may never be found.

A 12-week-old puppy can learn the *down* command, so if you have an older Chihuahua, do not fret. He is teachable too. Older puppies and adult dogs can master the *down-stay command*.

How to Teach It

1. Start with your Chihuahua when he is sitting. Hold a treat in front of him.
2. Slowly lower your hand with the treat next to his paws and say "Down."
3. If he goes into the *down* position, praise him with the treat and tell him that he is a good dog. If lowering your hand does not grab his attention, pull the treat forward, which may or may not produce the desired result. If he goes into the *down* position, great, he earns a reward.

Never use force to get the dog into the down position. You may cause physical harm. Secondly, he will not find the exercise pleasurable if it causes him pain or discomfort. Not every Chihuahua learns at the same pace. Some need more time than others. Once he grasps a concept you can move on to the next one.

Once he is good at the *down command*, add the *stay* command. Again, use positive reinforcement so that he understands the behavior.

1. Follow the above suggestions for the teaching the *down*. Once he is in the *down* position, ask him to stay.
2. Walk about 10 feet (3 m) away and see whether he holds the position.
3. Time him to see how long he can stay.

See whether he can hold it for at least one minute. That is about how long dogs must stay to pass the behavior test to become a registered therapy dog.

4. Reward him if he stays. If not, try again until he gets it.
5. Release him with an "Okay."
6. Add more time. See whether he can hold the *down*-stay position for two minutes. Always follow with a reward of a snack and/or praise to spur motivation.

Chihuahuas are so close to the ground anyway that teaching the *down-stay* sometimes is more work on the owners. They often have to crouch down to be level with the dog so that training goes smoothly. For those with a bad back, this lesson may be more stressful for the owner than the Chihuahua.

The *down-stay* position is a longer version of the *down* position.

Sit-Stay

Having a dog who obeys the *sit-stay* command indicates that the owner is in charge, not the dog. That is how it should be. No matter how much you love your dog, the owner should always have control. Chihuahuas have minds of their own and often do as they please. One minute a Chihuahua can be seated on his owner's lap in a dog park. But then he will clamp his teeth around a much larger dog's neck, putting himself in danger. For the Chihuahua's own protection, he should learn the *sit-stay* command and respond to it when told. It can spare his life or save him from being stitched up.

Teaching a dog to sit is a central component of training. If he does not know the *sit* command, it will be hard to teach anything else. When Grandma comes for Sunday dinner,

Multi-Dog Tip

Barking dogs can often be annoying to their owner and the neighbors. But a few Chihuahuas barked for a reason. On June 15, 2009, a trio of 3-pound (1.5-kg) Chihuahuas in southern California barked so loudly that they woke up their owner, Ana Lee Spray, who promptly investigated. Her three Chihuahuas fended off a mountain lion near the opening to her garage. According to KTLA News, the dogs refused to back off, cornering the big cat. When authorities arrived, they acted surprised that the Chihuahuas had fought off a mountain lion. (KTLA News 6/15/09)

Want to Know More?

To brush up on basic training skills, see Chapter 4: Training Your Chihuahua Puppy.

you do not want your dog jumping up on her. It is best if he sits nicely by your side as you greet Grandma. Admittedly, a leaping Chihuahua is not too disruptive, but he can still cause an elderly person or a small child to stumble. Learning the *sit-stay* command adds to his charm and makes him a polite little dog. You will be seen as a responsible owner.

How to Teach It

1. Hold a small treat in front of your Chihuahua.
2. Move the treat slightly above his nose. He will naturally raise his snout toward the treat.
3. Position your hand just over the dog's head and he will move himself into the *sit* position.
4. As he sits, say the word "Sit" and offer the treat. Make sure that he is seated before offering the reward.
5. Repeat this command several times and in several places in your home or yard or on your porch.

Teach him to sit inside the house as well as outside. He should be comfortable in both environments.

Adding the *stay* position to the sit position sounds complicated but is not. He already knows the two commands, *sit* and *stay*. You are just combining them as one.

To teach the *sit-stay* command:

1. Leash your dog and put him in the *heel* position.
2. Apply a little tension to the collar, but do not yank or pull him.

3. Face the dog and say the word "Stay," using a hand/palm motion that stops by his nose. Then step away from your dog. Hold the leash so that you cannot go far.
4. Count to ten and return to your dog's side. Praise him for being a good dog and release him with your release word.
5. Repeat the procedure several times.

Some Chihuahuas understand how to *sit-stay* right away; others need more time. Be patient. Eventually, every Chihuahua will be a master at the command and you will be a delighted owner.

Stand

Most dogs, including Chihuahuas, would rather cuddle up in a warm place, eat a bowl of kibble or munch on a treat, or just be with their families. Standing is not a typical position for them except when they are alerted to someone at the door. Then the Chihuahua investigates, yapping furiously. There may be times, however, when you want your Chihuahua to stand, so you should teach him this command.

Obeying the *stand* command is required in dog shows, so you may not think that it is important to teach your Chihuahua if you don't intend to enter him in conformation events. The *stand* command, however, serves other useful purposes. A visit to the veterinarian goes smoother if your dog stands up on command. The groomer has an easier time clipping his nails if he cooperates by standing up at your command.

How to Teach It

To teach the *stand*, your Chihuahua should be seated at your side, off leash.

1. Bend down to your dog's level because he is so small. You both should face forward.
2. Hold a treat at nose level about six inches

(15 cm) away from his face.
3. Say the word "Stand." As you say the word, move the treat away from your dog's face, being sure to keep the treat at nose level. As you move the treat away, your dog will stand in order to move forward and follow the treat.
4. As soon as your dog is on all fours, give him a treat.
5. Repeat this sequence until your dog is performing this behavior consistently and reliably. Step away while he holds the position for at least 60 seconds.

By the Numbers

Chihuahuas respond to positive reinforcement, including the use of treats during training. Too many snacks may lead to a portly pooch. Here are four alternatives to training with food:
1. Use only bite-sized snacks with Chihuahuas.
2. Buy only healthful brands of treats.
3. Try small pieces of carrots.
4. Dice chicken or cheese used as treats.

Remember that treats are an important part of training; so is verbal praise and stroking your dog when he responds favorably to commands. Do not overlook those training tools in your lessons.

CHAPTER 10

CHIHUAHUA PROBLEM BEHAVIORS

Incessant barking, shredding the rosebushes, and chewing on your new living room furniture. Does this sound like your Chihuahua? Problem behaviors can lead to apartment evictions, the cost of replacing damaged items, or neighbors who turn the other way when they see you walking your Chihuahua. Friends, coworkers, and family may decline invitations to your home because your dog is a pest.

Frustrated owners ignore the problem behaviors, confine the dog in a crate for long periods, throw him in the backyard, or abandon him to a shelter. None of those actions corrects the bad behavior. Neither the Chihuahua nor the owner is helped. If the Chihuahua ends up in an animal shelter, he may not be adopted and the owner, if she gets another dog, may face similar challenges with an equally mule-headed Chihuahua. Giving up should not be an option.

So if your Chihuahua puppy or adult starts to exhibit unacceptable behaviors, many of which are traced to boredom or bad breeding, step in and do something right away. Be proactive rather than reactive. Positive corrective training methods will teach your Chihuahua to give up gnawing on

your sofa, howling all day, or nipping at the neighbor's ankles. With your steady guidance he will let go of troubling habits and learn how to behave properly. Everyone will be content.

Discussed in this chapter are a number of common canine problem behaviors you may encounter with your Chihuahua. Corrective methods are suggested to help you and your Chihuahua overcome these hurdles.

AGGRESSION

Aggression can be the result of sloppy breeding, past physical or extreme verbal abuse, serious illness, or rough handling. Dogs who bite are always a problem. Biting is totally unacceptable. If your Chihuahua bites another animal or person, take that very seriously. Even though the Chihuahua is small, his dog bite is potentially dangerous and costly. Dogs are pack animals, and the Chihuahua may be trying to throw his weight around. Biting is not an appropriate way to achieve ranking or status in the pack.

An aggressive Chihuahua may display one or all of the following signs:
• growling
• snarling

- showing teeth
- tail hanging down between back legs
- fur rising on his back
- staring
- hunched-down position

Roughhousing with other dogs or the family cat can be natural for a dog at play. Puppies and young dogs, even toy dogs like Chihuahuas, enjoy chasing balls or chewing on squeeze toys. Dogs who live together share toys. Now and then there may be resistance when one grabs a toy from the other, but they generally learn and respect boundaries. Chihuahuas in particular favor their own kind. They hardly ever gripe when another Chihuahua swipes their toy.

If your Chihuahua lunges at another animal during play or sinks his teeth into the neck, be concerned. A larger dog with aggressive tendencies could retaliate and seriously harm your Chihuahua. On the other hand, if your Chihuahua is out of control he may hurt another toy dog, a puppy, or a cat. Worse yet, he may bite a human—and that lands you in big trouble.

How to Find a Reliable Behaviorist

Anyone can call themselves a dog behaviorist. To help find an experienced, ethical behaviorist, look for someone certified with the American Veterinary Society of Animal Behavior (www.avsabonline. org), The Animal Behavior Society (www.animalbehavior.org), or a trainer who specializes in behavior (www.ccpdt.org).

Any dog displaying signs of aggression should receive professional help.

How to Manage It

First and foremost, any dog displaying signs of aggression should receive professional help. But while employing the services of a professional, there are a few things you can do to understand and deal with the situation. First examine the aggression. What causes it? Are children or teens picking on your dog? Do other dogs at home push him around? Does someone at home resent his presence? Is he aggressive around food? Was he food- deprived in the past? Was he properly socialized as a puppy? Did he come from a puppy mill?

There are a number of ways to avoid and to deal with canine aggression.

- Always socialize your puppy or adopted dog. A dog who is part of the family is unlikely to become mean or aggressive.

- Never isolate your Chihuahua in the back yard or on a chain. Separating a dog from his family is cruel and inhumane.
- Neutering male dogs often reduces aggressive tendencies. Dog-bite cases sometimes end up in municipal courts. Judges may demand that the dog owner neuter the male dog as a precondition for release.
- Nursing moms normally protect their puppies. That is their natural instinct. Keep children and strangers away from a mother dog and her puppies. In their fascination with puppies, children may attempt to pick one up to cuddle. The mother dog may see the child as a threat and bite. In her view, mama is guarding her offspring from an unknown predator, even though that predator attends kindergarten or sucks his thumb. The dog does not know any better. We adults are more cognizant, so we have to be conscientious around children and nursing dogs.

Fear Biting

Some Chihuahuas fear bite, the result of poor breeding, lack of socialization, genetics, or past abuse. A fear biter should never be around children and should be seen by a professional dog trainer. The dog fears that he will be abused again, so he strikes out first. He may fear large men or even women with blond hair—whoever made him miserable. Modifying his behavior by slowly exposing him to these fears, bit by bit, should help him overcome them. For example, if he is terrified of men, the dog should be adopted into a female-only household. But at times men will enter his life, so he should get used to them. Let a friendly man talk to him and feed him treats or bits of kibble. If that works, then the friendly man can walk him. All of the moves

should be slow and supervised by the dog's owner or a dog trainer. Some dogs never overcome their fears, and they must be kept apart from the source.

Food Aggression

A Chihuahua who was food-deprived may be aggressive around his meals. There are several ways to handle food aggression. Everyone in the household should alternate feeding the puppy so that he is used to the entire family. If he snarls as you approach his food bowl, do not attempt to pick up his food. Back off because he could snap or bite. Next time feed him by hand. Chihuahuas are smart; they will not bite someone who feeds them. When you sense that he is more comfortable, drop a few bits of kibble into his bowl. After he eats it, drop a few more. He should become less protective of his food bowl. The process

Aggression: Consult a Professional

Consider enrolling your dog in obedience training with a professional trainer or at an animal shelter. If training tips and behavior modification efforts fail to control your Chihuahua's aggression, consult your veterinarian to rule out an underlying disease. An illness that causes discomfort, such as dental decay or arthritis, may cause him to nip or bite. Your Chihuahua has to know that you are in charge, not him. Do not ignore a dog who bites. You may end up in court, and a judge may order your dog to be euthanized. Always consult your veterinarian or a dog trainer about an aggressive dog.

Boredom can lead to excessive barking.

takes a little time, but the end result will be a calmer and better-adjusted Chihuahua.

If he lashes out at only one family or household member, let that person feed the dog. He will not starve himself by refusing the dog food. Giving him treats will also sweeten the pot. Until the relationship is smoothed, the Chihuahua should go for walks with the person he does not like.

BARKING (EXCESSIVE)

All dogs bark. That is how they communicate so that their owners know that they are hungry, have to eliminate, or to let them know that someone is approaching the home. Some dogs bark during play or even in spurts while asleep. Barking, however, can escalate to the point where it is out of control. Too much barking may violate local noise control ordinances. You could be slapped with a hefty fine by your condominium association or landlord. If enough neighbors complain or sign

a petition, you may be threatened with eviction or removal of your dog from the premises.

How to Manage It

Do not ignore uncontrollable incessant yapping or barking. You risk losing your dwelling and your dog. Help is available, but the barking behavior will not stop on its own.

Boredom often leads to excess barking. Examine your lifestyle. Do you live by yourself? Is the Chihuahua your only pet? How old is the Chihuahua? Does he spend eight to nine hours a day by himself? Does he have an abusive past? Was he a yard dog who had to bark for attention?

Determine whether your behavior or lifestyle causes the barking, especially if you have a young dog or puppy. Out of desperation, he may bark for attention if left alone too long. He may want to play or someone to cuddle with. The Chihuahua may even bark because he is hungry. What about your neighbors? Is there constant ruckus next door, such as kids playing, boisterous music, and people coming and going? Your Chihuahua responds to the commotion, which he sees as an invasion of his space.

Dogs naturally bark when guests rap on the door or ring the bell. In fact, barking may alert you to an intruder. In that case, barking is good.

To control excess barking, you have several options.

- Enroll your Chihuahua in doggy day care when you go out.
- Hire a dog-sitter to spend time with your dog while you are at work, or leave your Chihuahua with a trusted friend, neighbor, or family member.
- If your dog is crated, place his crate away from the window and door so that he is not

bothered by outside noise.

- Leave him with plenty of toys or chew bones to keep him occupied.
- Play soft music as a distraction while you are gone.

Finally, practice behavior modification. Knock on the door to elicit a bark. Say "Enough" in a firm voice. When he stops barking, reward him with a treat and praise. Every time there is a knock at the door, repeat the word "Enough. As soon as he is quiet, reward him. Food should distract him from barking and reinforce the cessation of barking on command, thus giving the owner more control.

If nothing stems the uncontrolled barking, consult your veterinarian or a professional dog trainer for further assistance.

CHEWING

A dog with nothing to do chews to pass the time. Teething puppies or untrained adult dogs can wreck entire households including new sofas, reclining chairs, leather purses, designer shoes, venetian blinds, lace curtains, and end tables. The list of items they can destroy is endless; some even surprising. Okay, the sofa that a Chihuahua chews apart will have more stuffing left inside than if a Mastiff got to it, but still, chewing is chewing.

Some dogs chew when they are nervous. Is tension smothering your household? Do you and your spouse bicker often? Perhaps your Chihuahua chews when he is uneasy or anxious.

How to Manage It

How do you deal with destructive chewing?

Crate training as mentioned in Chapter 4 is one of the most effective ways to curb destructive chewing. A puppy or adult dog has no way to rip apart your recliner if he is crated.

- Your dog should always have access to chew bones, like Nylabones, and toys. Chihuahuas, like most other dogs, easily tire of the same toys, so vary his playthings.
- Enroll your dog in an obedience training class.
- Exercise your dog regularly. A tired dog is less likely to be destructive while you are not home.
- Never give your dog old shoes or sneakers as playthings. He does not know the difference between an old ragged shoe ready for the Goodwill box and a brand-new pair of designer shoes. To him a shoe is a shoe. Dogs should play only with dog toys.
- If you see your dog with a favorite item in his mouth, do not tear it out. Tell him in a firm voice to "Drop it." Then praise him or reward him with a treat and replace the item with a toy or dog bone.
- Doggy day care or leaving your dog with friends or family may be an option until he overcomes the destructive chewing behavior.

Multi-Dog Tip

One dog walks nicely on a leash; the other does not. Do you leave the unruly dog home? Of course not. Practice daily leash walking inside your home or apartment a few steps at a time. If your dog still resists the leash, invest in a Gentle Leader, which is a collar that lessens or removes a dog's urge to pull. That restricts his movements and prevents him from pulling to the side. Then you can enjoy a peaceful morning walk with both Chihuahuas.

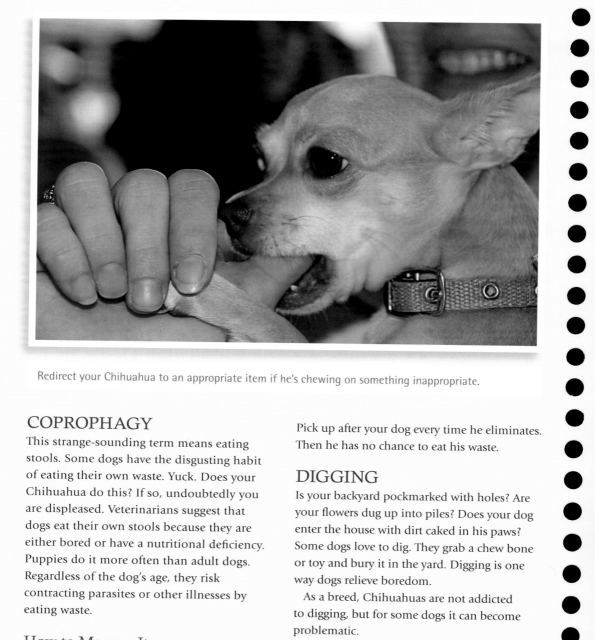

Redirect your Chihuahua to an appropriate item if he's chewing on something inappropriate.

COPROPHAGY

This strange-sounding term means eating stools. Some dogs have the disgusting habit of eating their own waste. Yuck. Does your Chihuahua do this? If so, undoubtedly you are displeased. Veterinarians suggest that dogs eat their own stools because they are either bored or have a nutritional deficiency. Puppies do it more often than adult dogs. Regardless of the dog's age, they risk contracting parasites or other illnesses by eating waste.

How to Manage It

To stop coprophagy, consult your veterinarian. Your dog may need digestive enzymes or Vitamin B added to his food. Another way to deal with coprophagy is to keep the yard clean.

Pick up after your dog every time he eliminates. Then he has no chance to eat his waste.

DIGGING

Is your backyard pockmarked with holes? Are your flowers dug up into piles? Does your dog enter the house with dirt caked in his paws? Some dogs love to dig. They grab a chew bone or toy and bury it in the yard. Digging is one way dogs relieve boredom.

As a breed, Chihuahuas are not addicted to digging, but for some dogs it can become problematic.

How to Manage It

You cannot take away a dog's natural digging instinct, but you can teach him how to control it. First, look at why and where he digs. If he is bored, provide him with stimulation. Give him toys to play with and rotate them so that he has a variety. Chihuahuas get bored with the same toys. Consider bringing home another dog as a playmate. Also, restrict him to one area of the yard. That is his space, so if he digs, you won't be upset.

Safety is a concern for dogs who dig. Some are such prodigious diggers that they paw their way under fences. Once they are away from home, they can be hit by cars or become lost forever. Chihuahuas are not especially likely to escape, but if you have a tenacious dog that digs under the fence, stop him from getting out. Bury rocks, bricks, or chicken wire near the fencing to discourage him.

Walk your dog before you leave in the morning. Tire him out so he sleeps most of the day. An exhausted dog is less likely to engage in destructive digging. Alternatively, hire a dog walker so that he gets out during the day for exercise.

Dogs also dig for another reason. Holes in the ground offer them an escape from the summer heat. If that is why your dog digs, provide him with adequate protection from the sun, such as an insulated dog house. Chihuahuas should not be outside dogs, however.

JUMPING UP

Dogs naturally race to the door when owners arrive home or company shows up. In fact, as soon as they hear the car door slam and keys jingle they are off and running. The canine greeting includes a tail wag, sometimes an excited bark, and nearly always jumping on you. They want your attention.

A Great Dane with no training is likely to flatten you at the front door. But a 4-pound (2-kg) Chihuahua? Toy breeds hardly have enough force to knock anyone over except

perhaps a small child or a frail senior. Owners have to decide whether they can live with jumping. Some can, while others cannot.

How to Manage It

Only consistency can modify jumping. Either it is okay or it is not. The Chihuahua does not understand that on Monday evening he can throw himself at the owner coming home from work but on Wednesday at noon he has to restrain himself when 78-year-old Uncle Joe visits from Omaha.

How do you discourage jumping? As soon as you or someone else enters the front door, order your dog firmly but gently to sit and stay. Bend down so that you are at his level and offer generous praise. Withhold praise and

Training Tidbit

Dogs with separation anxiety act out shortly after you leave. Fearful of being alone, they tear up furniture, books, lamps, or whatever is in sight. If crating or confinement is not possible, leave for a few minutes and then return. Assure the dog with generous physical praise. Repeat these steps several times. The dog will build up confidence because he believes that you are coming back. If you cannot visit during midday, ask a friend, neighbor, or relative to check on your dog. Constant reassurance helps the dog overcome separation anxiety. Dogs with extreme separation anxiety cannot be left alone for long periods.

You have to decide whether jumping up is a behavior you can live with.

attention if he jumps. If he sits, pay attention to him. Be consistent with jumping or your Chihuahua may become confused. Either he can jump on you or the behavior is not okay.

LEASH PULLING

Walking a dog who yanks, tugs, or simply refuses to be led on a leash is not enjoyable. Can an unruly Chihuahua knock you off balance or send you tumbling? Probably not, but your Chihuahua should walk nicely on a leash, a skill learned as a puppy. (We discussed leash training for puppies in Chapter 4.)

If you acquire your Chihuahua when he is an adult, he may already know how to walk on a leash. If not, he needs practice. Remember, some Chihuahuas may have spent their entire lives locked outside and never walked on a leash. Be patient and he will pick up leash training. In fact, a neglected Chihuahua will probably enjoy daily walks because no one paid attention to him before.

How to Manage It

Chihuahuas fit snugly into shoulder bags. Carrying your Chihuahua around is fine, but do not overlook the leash. Even if you live in a house and your Chihuahua uses the back yard to relieve himself, circumstances may change. You may move into an apartment or condo. Illness or injury may force you to have a neighbor walk your dog. Leash training then becomes crucial.

Leash your dog every day, even if it is just to walk around your apartment, condo grounds, or yard. Offer praise when the dog walks at a steady clip next to you. If he yanks or pulls, stop walking. Order him into the sit position. Wait a few seconds, then try walking again. If he whines or moans, ignore him—but never drag him by the leash. That can hurt his neck. Gently coax him to take a few steps; he may walk only a few steps at a time. Stay calm. With encouragement, praise, and the occasional treat, he will walk more each time. Eventually you and your dog will walk to the corner or around the block. He may even wake you up in the morning ready for his daily trot around the block.

For the recalcitrant dog who resists the leash, consider using a Gentle Leader. The Gentle Leader applies no pressure to the dog's throat and is a painless way to control a dog who has a tendency to lunge.

NIPPING

A teething puppy may nip when someone tries to pet him or pick him up. Rarely is this

Want to Know More?

For a refresher on how to teach the sit-stay, see Chapter 9: Chihuahua Training.

behavior aggressive, but end it while he is a pup. Grabbing hold of someone's hand is not acceptable when he is an adult, at which point he may bite. Then it is serious. He may be confined at a shelter for biting, and you may be hit with a costly lawsuit. Dogbite cases sometimes end up in court.

How to Manage It

When your pup tries to nip your hand or fingers, offer him a toy instead. If he lives with a family, everyone must be on board.

Consistent behavior is imperative. Do not slap or hit the pup for nipping. Rather, firmly tell him "No," but always offer him an alternative, such as a chew bone or squeak toy. You can also offer him a dog biscuit.

If the pup's nipping is accompanied by growling or snarling, consult your veterinarian. Perhaps there is an underlying medical issue that is causing his bad behavior. Aggression must be dealt with right away even though the Chihuahua weighs only a few pounds (kg). Do not ignore aggressive behavior in a puppy.

SEPARATION ANXIETY

Dogs with separation anxiety are often young, perfectly healthy, and full of love. Some are purebred, like your Chihuahua. They may

Carrying around your Chihuahua is fine, but he still needs to be leash trained.

end up in animal shelters because owners are frustrated by their unruly behavior. Not knowing that the destructive behavior can be turned around, owners either surrender them to shelters or chain them in the back yard. Neither solution serves the dog or the owner. The dog will probably be euthanized, and the owner may face separation anxiety with another dog.

Dogs with separation anxiety may bark as if competing for the first prize in a yapping contest. They may howl for hours, upsetting your neighbors, or exhibit some of the aforementioned destructive behaviors, such as digging, chewing, or nipping. They may even chew their own body parts, such as their tails or paws, inflicting serious damage. Some dogs dig inside the house, ripping up parts of the carpeting. Other dogs dig through screen doors, eat through drywall, or knock over bookcases. A really stricken dog may leap over the fence and get lost if you have a doggy door. A Chihuahua cannot knock over a bookcase or scale a 6- foot (2-m) fence, but if there is a hole in the wood or metal fencing, he can get out.

What causes separation anxiety? The puppy may have been removed from the litter far too early. As a rule, puppies should stay with their nursing moms until they are at least two months old. An adult dog may have been dumped by a thoughtless owner in a remote mountain region or at a city garbage site. Perhaps he fended for himself for weeks or months, scraping out a living by eating garbage. Maybe he survived snowstorms or the blistering desert heat of the southwest. A dog who faced weeks or months of extreme deprivation may fear starvation again when the owner leaves. He does not understand that you or someone else in the family will be home at the end of the day.

By the Numbers

Three- month-old puppies naturally teethe. They may chew or nip on your hand or fingers. Discourage such behavior by inserting a chew toy or Nylabone into the puppy's mouth. Say "No" in a firm voice if the puppy attempts to nip or chew on hands, but never use physical force to correct the behavior. It does not work. Only positive reinforcement shapes good behavior.

A dog's routine is upended when he lands in an animal shelter. He often cannot cope with the stress. Yes, dogs face stress when sent to shelters, because animal shelters are usually large, loud, and impersonal places. Shelter workers and volunteers provide the dog with his basic needs, namely food and water, but the dog is confused. All he wants is his home, complete with his bed, toys, and premium dog food. In most cases, however, going home is no longer possible. A dog with separation anxiety, regardless of age, causes most of the destruction as soon as you walk out the door. Later in the day, you return home to find the fluffy insides of your sofa scattered inside the living room or shards of pottery sitting by the coffee table. Scolding the dog at 5:00 p.m. does not help. Your Chihuahua will have no recollection of the massive damage he caused at 8:00 a.m. In fact, he'll be wagging his tail, showing how happy he is to see you. He'll expect you to serve him dinner when you feel like screaming, so do not yell or hit him. Physical punishment does not correct the bad behavior.

Separation anxiety can also be caused by boredom. The dog is lonely and sad without company. He has nothing to do and no one to entertain him. Dogs are pack animals. Without their pack around, they sometimes act out.

How to Manage It

How can you deal with separation anxiety?

- Crate the dog or confine him in a safe, secure space while you are out.
- Do not chain him outdoors. (It does not shape positive behavior.)
- Exercise him before leaving so that he is tired.
- Consider adding another dog or cat to the household so he has company.
- Leave on the radio so that he does not feel alone.
- Try doggy day care or leaving him with friends, family, or neighbors.
- If possible, take him to work.
- Talk to your veterinarian about herbal remedies or medication to combat stress.
- Leave the house and make no fuss. The dog should see your departure as normal.
- Enroll him in behavior training.
- Never punish him with physical force.
- Spend quality time with your dog when you are home.

THUNDERPHOBIA

Dogs fearful of thunderstorms can go into a panic at the first clap of thunder or flash of lightning. Some are so fearful that they crash through glass doors or windows. If they have access to the yard, they leap over the fence and flee in fear. A 5-pound (2.5-kg) Chihuahua does not have the strength to power through a glass patio door, but he can do a lot of damage to himself and your house if thunderstorms scare him. A storm may descend on your area while you are at work. What should you do?

How to Manage It

1. Keep your dog indoors all the time.
2. Make sure that doors and windows are locked.
3. Outside gates should be secure (in case you have a doggy door).
4. Consider Bach Flower remedy for stress relief.
5. Confine the dog to a small area if a storm is forecasted.
6. Consult your veterinarian for hard-to-manage cases.

Talk to your veterinarian about herbal remedies or medication to combat stress.

CHAPTER 11

CHIHUAHUA SPORTS AND ACTIVITIES

The world is changing for dogs. No longer confined to herding sheep or living in the barn, most dogs are part of the family. Shelter dogs find homes in greater numbers; fewer are euthanized. Owners are open to new ideas for entertaining themselves and their dogs. Sports are yet another activity that owners and dogs can share. Agility, flyball, lure coursing, etc., also give the overactive dogs a positive release for their energy. And these are sports for Chihuahuas too.

ACTIVITIES

The great outdoors appeals to millions of Americans. Every summer they pile into cars and head for the national parks to enjoy hiking, swimming, picnics, and camping. The family dog often comes along. Dogs are welcomed in most outdoor recreational areas as long as they are leashed, licensed, and under the owner's voice command. (And you should be a responsible owner and pick up your dog's poop. No one likes to step in poop—not even the small size that a Chihuahua makes!)

Chihuahuas may not be avid mountain hikers or joggers, but they can still be part of the family fun. For instance, include them on family picnics, camping trips, or short day walks in the park. Your Chihuahua will receive fresh air and exercise and you'll have a loyal companion at your side.

Animal-Assisted Therapy

Animal-assisted therapy, also known as pet therapy, has come a long way since the 1960s when Dr. Boris Levinson, a child psychiatrist, invited his own dog to be part of therapy sessions. Patients with problem behaviors displayed improvement when the dog was present, so Levinson pursued his novel approach despite a slew of critics. Today four-footed therapists provide therapy in hospitals, long-term care centers, schools, day care centers, domestic violence shelters, and crisis nurseries.

Therapy animals are mostly dogs, but other species, such as cats, horses, rabbits, goats, and birds, are registered with the Delta Society, a nonprofit organization whose focus is to improve human health and well-being through positive interactions with animals. Therapy Dogs International (TDI), another group, restricts itself to dogs and their handlers wherever they may be needed. Both groups, however, offer a valuable service to children and adults in need.

Before you go hiking, make sure your Chihuahua's ID tags are current.

Schools offer programs in which dogs help children learn to read. Volunteers and their registered pets visit hospice patients and their families to provide solace. Patients recovering from near-fatal car accidents find motivation from animal-assisted therapy. Abused children, confused and frightened, find a shred of hope in a tail-wagging therapist rubbing against them.

Chihuahuas are among the many breeds that serve as canine therapists. Not just any animal can do therapy work. To qualify, they all must:

- pass a behavior test
- have a veterinarian sign off on a health form
- be current on vaccinations
- show comfort around strangers
- always be clean and groomed
- enjoy being handled
- not be fearful of wheelchairs, walkers, or canes

If you think that your Chihuahua is up for therapy work, contact information is available in the Appendix. It is a commitment, however. Patients or students will depend on regular visits from you and your dog. The experience is rewarding and heartwarming, but do not sign up unless you are ready.

Camping

If your Chihuahua joins the family for camping trips, he should be healthy and in good shape. Leave older or sickly dogs home with family members or friends or in a reliable boarding kennel. Dogs terrified of thunder should stay home too. A sudden storm with booming thunder or crackling lightning that sweeps through the campsite may cause your dog to flee in panic. Tracking him down in strange territory may be impossible, especially in the pouring rain.

Your dog's license and ID must be current in the unlikely event that he becomes separated. Vaccinations should also be up to date. Check campgrounds before traveling to them to make sure that pets are allowed. Some may require an additional charge. It depends on the park. If travel to the campground requires an overnight motel stay, call a few chains to see which ones are pet friendly. Be alert and not caught off guard with no place to room with your Chihuahua.

Always check the camp's pet policies. Some campgrounds are privately owned. Others are on government property. Pet-friendly cabins may be limited. As a rule, dogs are allowed in most campsites, but some prohibit breeds with a known history of aggression. If your dog barks excessively or is disruptive, management may ask you to leave.

Nearly all campgrounds require dogs to be leashed or on tie-outs. Although I oppose chaining dogs and tethering them outside, tying them to a stakeout at a campground for a few hours is acceptable. Camp policy prohibits leaving your dog unattended, however. Pet theft happens everywhere, so someone in your party must always watch your Chihuahua. If you sleep in a tent at night, your dog should be snuggled next to you. Do not leave him alone outside. Wild animals such as bears sometimes roam through campgrounds, mostly searching for food. Your dog could be at risk if he is tied outside by himself.

In the summer, locking a Chihuahua inside a car or recreational vehicle is dangerous. Temperatures can rise rapidly in just minutes. Heatstroke, kidney failure, and even death can occur in a very short time. Always look for a safe alternative.

Determine the length of your camping trip and pack your dog's supplies accordingly. Among the items he will need are:

- food, bottled water, and treats
- food and water bowls (take plastic; they are easier to carry)
- bedding and toys
- leash and tie-out
- towels
- medication if applicable
- dog first-aid kit
- crate
- plastic poop bags
- current photo (in case he gets lost)

Training Tidbit

A Chihuahua named Belle, once sick and abandoned at an Arizona shelter, made her agility debut on December 5, 2009. She placed third in her category. On January 2, 2010, she stepped up and won first place in performance level 1 on a standard course. Not bad for a dog who faced an uncertain future just two years earlier. Belle lives a comfortable life with her owner Carole Weiner in Sun Lakes, Arizona.

Have fun. Camping trips can be wonderful. It is a chance for family and friends to bond. With a little bit of planning, your Chihuahua can be part of the festivities too.

Canine Good Citizen® Program

Developed in 1989 by the American Kennel Club (AKC), the Canine Good Citizen test is a ten-step program that evaluates all breeds for temperament, behavior, obedience, and other relevant skills. Dogs do not have to be agility champs or show stars to earn a certificate either. Any well-mannered dog, regardless of breed, age, or sex, can become a canine good citizen. The program has become so popular that apartment or condo managers may ask pet owners to produce the certificate before approving a rental agreement. It is usually mandatory for a dog to register as a therapy dog. Judges who rule in aggressive dog cases may order the owner to enroll the pet in a canine good citizenship class before dismissing the case.

The AKC maintains a list of certified dog trainers who teach the classes at animal shelters, pet stores, or their own facilities. 4-H clubs offer the classes so that children can learn proper dog-handling techniques. Upon completion, the dog earns a certificate naming him as an official Canine Good Citizen.

There are few requirements to enroll other than a current dog license and inoculation record. The dog's success depends on an owner willing to learn. Becoming a Canine Good Citizen is the first step involved in agility, obedience, conformation, and other dog activities. It shows a dog who responds to his owner and obeys basic commands.

Make sure that the trainer teaching the class is certified by the AKC; even if your dog passes the class, he won't earn his Canine Good Citizenship certificate unless the class is certified.

HIKING/WALKING

Chihuahuas generally enjoy snoozing on the couch or cuddled up next to their owners in the reclining chair. Hiking through a state park or jogging for 6 miles (9.5 km) is not a typical Chihuahua activity. Strenuous outdoor activity such as jogging taxes their small bodies. Healthy Chihuahuas, however, can enjoy short relaxing walks with their

If you walk your dog in the winter, dress him in a coat, sweater, or sweatshirt.

owners. They can stroll along city streets, leafy pathways in the park, or the boardwalk at the shore. Just do not expect your Chihuahua to exercise with the same vigor as a Border Collie. Understand his limitations and the both of you can spend quality time outdoors.

There is an alternative, however, for avid hikers to spend quality time outdoors with their Chihuahuas. Buy a suitable canvas pouch to carry your Chihuahua and you both can hike up to mountain summits! Always carry water. Your dog may get thirsty. Portable canvas water bowls are available at pet stores or where camping gear is sold.

If you walk your dog in the winter, dress him in a coat, sweater, or sweatshirt. Chihuahuas do not tolerate the cold, but dressed appropriately they can still enjoy a short brisk walk. Exercise keeps them fit and trim. Be careful in the summer. Never force your Chihuahua to walk in the midday sun. Take him out in the early morning or after dark. The sizzling sun heats up the pavement. In some places like the desert southwest, the sidewalk can burn a dog's pads.

SPORTS

Sports are a national American pastime. Some might even say they are an obsession. Magazines, clubs, media, and fans are devoted to football, baseball, soccer, golf, basketball, and other sports. Fans explode with joy when a local team wins a major championship. Popular athletes have celebrity status and earn millions from product endorsements.

There's a wide-open field for canine sporting activities. Purebreds and mixed breeds compete against each other for a prize or national title. Other times they do it just for fun. Whether your dog performs flawlessly to the applause of hundreds or stumbles on

Multi-Dog Tip

Have a house full of active Chihuahuas? Consider outdoor family activities such as regular visits to the local dog park. Cities large and small across the United States have dog parks, enclosed areas in public parks set aside just for dogs. Most are free and open to the public, but a few are for members only. Dog parks can be a great place for dogs to socialize, exercise, and release pent-up energy. Owners mingle with dog-friendly people and pick up behavior tips and advice about dog care. The best-selling author of *From Baghdad With Love*, the true story of a stray dog's rescue from Iraq, met his wife at a San Diego dog park.

the course, he must be obedience trained to compete. Many earn a Canine Good Citizen certificate. Unless a dog obeys his owner, he will never succeed in sports.

Before starting your dog in any canine sport, have him examined by a veterinarian first. Pre-existing conditions should be ruled out. Vaccinations must be current. Encourage your dog, but never force him to perform if he is fatigued, injured, or just not interested.

Recognize your dog's limits. Also, always take weather into consideration for outside activities. If it is too hot or cold for you, think about your dog—the weather is not suitable for him either.

Canine sports are not just about winning. They are about having fun and bonding w ith your dog and other owners. They are also about building friendships, both human

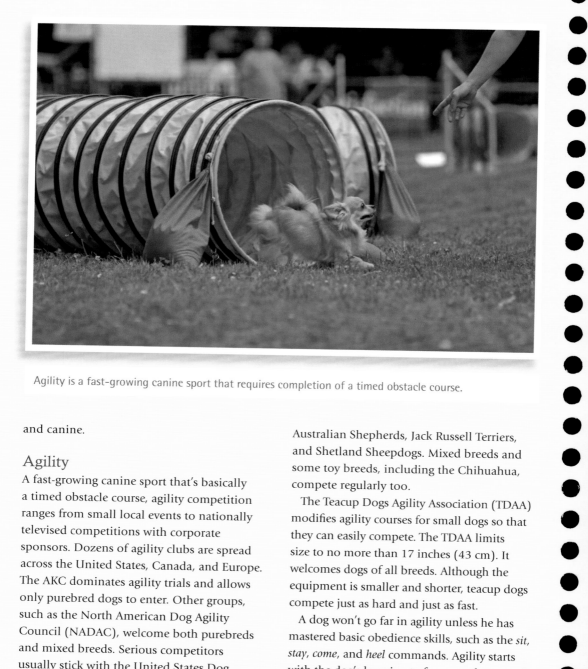

Agility is a fast-growing canine sport that requires completion of a timed obstacle course.

and canine.

Agility

A fast-growing canine sport that's basically a timed obstacle course, agility competition ranges from small local events to nationally televised competitions with corporate sponsors. Dozens of agility clubs are spread across the United States, Canada, and Europe. The AKC dominates agility trials and allows only purebred dogs to enter. Other groups, such as the North American Dog Agility Council (NADAC), welcome both purebreds and mixed breeds. Serious competitors usually stick with the United States Dog Agility Association (USDAA) because of its fast courses and high standards. Dogs on the agility circuit generally are Border Collies,

Australian Shepherds, Jack Russell Terriers, and Shetland Sheepdogs. Mixed breeds and some toy breeds, including the Chihuahua, compete regularly too.

The Teacup Dogs Agility Association (TDAA) modifies agility courses for small dogs so that they can easily compete. The TDAA limits size to no more than 17 inches (43 cm). It welcomes dogs of all breeds. Although the equipment is smaller and shorter, teacup dogs compete just as hard and just as fast.

A dog won't go far in agility unless he has mastered basic obedience skills, such as the *sit, stay, come,* and *heel* commands. Agility starts with the dog's learning to focus on the owner's voice and body language. Agility courses are fast, and there's only a slim margin of error. Success depends on excellent communication between the owner and dog. They work as a team. During training, owners introduce obstacles to their dogs one at a time. Successive obstacles become harder to overcome. Dogs jump over hurdles, run through weave poles, scamper across a teeter, and dash through a tunnel. In competition, judges deduct points for missed turns or not obeying the owner's command. Dogs who finish the course in the quickest time with the fewest deductions win. Each agility group has its own rules and regulations for competition.

An agility competition may be a trial in which dogs reach a certain level to compete at a more prestigious competition held at a later date. If they fail to earn a certain number of points, they do not move forward.

Some dog owners attend agility classes just for the experience. They never formally compete. Others devote considerable time and money into agility, traveling to weekend competitions for the chance to win a title. Regardless, agility requires dedication from the owner. Be prepared to spend a lot of time working with your dog. If you think that agility is for you and your dog, find an agility club near you. Clubs teach classes, have practice areas, and promote camaraderie.

Handlers say that agility is fun and rewarding. Owners meet people with similar interests and spend quality time with their dogs. Agility competitions are also a terrific form of entertainment.

Conformation

Conformation activity measures how well a dog lives up to standards of appearance and temperament that have been set for each breed; all show dogs must meet certain criteria. The American Kennel Club is the most well-known conformation show organization in the United States. During a conformation show,

Want to Know More?

If your Chihuahua gets especially dirty participating in a sport or activity, he may need a full-on grooming session. See Chapter 6: Chihuahua Grooming Needs for some pointers.

Chihuahuas pose while being examined. As the judge makes notes, the dog cannot move. That is an incredible accomplishment all by itself. In tandem with their handlers (who might or might not be their owners), the dogs circle the ring, showing off their poise and skill. Handlers and dogs who perform to near perfection are sometimes met with thunderous applause, yet a competing Chihuahua has to remain cool. The noise cannot rattle him.

The only disqualifications specific to all

If your Chihuahua loves to run and chase balls, the sport of flyball may be a great match.

Chihuahuas in the show ring are: 1.) Any dog over 6 pounds (2.5 kg) in weight; 2.) Floppy or cropped ears; 3.) Docked tail or bobtail. In addition, a disqualification for a long-coated Chihuahua is a too-thin coat that resembles bareness.

To be penalized as a serious fault are bites that are not level or scissors or any distortion of the jaws. The Chihuahua also has to be snappy-looking and stylish. If he is aggressive and growls or offers to bite the judge, he will be disqualified. Blind or deaf dogs and dogs having certain other disabilities are also not allowed in the show ring.

Owners who take care of their dogs and work with them can do well on the show circuit. Competition can be thrilling. It provides a good chance to meet other Chihuahua owners, but it requires hours of dedication and hard work. It also entails expenses, including travel expenses. Competition is not for everyone, but many people find it rewarding and worthwhile.

Flyball

In the 1970s a group of dog trainers added tennis balls to an obedience and scent-discrimination exercise. At first the addition seemed like no big deal, but dogs and their owners picked up on the intensity of the new sport, and it slowly built up a steady fan base. A performance on the Johnny Carson television show added to its popularity.

The National American Flyball Association (NAFA) reports membership of about

16,000. The field is small but growing as more people watch competitions.

A high-octane sport, flyball is especially suited for dogs who love to run and chase tennis balls. If you adopt or have a loving and smart but destructive dog, flyball might be the answer. Channel his negative energy into the sport and you might end up with a champion.

Owners must be fit and trim to handle the demands of flyball. You end up running as fast and as far as your dog. Each team has a minimum of five handlers and no more than six dogs. Four 51-feet-long (15.5-m) tracks are lined with mats. A flyball box at one end contains tennis balls. Hurdles are spaced 10 feet (3 m) apart. During competition, dogs leap over the hurdles and jump up and hit the flyball box with all four paws. The pressure releases a tennis ball, which the dog grabs. Pushing off the box, he leaps back over the hurdles, speeding toward the finish line. As one dog finishes, the next one is released. Speed is of the essence as these amazing speedsters fly through the course. The dog team with the fastest time wins the game.

Dogs of all breeds compete in flyball. Speedy dogs such as Border Collies, Greyhounds, and Australian Shepherds stand out, but other breeds such as Beagles, Jack Russells, Bichons, and Chihuahuas also join the fun. Flyball clubs report rescued dogs as members too. If your dog is active, loves to run and chase balls, and gets along with other dogs, flyball might be in his future.

As with other sports, a dog must obey basic commands, not show aggression, and be in good health to engage in flyball. Check NAFA for a flyball club near you. Training is demanding for both you and your dog. Expect to shell out money for tournament fees, dues, and equipment rental. But flyball handlers form close ties from working with each other.

Seeing their dogs compete and even sometimes win makes them proud.

Flying Disc

Flying disc contests started more than 30 years ago. Credit goes to a Whippet named Ashley who won a publicity stunt by soaring through the air catching flying discs thrown by her college-student owner. There are many contests held across the United States, Canada, and Europe, although no one organization sanctions flying disc contests. There are various levels of competition from novice to skilled.

Want to Know More?

A dog with three legs placed seventh at a 2007 flyball competition!

Dog owners everywhere toss flying discs to their dogs in parks, at the beach, or in their own yards. Very few dogs build up the skill and precision needed to win competitions. Most do it for fun or exercise. Watching the experts compete, however, can be breathtaking. Dogs perform acrobatic stunts as they leap and fly to grab those flying discs. Their stunts can be thrilling and seemingly impossible to perform. The sport is open to all dogs, regardless of breed, sex, age, or disability.

To get started, enroll your dog in basic obedience. He must listen to your commands to excel in this tough competitive sport. Then see whether there's a flying disc group near you. Sure, you can practice in your own back yard, but working with a team builds camaraderie. You learn from sharing experiences too.

Examples of flying disc organizations are Skyhoundz, Ashley Whippet Disc Dog Championships, and Flying Disc Dog Open. You can also ask a dog trainer or shelter in your area for more information. There are groups all around the United States.

Freestyle

Canine freestyle is sometimes called doggy dancing, but the sport is sophisticated, refined, and stylish. It is not just a bunch of owners hanging out with their dogs doing the boogie woogie. The handler and dog(s) perform obedience commands to music. No breed restrictions apply, and dogs must be six months old to compete.

As with other canine sports, dogs must be in shape and in trim and be masters at obedience. Owners must be dedicated and be willing to devote sufficient training time to the sport. If you are interested in canine freestyle, start by enrolling your dog in a basic obedience class. Then look for a dog trainer with an interest in canine freestyle who offers either a class or group/individual lessons. You can also purchase DVDs about canine freestyle to train at home.

Several professional organizations that sponsor events exist in the United States and Canada: the World Canine Freestyle Organization (WCFO), the US Freestyle Organization, and the Canadian Musical Canine Sports International (CMCSI).

Seeing owners perform with their dogs is beautiful, almost like attending a ballet.

Canine freestyle is a choreographed dance routine between dog and handler.

If you are traveling with your Chihuahua, make sure he's comfortable in his carrier.

In fluid motion, dogs follow their owners across the floor, performing acrobatic feats like turning and spinning. The sport is really starting to attract a following, albeit slowly. It probably won't be long before it has major sponsors, with competitions appearing regularly on television.

Obedience

Obedience is called a sport, but participants are so well trained that they might as well be part of a military drill team. During competition they are drilled on commands such as *sit*, *stay*, and *heel* as well as in scent discrimination and retrieving. To earn points, they must perform with precision. Owners are not allowed to interact with their dogs. It is as if the dog reads the owner's

mind and knows exactly what to do. And they do it very well.

Besides individual judging, each class of obedience (novice, open, or utility) competes against each other. With the handler absent, dogs cannot get up and walk away, nor can they interact with each other. Points are deducted if they do.

Obedience can be exhausting. To succeed, training must start with the puppy. Both the dog and his owner spend considerable time in training classes. Owners usually join a local obedience club, although some people train on their own. Expenses include training, equipment rental, travel to shows, and entry fees. Obedience trials and competitions sponsored by the AKC permit only purebreds, while the Mixed Breed Dog Club of America

(MBDA) welcomes any dog. Obedience is usually seen at popular shows like the Westminister Dog Show.

TRAVEL

If vacation plans include your Chihuahua, make sure that he is healthy enough to travel, whether it is by car or air. Dogs are not allowed on buses or boats unless they are certified to perform a vital service for a disabled person. A Chihuahua might be a registered hearing or seizure alert dog and in those cases would be permitted by federal law to accompany his owner on any form of public transportation.

Check with your veterinarian before embarking on a lengthy trip. Vaccinations and licenses should be up to date. Bring copies with you in case they are needed. Your Chihuahua should always have current identification that includes a microchip in case he gets away from you.

If your Chihuahua takes medication, pack enough to last for the duration of your trip. Carry your veterinarian's contact information for emergencies.

By Air

Each airline has different policies regarding travel with pets. Nearly all charge a fee. Before paying for a reservation, call the airline to determine its pet policy. Remember, airline policies are subject to change without notice. Because of the Chihuahua's small size, he may avoid being checked as baggage. The dog must, however, be in a proper-sized carrier with room to move around. The carrier has to fit underneath your seat.

Special requirements exist for foreign travel, even to neighboring countries such as Mexico and Canada. Call the U.S. State Department to find out what documents your dog needs. Some countries quarantine dogs from foreign countries for six months at the owner's expense. You may reconsider taking your Chihuahua to another country unless the move is permanent.

Tips for Air Travel

- Avoid connecting flights. This reduces the chances your pet will be lost.
- If the airline checks all dogs as baggage no matter the size of the breed, fly at night. If the plane gets stuck on the tarmac, the

By the Numbers

On May 2, 2009 Chihuahua lovers gathered in downtown Chandler, Arizona, for the annual Chihuahua races that are part of the Cinco de Mayo festivities. A hugely popular event attracting at least 1,000 adoring fans, the Cinco de Mayo Chihuahua races attract all kinds of Chihuahuas. Pedro, the reigning champion from 2008, mowed down the competition and seized the first-place trophy. Not all Chihuahuas took the race as seriously as Pedro. One dog stopped to sniff, another one lifted his leg on a clump of grass, while yet another one ran towards his owner sitting in the front row. Still, all of the Chihuahuas, whether adopted or from breeders, showed off their talents and provided the audience with an evening of fun.

The best person to watch your Chihuahua in your absence is a close friend or relative.

baggage compartment probably will be less hot than in the daytime..

- Check the airline's safety record of handling pets. Some display poor practices.
- Fly with your dog only if it is absolutely necessary. Every year pets die or get lost on commercial airlines flights.

By Car

If your Chihuahua is prone to motion sickness, your veterinarian can prescribe medications to help your dog cope with stop and go traffic, long drives, and the monotony of all-day confinement.

If you own a vehicle and your dog is not used to long-distance travel, take him on short drives so that he is acclimated to the car's motion. Always confine your puppy in a crate

or a special puppy seat when he is in the car. Do not allow him to be loose. He could be thrown off the seat if you brake suddenly or swerve. Alternatively, he might crawl around and slip underneath your feet while you are driving.

Rest stops along major highways set aside areas for dog walking. For safety, some are enclosed. Budget cuts, however, have forced the closure of highway rest stops in certain states and have reduced expenditures on maintenance in others. Bring your own waste bags in case none are provided, and always walk your dog on a leash. Stay away from the road's edge to avoid being hit by a car.

Your doggy bag should include food, snacks, water, and bowls. Take paper towels and plastic bags for clean-up. Always carry an extra leash

A Chihuahua is most comfortable in his own home.

in case the original one becomes misplaced. Include your Chihuahua's favorite toy and bed. Familiar items from home will help him adjust to being away. A canine first-aid kit is recommended too. If your plans include travel to cold weather areas, sweaters or coats are a must so that your dog is snug and warm.

Lodging

Hotels, motels, and bed & breakfast inns usually post pet policies on their websites or in brochures. Overnight stays are usually not a problem, especially along interstate highways. Sometimes there may be an additional charge for a dog or you may be given a room reserved for guests who smoke. Longer stays may

present a problem. A hotel may allow pets but require the dog to be with the owner at all times. Once travel plans are firm, call your choice of lodging and ask about its pet policy. Ask for a written confirmation so that there are no surprises upon arrival. Information posted on websites is sometimes inaccurate or outdated.

If Your Chihuahua Can't Come

The best person to watch your Chihuahua in your absence is a close friend or relative. A Chihuahua is most comfortable in his own home. If that is not possible, consider either a kennel, housesitter, or day care. Boarding kennels, reputable pet sitters, and day cares all require that your Chihuahua be licensed and current on vaccinations, which includes rabies, the 4-1, and bordetella. Nearly all boarding kennels and daycare owners have websites that post their requirements, fees, location, etc. If your Chihuahua has special needs, convey them before leaving. For example, if your dog is anxious around strangers, tell the sitter so that whoever it is can take precautions such as entering your home with treats. Also, let any facility or person know whether your Chihuahua takes medication.

Kennels

To find a reputable boarding kennel, do the following:

- Ask a friend, relative, coworker, veterinarian, or groomer for a recommendation.
- Visit the kennel and ask to inspect the premises. If the owner says no, continue looking.
- Make sure that the place is clean and the animals seem comfortable. A fresh smell is an indication that waste is picked up regularly.
- Get a confirmation on price and services in writing. Ask what the kennel's emergency plans are and ask for references.
- Leave a trusted contact to care for your Chihuahua in the event of a crisis.
- Call during your absence to check on your Chihuahua's status.
- Ask whether the facility is a member of the American Boarding Kennel Association (ABKA), the national trade organization.
- Ask whether complaints have been lodged against the kennel with the Better Business Bureau (BBB) or the consumer services division of the state attorney general's office.
- Make sure that the staff is courteous and friendly.

Housesitters

If someone will be housesitting your dog:

- Ask a friend, relative, coworker, veterinarian, dog owner, or groomer for a recommendation.
- Meet the sitter before you finalize vacation plans. After all, you are giving this person access to your home and to your beloved Chihuahua(s). The sitter has to be trustworthy and good around dogs. If the first meeting does not feel right to you or your dog, consider other arrangements. There's probably a reason for the unease.
- Request at least two references and call them.
- Find out how long the sitter has worked with dogs.
- See whether the person is bonded and insured.
- Find out if she is a member of the National Association of Professional Pet Sitters (NAPPS) or Pet Sitters International (PSI).

Day Cares

Day care is an option only if you will be gone for the day. Most day cares do not board overnight.

PART III

SENIOR YEARS

CHAPTER 12

FINDING YOUR CHIHUAHUA SENIOR

A puppy does not mesh with your lifestyle. You are gone too many hours during the day to properly housetrain a two-month old puppy or you are older and just want to avoid the chewing phase but you still want a Chihuahua. Plenty of unwanted Chihuahuas need you. According to the Humane Society of the United States (HSUS), at least 25 percent of all dogs in animal shelters are purebreds. So yes, Chihuahuas end up in shelters too, so consider adopting one. They make wonderful housepets. You'll do more than save a life, as important as that is; you'll alsoopen up space for another unwanted dog in either a shelter or rescue. Every single adoption makes a difference.

Experts seem to disagree on when a Chihuahua becomes a senior. The lowest estimate suggests 8 to 10 years, while the higher estimate says 12 to 13 years. It seems reasonable to say that by the time a Chihuahua reaches ten years of age, he has hit his twilight years.

ADVANTAGES OF SENIOR ADOPTION

As mentioned earlier, Chihuahuas normally have a life span of 12 to 17 years, so an 11- or 12-year-old dog can have plenty to offer. Senior dogs enjoy walks, can be registered as therapy animals, and will be trusted family friends. Do not let their age turn you off.

Senior dogs are nearly always housetrained and do not come with behavior problems like chewing, digging, or yanking on the leash. Some are already spayed and/or neutered. They are usually up to date on vaccinations. Unlike puppies, they can be left alone for longer periods. They do not need as much training or exercise, although some may need brushing up on their skills. Toys and chew bones may no longer interest them. Seniors may have shorter life spans than puppies, but an older dog will bring lots of joy and happiness to your life.

WHERE TO RESCUE YOUR CHIHUAHUA

There are many options for rescuing a senior Chihuahua, whether it's from a shelter/rescue, off-site adoption event, or breeder. Conscientious groups readily disclose all available information. If a group hedges about revealing the Chihuahua's past, find another group. Honesty really is the best policy. It is not fair or ethical to hide known health or behavior problems from potential owners.

Animal shelters and breed and pet rescues are always filled with older unwanted Chihuahuas. They are healthy, just lonely and in need of love. However, older dogs require the same patience as raising a puppy. Always ask the source about the dog's background, such as health and behavior history. Does the Chihuahua have medical and/or behavior issues? Will he need daily medication? Is special food part of his daily regimen? Does he have a bite history? Dogs with a bite history usually are not good candidates for adoption. Bites suggest a pattern of bad behavior based on careless breeding, abuse, or both.

Training Tidbit

An older dog may be set in his ways. For example, he spent the last 12 years sleeping in his owner's bed. The new owner loves his adopted Chihuahua but hedges about sharing his or her bed. And the Chihuahua is just as insistent that the owner's bed is where he belongs. What happens next? Provide the Chihuahua with his own soft, comfy bed. If needed, praise the dog for getting into his dog bed. Slip a treat inside as a way to make the dog bed appealing, but let him sleep inside your bedroom. Expecting him to sleep in a dog bed outside the bedroom may be too much of a change at once. Be patient with older dogs. Change should be gradual.

Shelter/Rescue

If you fall for a Chihuahua from a shelter or rescue, be ready to answer questions about your lifestyle, pet history, and willingness to make a long-term commitment. Although you may consider the questions to be intrusive, shelters and rescue groups want the Chihuahua in a forever home. Rescued Chihuahuas are often bounced around, perhaps even abused, and the shelter or rescue is trying to protect the dog from further trauma. Some groups may even require a home visit or reference check. Please be patient. The process may take longer than buying from a breeder, but you are saving an unwanted Chihuahua's life.

At the same time, you have a right to ask questions about the care of the Chihuahuas in the shelter or rescue. Were they fed daily? Did they live in a clean, sanitary environment? How was disease controlled? Did staff and volunteers treat the animals with kindness? Was the shelter properly heated or cooled? Did the shelter and/or rescue have a history of complaints? Were the complaints serious? Deal only with a reputable shelter and/or rescue. Unless you live in a rural community, there is usually more than one shelter or rescue around.

Remember, you incur expenses for a Chihuahua whether you buy from a breeder or adopt. Not all adopted Chihuahuas come with problems, behavioral or medical. Some adult Chihuahuas were given up because elderly owners died or entered nursing homes. Other dogs, however, were abused or beaten and removed as part of cruelty investigations. A few lost Chihuahuas entered animal shelters as strays and were not reclaimed. Still others were saved from a bleak, miserable existence at puppy mills and given second chances. All Chihuahuas have their own unique needs.

Multi-Dog Tip

Tina Eacret, volunteer manager for the Arizona Animal Welfare League, has nine rescued dogs (eight Chihuahuas and one Pomeranian) and three cats. She regularly scans the euthanasia list posted at Maricopa County Animal Care and Control and then deletes it. On February 5, 2009, for unknown reasons, she read the list and her eyes stuck to the words "Kennel 429, 15 y.o. F Chihuahua, no teeth."

"I'm a hopeless Chihuahua lover, so I opened the attached picture," Eacret says. "There was Mabel, old and toothless. I couldn't let her die in the shelter, not after living 15 years." Eacret called her husband Steve, whom she describes as patient and understanding, to say that she was going to foster a Chihuahua. He probably knew the foster was really an adoption. That evening, Eacret drove to the Mesa shelter and picked up Mabel.

Mabel had a heart murmur and no lower jaw, and she wasn't spayed. But she pulled through all of the medical procedures and now lives a comfortable life with Eacret, her husband Tim, and their multi-pet household. She also spends most days at the Welfare League, sleeping in a softy cozy bed in Eacret's office. Now and then she greets visitors with a tail wag. Mabel may be older than most adopted Chihuahuas, but she is full of love and has a special place in Eacret's heart. (Chihuahua Connection Holiday 2009).

To find a shelter or rescue near you, visit petfinder.com, an online database with thousands of animals, mostly dogs and cats, searching for good homes. It is also a directory of animal shelters and rescue groups in the United States, Canada, and Mexico.

Off-Site Adoption

Off-site adoption events are another reliable source to find an adult Chihuahua. Some communities host adoption events at public places like churches, community centers, or libraries. Shelters and rescue groups are invited to bring adoptable animals so that they can find good loving homes. A Chihuahua rescue group may attend with unwanted dogs available for adoption. Check your local press for such an adoption event like this in your community.

Breeders

Lastly, once in a while a reputable breeder has adult Chihuahuas available for adoption. The breeder will take back dogs that he or she bred, even if they are seven years old. An owner may have died, faced foreclosure, or fled an abusive marriage. The breeder will offer older dogs for adoption but does not expect them to be used for breeding. Before adoption, the adult dogs will be spayed or neutered. A responsible breeder will screen potential homes with the same vigor as expended with her puppies. The senior Chihuahua will not go home with just anyone.

There are many options for rescuing a senior Chihuahua, including shelters, rescues, adoption events, and breeders.

INTRODUCING YOUR NEW CHIHUAHUA

If you already have a Chihuahua at home, introductions to another Chihuahua are usually smooth and uneventful. Chihuahuas typically get along with their own kind, rarely offering resistance. If you have a different breed, let all of the dogs meet in a neutral setting, such as a public park, before bringing the new Chihuahua home. If the dog you already have has a known aggression problem with other dogs, it is not a good idea to bring home a Chihuahua. They will probably fight, especially if both are males.

Find out whether the prospective adoptee Chihuahua is feline friendly if you have a cat at home. If the shelter or rescue does not know the Chihuahua's history with cats, arrange a dog/cat meeting before sealing the adoption.

Everyone in the household should agree on the adoption. The Chihuahua should become part of the family and not be dumped in the yard. Each member, including the children, should interact with the Chihuahua before the adoption becomes final. If someone is edgy about the adoption, shelve plans until everyone is on board. Otherwise, problems may arise later. The Chihuahua will pick up on the resentment, and the family dynamic will be unsettled. Until everyone says yes about adopting a Chihuahua, take time to think about the choice for a few days or even weeks. You might also look at other available Chihuahuas or foster a Chihuahua for a shelter or rescue.

FOSTERING A CHIHUAHUA

As a foster, you achieve two goals. You help a dog in need. Rescues are typically short of cash and foster homes. Approved foster homes allow them to save more animals. As a foster, you spend time with one particular Chihuahua before making a commitment. You can determine whether the dog has behavior problems, is shy, or is moody and temperamental. If the match does not seem to fit, you can continue to foster the Chihuahua until he finds a permanent placement and you keep looking for a dog to match your needs. And you help the rescue in the meantime by keeping the Chihuahua out of an animal shelter or boarding kennel.

ADOPTION AGREEMENTS

Adoption agreements vary, but they are all in writing. The majority of shelters and rescues will ask you to provide your Chihuahua with a permanent and loving home. You will be asked to return the Chihuahua to them if you can no longer care for him, regardless of the reason. Some offer a health guarantee for the first 30 days. Some offer longer terms, while some give no assurances at all. Still others give one free medical exam with a licensed private veterinarian. Find out whether the rescue or shelter offers follow-up services should your adopted dog develop adjustment problems. Some have trainers, either staff or volunteers, available to take your questions and to help out. The range of services depends on the resources of the shelter or rescue. Resources change, depending on volunteers, donations, and grants.

Some shelters offer reduced prices to adopt older dogs or dogs with special needs (blind, deaf, or missing a limb). Special needs dogs and senior dogs are harder to place and generally linger in shelters longer than puppies and younger dogs. Senior citizens are once in a while given a discount to adopt senior dogs. Ask your local shelter if it offers discounted

Multi-Dog Tip

Thinking about a puppy around a senior? Not so fast. If you have a senior dog, he may or may not welcome a puppy. Old dogs are set in their ways. Play rarely interests them. They expect meals at a certain time. Chronic ailments such as heart disease or arthritis may cause pain or discomfort. Sometimes they might be cranky or irritable. Adding a playful, rambunctious puppy will alter the aging dog's routine. It will probably not breathe new life into a sick old dog. Let a grouchy old dog enjoy his twilight years without a puppy pestering him to play. He'd likely rather sleep. Wait until your older dog has passed before introducing a new puppy into the household.

rates to adopt older dogs.

Older dogs generally are good matches for older people because they do not require a lot of exercise, they do not tug on the leash, and they can be accommodated in senior housing or assisted living centers.

The Cost to Adopt

Costs to acquire rescued Chihuahuas are considerably less than for purebred puppies from a breeder and usually include the spay/neuter surgery, vaccinations, and a microchip. A license is part of the adoption package at some shelters. Depending on the availability of donations, shelters and/or rescues may give you a leash, collar, or a bag of dog food/snacks with your new Chihuahua. Nearly all will give you handouts about dog behavior, feeding, and health.

CHAPTER 13

CARING FOR YOUR CHIHUAHUA SENIOR

Take a peek at the daily activity schedule inside a senior citizen center. The list is probably long and may include squared ancing, sightseeing, chess, and hiking. Seniors typically retire at 65, but they do not stop living. Most remain active with volunteer work, part-time jobs, and leisure activities. Old dogs are like old people. Aging Chihuahuas may be a little cranky, grayer around the edges, and sleepier than they once were, but they still have plenty to give. Make a few adjustments that are discussed in this section and your older Chihuahua can go on daily walks, family vacations, Fourth of July picnics, and visits to the dog park.

When does a Chihuahua officially become a senior dog? Experts generally agree that toy breeds, including the Chihuahua, enter their twilight time around ten years of age. Toy dogs can live as long as 20 years.

SIGNS OF AN AGING CHIHUAHUA

One day you wake up and glance at your beloved Chihuahua cuddled up in his bed. He seems so peaceful as he sleeps, but then you realize that his youth has slipped away. Maybe he is now 12 or 13 years old. By official standards, he is a senior canine citizen. If he were human, he would be eligible for Social Security and Medicare. He is a dog, but you can still help him age gracefully. Make his twilight years comfy and cozy.

The following signs are typical of aging in dogs:

- advanced dental disease
- arthritis
- diminished sense of taste, sight, hearing
- gray or white muzzle
- increased sleep
- lackluster coat (thinner and drier)
- less tolerance for cold
- slower gait
- tremors
- urinary incontinence

Indoor dogs who received routine veterinary care, ate good-quality dog food, maintained their recommended weight, lived in a smoke-free environment, and were treated like part of the family generally show fewer signs of aging than neglected or outdoor Chihuahuas. Old-dog diseases, however, may still creep up on them. Renal failure, cancer, and heart disease are common in all senior dogs. After working for all of those years, some organs just tire out and quit working.

There is a lot you can do to keep your senior dog comfortable, happy, and safe.

Aging naturally affects even the best-kept Chihuahuas who were spruced up at doggy spas or were fussed over and primped by fastidious owners. Age notwithstanding, there is a lot you can do to see your dog through his silver years so that he is comfortable, happy, and safe. No Chihuahua lives forever, but he can live pretty darn well for a long time— with your help of course.

FEEDING

A dog's metabolism fades as he ages, making him prone to weight gain. Owners face the same issues as they age. Switch your older Chihuahua to a senior food because the ingredients are designed for the older, not so perky dog. Easier to digest senior brands contain less fat because the older dog requires less, and fat is an energy source. The older dog needs less food to prevent weight gain. As his metabolism slows down, he exercises less. His daily walk may consist of taking a few steps to the next house rather than the four blocks he once covered. Eating the same amount of food leads to a plump little pooch. Older dogs are also less energetic. More bran and fiber are mixed in senior food to prevent constipation, another common issue for older dogs. As the Chihuahua ages, his coat loses its luster and shine. Senior food is blended with additional vitamins and minerals to keep the coat shiny and smooth. The supplements help prevent flaky skin because a dog's skin loses elasticity with age.

Feeding Schedule

Stick to the same feeding schedule of twice-daily meals, but cut down on the intake amount. Do not starve him—just reduce the amount a little. Ask your veterinarian to suggest the appropriate amount to feed your old dog. Small dogs need no extra padding, so avoid the temptation to feed him a third meal, unless of course your veterinarian recommends it. If you disagree, talk to your veterinarian or ask for a second medical opinion.

Make the Food More Appetizing

If your dog has trouble chewing the small-breed kibble because of dental decay, add a splash of warm water, meaty broth, or dog food sauce to soften the kibble. That should make it more appetizing to him and easier to eat. Too much liquid, however, will make it mushy and unappealing.

How to Give a Pill

- Hold the pill with your forefinger and thumb.
- Gently open your dog's mouth.
- Place the pill as far back as possible.
- Hold his snout until he swallows the pill.

Some Chihuahuas resist taking their medicine. They spit out the pills when you turn your back. As an alternative, place the pill inside a tiny dot of peanut butter or on a sliver of cheese. That almost always works like a dream and the pill gets swallowed.

Add Variety

For years your Chihuahua faithfully rushed to his food dish as soon as it hit the floor. He licked the bowl dry and wagged his tail for more. Now he eats a few bites and then walks away. Humor your old dog—he deserves special treatment. Add variety to his food with a touch of cooked white rice, chopped hard-boiled eggs, steamed carrots, a tablespoon of baby food or cereal, or a little canned dog food and then stir it around in his dried food. Avoid switching to all soft food unless he loses all or most of his teeth. As long as he can still eat kibble, maintain his diet of dried food. That is best for him. If you live alone, this presents no problem.

However, if you live in a multi-pet household, the other dogs or cats may demand the same variety. Their noses tell them that the older dog gets treated to something they do not. So use your judgment about spicing up your old dog's food. You may stick with broth or dog food sauce to avoid competition from other dogs or cats who smell the more appealing rice, canned food, or hard-boiled eggs.

Supplements

Consider adding nutritional supplements to your Chihuahua's food if your veterinarian agrees. Glucosamine, for instance, benefits dogs with arthritis. It is said to improve their mobility. Arginine, an essential amino acid, stimulates the old dog's immune function. Omega-3 fatty acids are good for the brain and nervous system. Vitamin E adds sheen to his drying skin and coat. Before starting your dog on vitamins or supplements, discuss them with your veterinarian to determine the proper dosage. Most vitamins and supplements are manufactured for human usage. Carefully taper the dose for your 3- to 6-pound (1.5- to 2.5-kg) Chihuahua. Too much can be harmful or toxic for such a small dog.

Treats

Despite age and chronic ailments, many senior dogs retain their taste for treats. Consider buying biscuits for the older dog; manufacturers have made a variety of them available. For the dog with dental issues, buy soft, easier-to-chew treats. Make sure that they are sized appropriately for the Chihuahua. Do not overfeed snacks to a less active senior dog, no matter how much he begs or whines for more. One or two biscuits a day is sufficient.

Water

Always keep a bowl of fresh clean water available. Water is essential for all dogs. Senior dogs drink less water, but they still need access to it. Because the senior dog sometimes becomes forgetful, do not move his bowl to a new place. Keep his lifestyle as routine as possible. At this stage, he is quite settled in his habits. Avoid any changes that will unsettle

Consider adding nutritional supplements to your Chihuahua's food if your veterinarian agrees.

him, and that includes moving his food or water bowls.

GROOMING

Grooming remains an important part of a geriatric dog's overall care. Age does not diminish the need for brushing, bathing, nail trimming, or dental care. An old dog still likes to smell fresh and look chipper. Regular grooming sessions also offer owners the chance to examine older Chihuahuas for lumps and bumps. Most lesions are benign, but now

and then one may be malignant. If you find a suspicious lump or bump on your dog, make an appointment with your veterinarian.

If your dog tires while grooming him, let him rest. Do not make him uncomfortable. Or trim his nails on Monday, comb him on Tuesday, and brush his teeth on Friday. He may be old and cranky, so humor him.

Combing/Brushing

Do not groom an old dog in a cold, drafty room. Turn up the heat so that it is toasty and warm. Close all windows and doors.

Dry skin sometimes afflicts old dogs, so continue so comb him often. Long-coated Chihuahuas still need frequent brushing, even at their advanced ages. Dirt, debris, and external parasites can cling to their coats when they are out in the yard or on a daily walk. Their skin may be sensitive, so use care when combing/brushing. If the bristle brush or hard comb is too rough on his skin, use a soft comb or brush. Brushing/combing stimulates the oils in the dog's skin and should help ease the dryness and flaking that comes with age.

Clean your dog's brushes and combs now and then. Use the comb to pull out excess fur from the brush. Soak combs and brushes in a soapy solution overnight. Unless the combs pick up fleas or other parasites, warm soapy water is sufficient to wash your dog's combs and brushes. Rinse them thoroughly to make sure that all of the soap is gone.

If the combs and brushes appear worn out in your Chihuahua's old age, it is time to spring for a new set. He may live to be 20 years old!

Bathing

Before dipping your dog in the water, test it first. The water should be warm but not hot enough to scald your dog or your own hands.

Travel

Unless it is absolutely necessary, leave your older dog at home; he will be more comfortable. Ask a trusted friend, neighbor, or relative to care for him while you are on vacation or business. Traveling long distances in a car is rough on the older dog, especially if he has chronic illnesses such as heart disease, arthritis, or incontinence. Airplane travel is not recommended for senior dogs unless the owner is relocating and has no other way to move with the Chihuahua. Plenty of boarding kennels can safely accommodate the needs of older dogs.

After his bath, let him shake off excess water, then thoroughly towel dry him. In winter, use a blow-dryer to make sure that he is completely dry. Keep him indoors for a few hours so that he does not catch a chill. Take him outside to go potty before giving him a bath. You don't want a bath interrupted by a dog who needs to go outdoors, particularly in the winter when it might be raining, snowing, or very cold. Do not bathe an older dog more than once a month. Age brings about a loss of shine. Excess bathing washes away the little bit of oils that are left.

Nail Care

Trim his nails regularly. He walks less, so his nails will grow longer. After all of these years, he should be accustomed to the nail clipper. If he never developed a liking for it, take him to the dog groomer for routine nail clipping. Most groomers do not require an appointment for a simple nail trim. They accept walk-ins for a modest fee. And, of course, your veterinarian can trim his nails as well.

Dental Care

Continue to brush your dog's teeth regularly in his twilight years. At his age, there is plaque buildup, so brushing keeps it in check. Your veterinarian always looks at his teeth at the annual examination. A professional annual cleaning is recommended, even in the dog's old age.

HEALTH

Help your Chihuahua grow old gracefully. As with humans, dogs are more susceptible to disease as they age. With regular veterinary care, proper nutrition, and exercise, your Chihuahua can maintain good health well into his twilight years.

Preventive Care: Senior Checkups

Geriatric wellness programs for senior pets are common at most veterinarians' offices and animal hospitals. These age-specific

A senior Chihuahua's skin may be extra sensitive.

programs are geared to keep the older dog in good health because seniors tend to get sicker more often, and their recovery rate is slower. Preventing disease is vital for the senior dog. An initial exam includes a measure of the dog's weight and temperature. The following baseline diagnostic tests are usually taken:

- blood pressure
- complete blood panel
- EKG
- fecal examination
- urinalysis
- X-rays

In prior years, taking a dog's blood pressure was awkward and cumbersome. Now, with the availability of newer instruments, the process is simpler for the veterinarian and easier on the dog. Elevated blood pressure in a senior dog is usually a sign of cardiac disease and should be explored further with your veterinarian. Ideally, old dogs should go for checkups twice a year. If that is not possible, keep them to the annual visit.

On a geriatric wellness examination, a veterinarian will look for the following symptoms that could be a sign of a serious disorder:

- abdominal swelling
- abnormal breath sounds
- behavior changes
- ocular changes or discharge
- rapid weight gain or loss
- rectal abnormalities
- skin lesions
- swelling or bleeding

Assuming that all of the laboratory test results come back normal, your old dog is in remarkably good health. That is an indication of your excellent work taking care of your dog. Keep up the same routine; it is obviously working. If there are negative findings, your veterinarian will discuss them with you and describe available treatment plans for your dog.

Many veterinarians do not vaccinate senior dogs. Annual vaccinations over the years sufficiently built up his immunity. Further vaccinations are not needed. The DHPP vaccine is recommended but not required by law. Rabies vaccinations, on the other hand, are mandated in all 50 states. If your veterinarian considers it too risky to vaccinate your dog against rabies, contact local animal control. Ask whether a letter signed by your veterinarian excuses your elderly dog from the rabies requirement. If it does not, comply with local regulations in the slim chance your old dog bites someone. An unvaccinated dog is always kept confined at either the shelter or a boarding kennel, regardless of age.

Want to Know More?

Playing with a senior Chihuahua? Yes, play keeps an older dog mentally and physically fit. Indeed, an old dog cannot chase down a ball with the same speed as a young pup, but he may enjoy a game of fetch, even at his age. (See Chapter 11 for some activities ideas.) Do not rule out play in a senior dog's life. Toys and chew bones do not have the same allure as they once did, but old dogs still like to have fun.

Arthritis

Arthritis, also known as an inflammation of the joints, can afflict young dogs but usually flares up in older dogs. It also affects dogs after bone or joint injuries. If your dog struggles to stand up, drags his way around the block on his daily jaunt, or winces in pain as he walks up the stairs, he is probably arthritic. Loss of appetite is another sign of arthritis. Dogs in pain often refuse to eat, even when tempted with treats. Your veterinarian will confirm the diagnosis with x-rays of the afflicted joints and a complete physical examination.

The disease does not discriminate, but it is more common in large, portly dogs, especially ones who spent their lives outside. Chihuahuas, however, can still become arthritic. Symptoms are often exacerbated by cold, soggy weather. Treatments to ease the pain and discomfort include prescription drugs as well as holistic options, such as the supplement glucosamine, acupuncture, chiropractic, whirlpool baths, and massage.

Even if you do not spring for a heated bed with extra padding for your arthritic dog, make sure that he has a soft, comfortable place to rest. During the winter, his space should always be warm and cozy. An arthritic dog should never live outside in any weather. That would be cruel and inhumane.

Some Chihuahuas spend time with their owners on the patio on warm sunny days. Your old Chihuahua can still hang with the family outside on those balmy afternoons or evenings, but he needs a snug cozy bed, perhaps with a towel or baby blanket inside for extra comfort.

Continue to exercise your arthritic dog within his limitations. He may only be able to walk half a block, but modest exercise will keep his joints limber. No exercise at all will worsen his condition. His pace will be slower, but do not rush him. Forcing him to move faster will exacerbate the arthritis and increase his pain level.

If your dog is overweight, he must slim down. Only you can help him. Switch to lite or low-calorie dog food, feed no table scraps, and reduce his treats. Less weight is a significant benefit to an arthritic dog.

A portable ramp may be needed to help him get up stairs or into your van. Ramps are sold in most large retail pet stores.

Canine Cognitive Disorder (CCD)

The changes started so slowly you almost failed to notice. During a pounding rainstorm, your Chihuahua remained in the soggy yard rather than dashing through the doggy door for the comfort of the dry house. You had to run outside, grab him, then dry him off. He looked confused. Then there was the time you called him for dinner but he huddled behind the television set, staring into space. He ignored his dinner. You picked him up, but he did not seem to notice you.

Older dogs, even those who were well cared for and loved, can become afflicted with canine cognitive disorder (CCD), the doggy version

Make sure that your senior has a soft, comfortable place to rest.

of Alzheimer's disease. The following are signs of canine cognitive disorder, similar to Alzheimer's disease:

- cannot find the food or water bowl.
- stands in a corner staring into space
- soils himself
- forgets to come in after taking care of business in the back yard
- fails to recognize familiar people or places
- scares easily
- wanders off if left alone

If your dog exhibits any of these symptoms, he probably has CCD. CCD is a heartless disease because it disrupts the memory and reasoning patterns of otherwise healthy seniors. Alzheimer's now and then targets someone younger, in his 50s. CCD follows the same progression, afflicting mostly old dogs, but occasionally it strikes a dog in his prime.

CCD can mimic other neurological disorders, such as brain cancer or a tumor, so your veterinarian will perform a thorough examination to rule out other neurological causes. Tests may include a complete blood panel and urine analysis. Medical options for CCD are few. Some medications enhance dopamine levels, and holistic treatments alleviate some symptoms so that your Chihuahua is comfortable, but no cure exists for CCD.

A dog can live with CCD for a while, but the owner has to make changes at home for the dog's safety. Do not rearrange furniture, because even the slightest change will rattle him. Take him out more often to avoid accidents. He may forget how to use a doggy door. Avoid giving him full access to the house while you are out, or he may hurt himself by falling down the stairs. A pool should be gated so that he does not fall in and drown. For his own safety, lock him in a crate or laundry room when no one is home. Make sure that he has soft bedding so that he is comfortable. His ID tags should always be current in the unlikely event that he slips out of your home. He may need extra tender loving care to cope with this scary disorder. Comfort him more often so that he feels safe and secure. His world is changing, and he may not understand what is going on.

CCD is a big change for the owners too. Their Chihuahua is not the same anymore. He is old and frail. He forgets to come when called. He stares at the wall or sits in a corner. He may soil his bed and then lie in it. Slight noises and strangers may frighten him.

The end may come sooner than the owner had expected, and he or she may start to think about euthanasia, an emotionally wrenching part of pet ownership. The owner has to decide how long he or she can live with a dog afflicted with CCD.

Cataracts

At the dinner table your Chihuahua sits by your feet. Looking into his eyes, you notice a difference: His eyes are cloudy. Cataracts can force senior citizens to surrender their driver's licenses and restrict their lifestyles. With an old dog, cataracts are a major cause of blindness, while some dogs become only visually impaired. Dense white spots that cover the eye lens, canine cataracts can be inherited or

Canine cognitive disorder is similar to Alzheimer's in humans.

caused by illnesses such as diabetes. Cataracts are seen more in purebreds than mixed breeds, but Chihuahuas are not highly susceptible.

Dogs with cataracts should not be bred, as cataracts can be passed along to the offspring. A reputable breeder spays or neuters these dogs and ends their breeding cycles.

Treatment includes surgical removal, similar to cataract treatment in people. Assuming the dog had no previous eye problems, the simple operation usually restores vision. Expect a cost, though. Veterinary ophthalmologists are highly skilled, and the surgical technique is specialized.

For dogs who live with cataracts, whether they are blind or just visually impaired, they can maintain normal lives with some modifications at home. Teach them how to find the doggy door, and do not move the furniture. Leave your Chihuahua's food and water bowls as well as his bed in the accustomed places. He will adjust to the routine. He may also bump into things, so remove any valuable pottery or lamps that lie in his path. Also, block his access to stairs or a pool. Do not leave clutter around blind or visually impaired dogs. They can get tied up in the mess and hurt themselves.

Blind dogs can still exercise. In fact, they may enjoy a hearty walk around the block. Leash the dog and take him outside for exercise and fresh air. Never let a blind dog off the leash, even if he is under voice control. That is far too dangerous for a dog who cannot see.

There are support groups around the United States for owners of blind dogs to share experiences and information about their dogs' condition. Blind dogs make wonderful family pets. They see with their hearts.

By the Numbers

Old dogs, like old people, are prone to gain weight. That can negatively impact their health. Here are eight ways to keep your senior Chihuahua fit and trim:

1. Buy good-quality food.
2. Limit intake of wet food.
3. Feed only the daily recommended amount.
4. Avoid table scraps.
5. Be sparing with snacks and treats.
6. Walk him at least once a day, even if it is only to the corner and back.
7. Keep his water bowl full.
8. Take him for an annual veterinary checkup.

Cushing's Disease

The pituitary gland secretes a variety of hormones, most of which regulate other organs in the body. One of the hormones is ACTH, which stimulates the adrenal gland to produce glucocorticoids. With Cushing's, the pituitary gland sends out the wrong signal to the adrenal gland and the dog ends up with more glucocorticoids than his body can process. Overproduction is a problem that must be addressed. In some cases, a tumor of the pituitary gland is the problem; in others, a tumor of the adrenal gland causes Cushing's. Tumors may be benign, although some can be malignant. The cause is unknown and the disease is not widely understood.

Symptoms include increased thirst and appetite, a bloated abdomen, and hair loss. Cushing's typically affects middle aged to older dogs. Onset is around ten years of age. The disease is common in Toy breeds. Chihuahuas are rarely affected, however.

Diagnosis includes urine analysis, complete blood count, and the ACTH (hormone) stimulation test. If your veterinarian suspects Cushing's, she will lay out a diagnostic and treatment plan with you. Medication suppresses symptoms so dogs can live with Cushing's for one to two years, sometimes longer. Surgical removal may be advised for adrenal tumors, especially if they are cancerous, but surgery for pituitary tumors is not practical. Cushing's disease shortens a dog's life span. A dog can survive with Cushing's for about two years.

Dental Disease

Appetite loss may be a sign of dental disease, namely tooth decay or gum infection. Both cause pain and discomfort. Examine the insides of your dog's mouth and teeth. If his breath smells like a camel or his teeth are darkened or stained, make an appointment with your veterinarian. If your dog's mouth hurts, he may not eat. Old dogs may require tooth extractions and antibiotics if the decay is widespread, but only your veterinarian will know for sure. Toothless old dogs can live for years eating canned food and soft treats. Some can even eat kibble if it is softened with water, broth, or dog food sauce. They will eat a bowl of mushy dog food. Ignoring dental decay is not an option. Gum disease and rotten teeth do not heal themselves without professional treatment.

Hypothyroidism

Older dogs sometimes face hypothyroidism, an underactive thyroid gland. Every dog has a thyroid gland, two butterfly-shaped lobes in the neck area. When the gland becomes

Cushing's disease typically affects middle-aged to older dogs.

underactive, the dog usually gains weight. Other symptoms include dry skin, patchy hair loss, less tolerance for cold, and lethargy. The condition is not common in toy breeds, but it can happen, especially in an older Chihuahua. If you suspect that your Chihuahua may have a thyroid condition, call your veterinarian for an appointment. A blood test will confirm whether the disease is present. Treatment is available, and daily medication with a synthetic thyroid hormone will generally restore an affected Chihuahua's health and allow the dog to live a normal, complete life with few side effects. He should lose the gained weight with exercise and diet control,

A senior dog may have diminished senses.

and the fur will grow back. Routine follow-up care with blood testing is recommended, but hypothyroidism is not life threatening to your Chihuahua.

Congestive Heart Failure (CHF)

Congestive heart failure (CHF) is typically related to lifestyle: the dog is older, has a history of little or no exercise, and is obese. He ate a nutritionally imbalanced diet. CHF interferes with blood flow from the heart through the rest of the body. The results are often devastating to dogs, just as they are to humans. Oxygen-starved organs malfunction, leading to a variety of discomforting symptoms that may include coughing, difficulty in breathing, fluid in the lungs or abdomen, or an enlarged spleen.

Diagnosis is usually done by X-rays, physical examination, ultrasound, or a combination of these. The veterinarian looks for an enlarged heart or fluid accumulation around the heart. The chest area may be enlarged, indicating the presence of fluids.

No cure exists for CHF. Treatment includes medication to eliminate excess fluids and improve blood flow. Diets are restricted to low-sodium specialty dog foods. Owners of overweight dogs are strongly encouraged to help their pets trim down. Modest exercise is recommended for weight control and to maintain healthy cardiac function.

CHF cuts a dog's life short, but the disease can be prevented with regular exercise, proper diet, and regular veterinary care. No one can say how long your dog will live with the disease, but be proactive. A change in his lifestyle will give him more quality time.

TRAINING

Senior dogs generally do not need a lot of training. Adopted dogs may need brushing up on their housetraining skills because of confinement in an animal shelter or boarding kennel. Before rescue, some older dogs may have been shut outside their entire lives, depriving them of valuable socialization. Living indoors will be strange at first, but most dogs will get used to the comforts right away.

The senior dog may have issues with diminished or lost senses. If age or disease takes away his hearing or sight, retraining issues then become apparent. For example, teach your blind dog how to find the doggy door or the water bowl. Do not move furniture around. Blind dogs find their way around by feel or smell. Their working senses help them remember whether the doggy door is by the couch. If the couch suddenly disappears, the dog may become confused and have an accident.

Problem behaviors are rare with older dogs, but sometimes they happen. Perhaps a senior dog barks too much. Look at what sets off the barking. Is it to alert you? The Chihuahua is a very protective dog despite his small size. Even old dogs protect their families, new or old. For example, does he bark when the doorbell rings or if he sees people pass by the front window? Is he afraid of your male house guests, a sign of past abuse? Controlling excessive barking is possible, but only if you know the cause. Older dogs are trainable, and bad behaviors can be reshaped so that the outcome is positive. Good results may take more time and patience, but nothing is impossible to accomplish with a Chihuahua, including seniors.

If you adopt or acquire an older Chihuahua with behavior issues, enroll him in a training class. You will not be the only dog owner with a senior in the class. Most canine students are younger, but old dogs are often enrolled. you *can* teach an old dog new tricks.

Training Tidbit

A senior Chihuahua who loses all or part of his sight or hearing can still have a quality life. Owners should consider the following precautions to make their dog's life easier:
- Do not rearrange the furniture.
- Keep his food and water bowls in the same place
- Stick to his usual feeding schedule.
- Make sure that the ID is current.
- Block access to stairs.
- Gate or otherwise restrict access to the pool.
- Do not allow in garage.
- Take him for veterinary exams.
- Spend extra time with him.

Avoid long separations from old blind dogs. If you go away on vacation or a business trip, ask a trusted friend or neighbor to watch your dog. A boarding kennel might be too stressful for an old blind dog.

CHAPTER 14

END-OF-LIFE ISSUES

Saying good-bye to a treasured Chihuahua can reduce the owner to emotional shambles. Big strapping men weep uncontrollably. Bereft owners call in sick to their jobs. Your dog's death is the hardest part of dog ownership. Your Chihuahua may die unexpectedly in his sleep at five years of age from heart disease, or he may live until your oldest child graduates from college. But death at some point is inevitable. And it is a crushing moment when it happens.

Since he was a scrappy puppy, your Chihuahua has been a loyal, loving, and devoted companion. At Christmas season he sat on Santa's lap and the cost of his photo benefited your local animal shelter or Chihuahua rescue. He joined you on family picnics and scarfed down hot dogs. On cold blustery nights in the dead of winter, he cuddled next to you in bed. Every payday, you treated him to a box of special treats. And once in a while you bought him a steak. He greeted you with the same enthusiastic tail wag whether you were gone for ten minutes or six hours. You adored him.

After 15 years, though, he lost his spry step. He no longer jumped up to eat his meals. A

By the Numbers

Here are eight tips to help you handle grief:
1. Cry if you want to—it's okay.
2. Assemble an album with your pet's photos.
3. Scatter his ashes in a favorite place.
4. Send a donation in his name to an animal shelter or rescue.
5. Keep his food dish, bowl, and leash for the memory.
6. Talk to friends and family about your good times.
7. Read a book about pet grief.
8. Give unused food and snacks to an animal shelter or rescue.

Your veterinarian is the best source with whom to discuss end-of-life issues.

treat no longer interested him. Heart disease caused a dry hacking cough. The twinkle in his eyes dimmed long ago. He slept nearly all day long.

WHEN IT'S TIME

At some point, every dog owner faces that dreaded decision—when to let go. That choice will face you too. Chihuahuas live a long time, but they do not last forever. Your veterinarian is the best source to discuss end-of-life issues, palliative care, and when it is time for euthanasia. Always keep an open line of communication with your veterinarian about your dog's medical condition. Do not have unrealistic expectations, however. No doubt you love your dog and want him to live as long as possible. Your veterinarian cares too.

After all, the vet has treated your dog for a long time. In many cases, he or she has known your Chihuahua since you brought him home from the breeder. Now the vet can only dispense pain medications and others to make your dog comfortable, but he or she cannot cure a dog with end-stage bone cancer, cardiomyopathy, or renal failure. Veterinary medicine has come a long way, but it has limitations.

You may feel angry that you provided excellent care for your Chihuahua throughout his life yet he is now gravely ill. He ate premium dog food for years and had annual checkups. He lived indoors. Yet your neighbor's dog always lived in a cluttered yard for 12 years, never saw a veterinarian, and is quite healthy. Life is not always fair.

Alternatively, you may feel guilty that you

could not pay for more expensive procedures or medications because you just don't have the money. It is natural to feel that way; you loved and cared for your dog. You provided your Chihuahua with a wonderful loving home. You did your very best. Your Chihuahua loves you.

EUTHANASIA

Your dog will probably tell you when he is ready to let go. He may stop eating. He may be unable to stand. His breathing may be so labored that he can barely lift his head.

When the dog's quality of life fades and he is no longer himself, that is the time all dog owners dread. No one wants to say good-bye, but euthanasia releases a dog from pain and suffering in a peaceful, dignified manner. It is usually performed in a quiet room at the veterinarian's office. If you cannot handle the emotional trauma alone, ask a friend or family member to join you. The veterinarian will understand your feelings.

Some veterinarians make house calls so that the dog can go to his final resting place surrounded by loving family and friends in the comfort and dignity of his home. Check with your veterinarian to see whether this is an option.

Euthanasia is emotionally crushing for the owner, but it is painless for your dog. First, the

Multi-Dog Tip

Best Friend's Animal Sanctuary in Kanab, Utah, the nation's largest no–kill animal shelter, set aside an area called Angel's Rest for resident and staff pets when they die. Some shelter animals spend their entire lives at the Sanctuary, and staff members are quite attached to them. Naturally, they mourn these losses. Members of the public can also bury their pets or their pet's ashes at Angel's Rest. Donations benefit Best Friends. Angel's Rest is a place of comfort, solace, and healing for the staff and visitors at the Sanctuary (Courtesy of Best Friend's Animal Sanctuary).

It's natural to feel profound grief when losing a beloved pet.

veterinarian injects a sedative to relax and calm him. Then the two of you spend your last minutes alone while the sedative induces a deep sleep. A few minutes later, the veterinarian and a technician return. As you hold and gently stroke your dog, telling him that you will miss him, the veterinarian will inject a vein in the dog's leg with an overdose of a barbiturate. In about 15 to 20 seconds, his heart will stop beating. He is at peace.

If you need more time, the veterinarian will leave you alone with your dog. Sometimes the entire family attends the euthanasia; sometimes only one person does. It is a deeply moving and personal experience. It is usually tearful. An alert and sensitive veterinarian has tissues available.

The veterinarian's receptionist is sensitive to pet loss, but she must ask you about your pet's remains. Do you want cremation? Burial? She can help you with these delicate arrangements. And of course she has to ask you for payment. Be prepared to deal with payment issues.

For owners who cannot afford euthanasia either in the home or at a veterinarian's office, most animal shelters provide this service. Generally it is not free, but the rates are reduced.

GRIEF

Some owners are so profoundly depressed by the experience that they never live with another dog. Others love dogs so much that they visit either a breeder or animal shelter

⊙ *Training Tidbit*

Loving your Chihuahua means that someday you will let him go. Nearly all of us outlive our pets and have to decide when their time has come. Consider the following:

- Is he in considerable pain?
- Has he stopped eating?
- Are his seizures uncontrolled?
- Is he unable to stand?
- Is there bleeding?

If your dog exhibits any or all of these end-of-life symptoms, he is ready for euthanasia, a merciful death. Call your veterinarian to discuss arrangements.

the next day. Some do it the same day. Each person experiences grief at his or her own pace.

Expressing feeling about pet loss is no longer a social taboo. Dogs are frequently an elderly person's only companion. For children, a pet's loss may be their first experience with death. In some families, dogs are integral members loved by all. Their loss changes the family dynamic, so they usually add another dog.

Do not look to replace the Chihuahua who just died. He was your friend and had his own unique personality. Nothing can replace him or the fond memories you shared over many years. A new dog, whether adopted or from a breeder, will be different. Love the new dog for who he is. He too will bring joy and happiness into your life.

Allow yourself ample time to mourn. You experienced a significant loss, and as a devoted pet lover you will experience feelings of grief and sadness. It is normal to cry and feel sad and empty. You will miss your Chihuahua for a long time. He was special. Maybe he was your first puppy or was a stray without tags who just straggled into your yard. You shared years of warm, tender memories. As each day passes, though, the loss will sting just a little bit less and your heart will slowly start to heal.

Never minimize your feelings, even if others scoff at you by saying, "It was just a dog. You'll get over it." You have a right to your feelings. Your Chihuahua was a valued member of your family and an integral part of your life. But if the grief interferes with your personal or professional relationships, seek professional intervention. Pet loss therapy is available. Mental health workers, nurses, and veterinarians counsel bereaved pet owners at shelters, hospices, and mental health clinics. Some pet owners may attend a few sessions, while others may require professional intervention that includes medication.

50 FUN FACTS EVERY CHIHUAHUA OWNER SHOULD KNOW

1. Chihuahuas are better than Prozac.

2. Chihuahuas are small dogs with big attitudes.

3. Chihuahuas are fearless.

4. Chihuahuas are loyal; they don't ask for a divorce.

5. Chihuahuas are couch potatoes.

6. Chihuahuas fit into a purse but they prefer to walk.

7. Chihuahuas are not toys; they are companion animals.

8. Chihuahuas prefer other Chihuahuas.

9. Chihuahuas can excel in agility trials.

10. Chihuahuas come in different colors.

11. Chihuahuas add zest to a dull existence.

12. Chihuahuas are strong-willed but trainable.

13. Chihuahuas enjoy pampering.

14. Chihuahuas are photogenic.

15. Chihuahuas are smarter than humans; we go to work and they relax all day.

16. Chihuahuas are fun-loving and fun to love.

17. Chihuahuas are protective.

18. Chihuahuas are part of the family.

19. Chihuahuas should eat nutritionally complete meals but not overindulge with table scraps or snacks.

20. Chihuahuas are a healthy breed, but don't overlook annual exams.

21. Chihuahuas are easy to maintain, but they still need grooming.

22. Chihuahuas are fragile. Be careful handling them.

23. Chihuahuas chill easily. Remember their sweater or coat.

24. Chihuahua nails grow quickly, so keep them trimmed.

25. Older Chihuahuas are set in their ways. Humor them if you have to.

26. Chihuahua puppies are fun. Entertain them with games.

27. Never isolate your Chihuahua in the yard away from the family.

28. Chihuahuas need their teeth cleaned even as puppies.

29. Chihuahuas have a gentle, caring side.

30. Chihuahuas can learn obedience, even advanced skills.

31. Chihuahua puppies can be mischievous but playful.

32. Chihuahuas can get lost. Don't let them roam at large.

33. Always make sure that your Chihuahua wears current identification.

34. Reward your Chihuahua puppy with praise and treats to shape positive behavior.

35. Chihuahuas star in movies, Broadway plays, and television commercials.

36. Famous celebrities own Chihuahuas.

37. Chihuahuas should be house pets, not relegated to the back yard.

38. Crate training a Chihuahua is not cruel. Just don't lock him up for long periods.

39. Chihuahuas like a good belly rub every day.

40. Never abuse a Chihuahua.

41. Expose your Chihuahua puppy to your social network.

42. Biting, even in play, is a serious problem. Do not ignore it.

43. Chihuahuas can be therapy dogs and visit seniors in nursing homes or hospitals.

44. Chihuahuas love to give kisses.

45. Chihuahuas can show off their natural beauty on the show circuit.

46. Chihuahuas bask in the comfort of a cozy bed.

47. Chihuahuas who live indoors can still become infested with fleas.

48. Take your Chihuahua for a daily walk.

49. Consider adopting an unwanted Chihuahua.

50. Do not add to pet overpopulation—spay/neuter your Chihuahua. Shelters are loaded with Chihuahuas and Chihuahua mixes.

RESOURCES

ASSOCIATIONS AND ORGANIZATIONS

Breed Clubs

American Kennel Club (AKC)
5580 Centerview Drive
Raleigh, NC 27606
Telephone: (919) 233-9767
Fax: (919) 233-3627
E-Mail: info@akc.org
www.akc.org

British Chihuahua Club
www.the-british-chihuahua-club.org.uk

Canadian Kennel Club (CKC)
89 Skyway Avenue, Suite 100
Etobicoke, Ontario M9W 6R4
Telephone: (416) 675-5511
Fax: (416) 675-6506
E-Mail: information@ckc.ca
www.ckc.ca

Chihuahua Club of America (CCA)
www.chihuahuaclubofamerica.com

Federation Cynologique Internationale (FCI)
Secretariat General de la FCI
Place Albert 1er, 13
B – 6530 Thuin
Belqique
www.fci.be

The Kennel Club
1 Clarges Street
London
W1J 8AB
Telephone: 0870 606 6750
Fax: 0207 518 1058
www.the-kennel-club.org.uk

United Kennel Club (UKC)
100 E. Kilgore Road
Kalamazoo, MI 49002-5584
Telephone: (269) 343-9020
Fax: (269) 343-7037
E-Mail: pbickell@ukcdogs.com
www.ukcdogs.com

Pet Sitters

National Association of Professional Pet Sitters
15000 Commerce Parkway, Suite C
Mt. Laurel, New Jersey 08054
Telephone: (856) 439-0324
Fax: (856) 439-0525
E-Mail: napps@ahint.com
www.petsitters.org

Pet Sitters International
201 East King Street
King, NC 27021-9161
Telephone: (336) 983-9222
Fax: (336) 983-5266
E-Mail: info@petsit.com
www.petsit.com

Rescue Organizations and Animal Welfare Groups

American Humane Association (AHA)
63 Inverness Drive East
Englewood, CO 80112
Telephone: (303) 792-9900
Fax: 792-5333
www.americanhumane.org

American Society for the Prevention of Cruelty to Animals (ASPCA)
424 E. 92nd Street
New York, NY 10128-6804
Telephone: (212) 876-7700
www.aspca.org

Gabriel's Angels
www.gabrielsangels.org

The Humane Society of the United States (HSUS)
2100 L Street, NW
Washington DC 20037
Telephone: (202) 452-1100
www.hsus.org

Royal Society for the Prevention of Cruelty to Animals (RSPCA)
RSPCA Enquiries Service
Wilberforce Way, Southwater,
Horsham, West Sussex RH13 9RS
United Kingdom
Telephone: 0870 3335 999
Fax: 0870 7530 284
www.rspca.org.uk

Sports

International Agility Link (IAL)
Global Administrator: Steve Drinkwater
E-Mail: yunde@powerup.au
www.agilityclick.com/~ial

The World Canine Freestyle Organization, Inc.
P.O. Box 350122
Brooklyn, NY 11235
Telephone: (718) 332-8336
Fax: (718) 646-2686
E-Mail: WCFODOGS@aol.com
www.worldcaninefreestyle.org

Therapy

Delta Society
875 124th Ave, NE, Suite 101
Bellevue, WA 98005
Telephone: (425) 679-5500
Fax: (425) 679-5539
E-Mail: info@DeltaSociety.org
www.deltasociety.org

Therapy Dogs Inc.
P.O. Box 20227
Cheyenne WY 82003
Telephone: (877) 843-7364
Fax: (307) 638-2079
E-Mail: therapydogsinc@
qwestoffice.net
www.therapydogs.com

**Therapy Dogs International
(TDI)**
88 Bartley Road
Flanders, NJ 07836
Telephone: (973) 252-9800
Fax: (973) 252-7171
E-Mail: tdi@gti.net
www.tdi-dog.org

Training

**Association of Pet Dog
Trainers (APDT)**
150 Executive Center Drive
Box 35
Greenville, SC 29615
Telephone: (800) PET-DOGS
Fax: (864) 331-0767
E-Mail: information@apdt.
com
www.apdt.com

**International Association of
Animal Behavior Consultants
(IAABC)**
565 Callery Road
Cranberry Township, PA 16066
E-Mail: info@iaabc.org
www.iaabc.org

**National Association of
Dog Obedience Instructors
(NADOI)**
PMB 369
729 Grapevine Hwy.
Hurst, TX 76054-2085
www.nadoi.org

Veterinary and Health Resources

Academy of Veterinary Homeopathy (AVH)
P.O. Box 9280
Wilmington, DE 19809
Telephone: (866) 652-1590
Fax: (866) 652-1590
www.theavh.org

American Academy of Veterinary Acupuncture (AAVA)
P.O. Box 1058
Glastonbury, CT 06033
Telephone: (860) 632-9911
Fax: (860) 659-8772
www.aava.org

American Animal Hospital Association (AAHA)
12575 W. Bayaud Ave.
Lakewood, CO 80228
Telephone: (303) 986-2800
Fax: (303) 986-1700
E-Mail: info@aahanet.org
www.aahanet.org/index.cfm

American College of Veterinary Internal Medicine (ACVIM)
1997 Wadsworth Blvd., Suite A
Lakewood, CO 80214-5293
Telephone: (800) 245-9081
Fax: (303) 231-0880
Email: ACVIM@ACVIM.org
www.acvim.org

American College of Veterinary Ophthalmologists (ACVO)
P.O. Box 1311
Meridian, ID 83860
Telephone: (208) 466-7624
Fax: (208) 466-7693
E-Mail: office09@acvo.com
www.acvo.com

American Holistic Veterinary Medical Association (AHVMA)
2218 Old Emmorton Road
Bel Air, MD 21015
Telephone: (410) 569-0795
Fax: (410) 569-2346
E-Mail: office@ahvma.org
www.ahvma.org

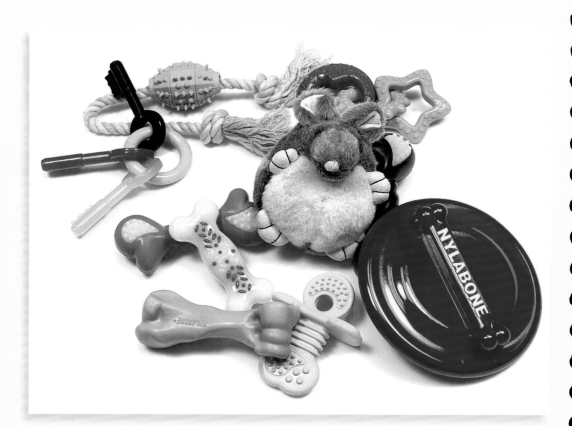

American Veterinary Medical Association (AVMA)
1931 North Meacham Road,
Suite 100
Schaumburg, IL 60173-4360
Telephone: (847) 925-8070
Fax: (847) 925-1329
E-Mail: avmainfo@avma.org
www.avma.org

ASPCA Animal Poison Control Center
Telephone: (888) 426-4435
www.aspca.org

British Veterinary Association (BVA)
7 Mansfield Street
London
W1G 9NQ
Telephone: 0207 636 6541
Fax: 0207 908 6349
E-Mail: bvahq@bva.co.uk
www.bva.co.uk

Canine Eye Registration Foundation (CERF)
VMDB/CERF
1717 Philo Rd
P O Box 3007
Urbana, IL 61803-3007
Telephone: (217) 693-4800
Fax: (217) 693-4801
E-Mail: CERF@vmbd.org
www.vmdb.org

Orthopedic Foundation for Animals (OFA)
2300 NE Nifong Blvd
Columbus, Missouri 65201-3856
Telephone: (573) 442-0418
Fax: (573) 875-5073
Email: ofa@offa.org
www.offa.org

US Food and Drug Administration Center for Veterinary Medicine (CVM)
7519 Standish Place
HFV-12
Rockville, MD 20855-0001
Telephone: (240) 276-9300 or (888) INFO-FDA
http://www.fda.gov/cvm

PUBLICATIONS

Books
Anderson, Teoti. *The Super Simple Guide to Housetraining*. Neptune City: TFH Publications, 2004.

Anne, Jonna, with Mary Straus. *The Healthy Dog Cookbook: 50 Nutritious and Delicious Recipes Your Dog Will Love*. UK: Ivy Press Limited, 2008.

Dainty, Suellen. *50 Games to Play With Your Dog*. UK: Ivy Press Limited, 2007.

Gagne, Tammy. *The Chihuahua*. Neptune City: TFH Publications, 2005.

Miller with Morgan. *Chihuahuas*. Neptune City: TFH Publications, 2006.

Morgan, Diane. *Good Dogkeeping*. Neptune City: TFH Publications, 2005.

Magazines
AKC Family Dog
American Kennel Club
260 Madison Avenue
New York, NY 10016
Telephone: (800) 490-5675
E-Mail: familydog@akc.org
www.akc.org/pubs/familydog

AKC Gazette
American Kennel Club
260 Madison Avenue
New York, NY 10016
Telephone: (800) 533-7323
E-Mail: gazette@akc.org
www.akc.org/pubs/gazette

The Chihuahua Connection
www.tazchi.com

Dog & Kennel
Pet Publishing, Inc.
7-L Dundas Circle
Greensboro, NC 27407
Telephone: (336) 292-4272
Fax: (336) 292-4272
E-Mail: info@petpublishing.com
www.dogandkennel.com

Dogs Monthly
Ascot House
High Street, Ascot,
Berkshire SL5 7JG
United Kingdom
Telephone: 0870 730 8433
Fax: 0870 730 8431
E-Mail: admin@rtc-associates.freeserve.co.uk
www.corsini.co.uk/dogsmonthly

Websites
Nylabone
www.nylabone.com

TFH Publications, Inc.
www.tfh.com

INDEX

Boldfaced numbers indicate illustrations.

A

AAFCO (American Association of Feed Control Officials), 102, 103, 106
AAHA (American Animal Hospital Association), 49, 202
AAVA (American Academy of Veterinary Acupuncture), 202
abdominal area, care of, 112
ABKA (American Boarding Kennel Association), 169
Academy of Veterinary Homeopathy (AVH), 126
accidents, housetraining, 66–67, **66**
activities
  agility, 157, 160–161, **160**
  animal-assisted therapy, 40, 134, 155–156
  camping, 157–158
  Canine Good Citizen program, 158
  conformation, 161–162
  flyball, 162–163
  flying disc competition, 163–164
  freestyle, 164–165
  hiking, **156**, 158–159
  obedience competition, 165–166
  sports, 159–166
  traveling, 166–169, **167**, **168**, 183
  walking, 158–159, **158**

acupuncture, 125–126
ACVIM (American College of Veterinary Internal Medicine), 202
ACVO (American College of Veterinary Ophthalmologist), 201, 202
adoption of adult dogs
  agreements for, 176–177
  breeders and, 175, **176**
  costs for, 177
  foster care for, 77, 81, 175, 176
  homecoming expectations, 81
  in multi-dog environment, 76, **76**, **80**, 81
  in multi-pet environment, 176
  off-site adoptions, 175
  reasons for, 75–76, 173
  rescue groups, 76–77, **78**, 79–81, 173–175, **176**
  retraining and, 75
  shelters for, 76–81, **78**, **80**, 173–175, **176**
  training for, 75, 79
ADPT (Association of Professional Dog Trainers), 59
adult dogs
  adopting, 75–81, **76**, **80**, 173–177, **176**
  breeders and, 175, **176**
  fostering, 77, 81, 175, 176
  homecoming expectations, 81
  in multi-dog

environment, 76, **76**, **80**, 81
  rescue groups for, 76–77, **78**, 79–81, 173–175, **176**
  retraining and, 75
  shelters for, 76–81, **78**, **80**, 173–175, **176**
  training for, 75, 79
African fox, 11
aggression, 143–146, **144**
agility, 157, 160–161, **160**
aging, signs of, 179–180, **180**
agreements
  for adoption, 176–177
  for health details, 25
AHA (American Humane Association), 200
AHVMA (American Holistic Veterinary Medical Association), 202
air travel, 166–167, 183
AKC. *See* American Kennel Club (AKC)
AKC Family Dog (magazine), 203
AKC Gazette (magazine), 203
All American Pet Brands, 15
allergies, 122–123, **122**
alternative therapies, 125–128, **125**
Alzheimer's disease, 186, 187
American Academy of Veterinary Acupuncture (AAVA), 202
American Animal Hospital Association (AAHA), 49, 202

American Association of Feed Control Officials (AAFCO), 102, 103, 106

American Boarding Kennel Association (ABKA), 169

American College of Veterinary Internal Medicine (ACVIM), 202

American College of Veterinary Ophthalmologist (ACVO), 202

American Holistic Veterinary Medical Association (AHVMA), 202

American Humane Association (AHA), 200

American Kennel Club (AKC), **10**, 12, 20, 31, 33, 158, 161, 165, 200

American Society for the Prevention of Cruelty to Animals (ASPCA), 200

American Veterinary Chiropractic Association (AVCA), 126

American Veterinary Dental Society (AVDS), 92

American Veterinary Medical Association (AVMA), 202

anaplasmosis, canine, 119

Ancylostoma braziliense (hookworm), 114

Ancylostoma caninum (hookworm), 114

Anderson, Teoti, 203

Angel's Rest, animal sanctuary, 195

animal welfare groups, 200

animal-assisted therapy, 40, 134, 155–156

Anne, Jonna, 203

annual health visits, 111–113, **112**

anticonvulsive medication, 121–122

antifungal drugs, 119

anti-parasitic treatments, 123

anxiety, separation, 149, 151–153, **153**

APDT (Association of Pet Dog Trainers), 201

Arizona Animal Welfare League, 175
arthritis, 185
Ashley (Whippet), 163
Ashley Whippet Disc Dog Championships, 164
ASPCA (American Society for the Prevention of Cruelty to Animals), 200
ASPCA Animal Poison Control Center, 202
Association of Pet Dog Trainers (APDT), 201
Association of Professional Dog Trainers (ADPT), 59
associations, list of, 200–203
AVCA (American Veterinary Chiropractic Association), 126
AVDS (American Veterinary Dental Society), 92
AVH (Academy of Veterinary Homeopathy), 126, 201
AVMA (American Veterinary Medical Association), 202

B
baby teeth, retained, 121
Bach Flower, 126
backyard breeders, 34–35, 54
Banchero, Natalio, 15
BARF (bones and raw food) diet, 104–105
bargain brand vs. premium foods, 46–47, 97, 126
barking, excessive, 146–147, **146**
barking dogs story, 140
bathing
    frequency of, 88
    process for, 24, **87**, 88–89
    supplies for, 88
    temperature and, 182–

183, **183**
    tick baths and, 89
bedding, 39, **116**, 174, **186**
bee stings, 129
behavior classes, 29
behavior problems
    aggression, 143–146, **144**
    barking, excessive, 146–147, **146**
    biting, 143, 145
    chewing, 147, **148**
    coprophagy, 148
    digging, 148–149
    jumping up, 149–150, **150**
    leash pulling, 147, 150, **151**
    nipping, 150–151
    separation anxiety, 149, 151–153, **153**
    thunderphobia, 153
behaviorist, 144
Belle (Chihuahua), 157
Best Friends Animal Sanctuary, 195
Beverly Hills Chihuahua (Disney film with Chihuahua star), 14
Big Mama's House 2 (movie with Chihuahua star), 14
bites, on Chihuahuas, **128**, 129
biting, 143, 145
bleeding, 129
blindness, 188, 191
blow-drying, coat/hair, 88–89
bobtails, 162
body structure, 20–23
bones
    broken, 129–130
    feeding, 107–108
    as toys, 41
bones and raw food (BARF) diet, 104–105

booties (clothing), 64, **158**, **183**
Boredella burgdorferi (Lyme disease), 52–53
bowls, food and water, 41, 159
breed characteristics, 19–20, 198–199
breed clubs, 12–13, 200
breeders
    adult dogs and, 175, **176**
    documents from, 36
    health agreements and, 25
    responsible traits of, 33–37, **34**
    visiting, 35–36, **35**
breed-specific disorders, 120–122
British Kennel Club, 12–13, **14**, 200
British Veterinary Association (BVA), 202
Bruiser (Chihuahua), 14
brushing
    coat, 24, **24**, 84–88, **86**, 182
    teeth, 93
BVA (British Veterinary Association), 202

C
camping, 157–158
Canadian Kennel Club (CKC), 200
Canadian Musical Canine Sports International (CMCSI), 164
cancer, 123
canine anaplasmosis, 119
canine cognitive disorder (CCD), 185–187, **187**
Canine Eye Registration Foundation (CERF), 202
Canine Good Citizen program, 158

canned foods, 102, **103**
Capin, Leslie, 15
car travel, 167–168, 183
carbohydrates in diet, 99
cataracts, 187–188
CCA (Chihuahua Club of America), 12, 33, 200
CCD (canine cognitive disorder), 185–187, **187**
Center for Disease Control, 119–120

CERF (Canine Eye Registration Foundation), 202
characteristics of breed, 19–20, 198–199
checkups, 50–51, 52, 111–113, **112**, 183–184
chewing, 147, **148**
CHF (congestive heart failure), 190–191
The Chihuahua (Gagne), 203

Chihuahua (Miller & Morgan), 203
Chihuahua Club of America (CCA), 12, 33, 200
The Chihuahua Connection (magazine), 203
children and Chihuahuas, 25–26, **26**, 49
China, history of Chihuahuas in, 10
chiropractic therapy, 126

Chloe (Chihuahua), 15
chondroitin supplements, 126
CKC (Canadian Kennel Club), 200
classes, behavior/training, 29, 70–71
cleft palate, 55
clothing for Chihuahuas, 41–42, 64, **64**, **136**, **144**, **158**, 159, **183**
CMCSI (Canadian Musical Canine Sports International), 164
coat/hair
   blow-drying, 88–89
   types of, 21–22
coats (clothing), 41–42, 64, **64**, **136**, **158**, 159
Coco (Chihuahua), 14
collars, 39–40, **39**, 147
color, coat and eyes, 22
combing, 86, 182
Come command, 68–69
commands. *See also specific commands*
   basic, 67–71
   intermediate, 135–141
commercial diets, 101–103
conformation competition, 161–162
congestive heart failure (CHF), 190–191
contagious diseases, 51–54, **51**
coprophagy, 148
costs
   adoption, 76, 177
   maintenance, 23
crate training, 28–29, 61–62, **62**
crates, 40, 42
cropped ears, 162
Ctenocephalides canis (flea), 117

Cushing's disease, 109, 188–189, **189**
CVM (US Food and Drug Administration Center for Veterinary Medicine), 203

D
Dainty, Suellen, 203
day care, doggy, 169
DDFL (Denver Dumb Friends League), 15
deer ticks, 52–53
Delta Society, 40, 155, 200
dental
   care, 92–94, **92**, 183
   problems, 189
Denver Dumb Friends League (DDFL), 15
Dermatophytes (fungus), 117–119
de-worming, 50, 114, 116
DHLPP vaccination, 51
diagnostic tests for seniors dogs, 184
diet. *See* feeding
digging, 148–149
Dipylidium caninum (tapeworm), 115–116
Dirofilaria immitis (heartworm), 114
diseases, 52–54. *See also* health issues
distemper, 52
docked tails, 162
documents from breeders, 36
Dog & Kennel (magazine), 203
dog parks, 27, 70–71, 159
dog tick fever, 119
The Dog Whisperer (television series with Chihuahua), 14
doggy day care, 169
doggy doors, 65, 107

Dogs Monthly (magazine), 203
domestication of the dog, 7–8, **8**
Down command, 69–70
Down-stay command, 138–139, **139**
Dr. Papidies (Chihuahua), 15
dried foods (kibble), 101–102
Duff, Hilary, 14

E
Eacret, Tina, 175
ears
   care of, 89–91, **89**, 112
   characteristics of, 22
   problems with, 119, 123–124
ehrlichiosis, 119
emergency care, 49, 128–131
end-of-life issues
   euthanasia, 195–196
   grief, coping with, 173, 196–197, **196**
   letting go, 194–195, **194**, 197
entropion, 120
environment requirements, 19, 23, 38
epileptic. *See* seizures
Europe, history of Chihuahuas in, 10
euthanasia, 195–196
evacuation plan for natural disasters, 124
exercise
   health issues and, 109, **113**
   requirements, 24, 31, 81
exercise pens, 38, 62
eyes
   care of, **90**, 91–92, 112

characteristics of, 22
problems with, 124,
187–188

F

famous Chihuahuas, 13–15,
13
fats in diet, 97–98
FCI (Federation
Cynologique
International), 200
fear biting, 145
Federation Cynologique
International (FCI), 200

feeding. *See also* nutrition
bargain brand vs.
premium foods, 46–47,
97, 126
bones, 107–108
bones and raw food
(BARF) diet, 104–105
canned foods, 102
commercial diets, 101–
103
dried foods (kibble),
101–102
foods, types of
bargain brand vs.

premium foods,
46–47, 97, 126
canned foods, 102
dried foods (kibble),
101–102
holistic foods, 106–
107
raw food diets,
104–105
semi-moist foods, 103
wet foods, 102
free-feeding, 108–109
frequency of, 45, 46, **46**,
106

holistic foods, 106–107
kibble (dried foods), 46, 101–102
noncommercial diets, 103–105
obesity and, 102, 109, 188
puppies, 45–48
quantity, 47–48
raw food diets, 104–105
schedules, 47, **48**, 108–109, 180
semi-moist foods, 103
seniors dogs, 180–182
small-breed kibble, 46
specialty diets, 105–107
treats, 107, 141, 181
types of foods, 46–47, 97, 101–107, 126
wet foods, 102
female vs. male Chihuahuas, 23
50 Games to Play With Your Dog (Dainty), 203
flea combs, 86
fleas, 117, **118**, 121
flea/tick control, 40
floppy ears, 22–23, 162
flyball, 162–163, **162**
flying disc competition, 163–164
Flying Disc Dog Open, 164
food aggression, 145–146
food bowls, 41
food storage, 101–102
fostering a Chihuahua, 77, 81, 175, 176
fox, African, 11
free-feeding, 108–109
Freestyle, 164–165, **164**
From Baghdad With Love, 159
frostbite, 130
fur mats, removing, 87–88

G
Gabriel's Angles, 200
Gagne, Tammy, 203
Gentle Leader collars, 147
Gigdet (Chihuahua), 13
gingivitis, 92
glucosamine supplements, 126
Good Dogkeeping (Morgan), 203
grand mal seizures, 121
grief, coping with, 193, 196–197, **196**
groomers, professional, 94–95, **94**
grooming
    as health check, 85
    importance of, 83–84
    preparation for, 91, 93
    puppies, 48
    requirements, 24, **24**
    seniors dogs, 182–183
    supplies, 40, 84

H
handling your Chihuahua, 24–25, 35–36
head characteristics, 22
health agreements from breeders, 25
health care
    dental, 92–94, **92**, 183
    ears, 89–91, **89**, 112
    emergency care, 128–131
    eyes, **90**, 91–92, 112
    general issues, 48–51, 111–113
    lungs, 112
    mouth, 111–112
    preventative care, **50**, 183–184
    teeth, 92–94, **92**
    testicles, 112
health issues
    allergies, 122–123, **122**

Alzheimer's disease, 186, **187**
Ancylostoma braziliense (hookworm), 114
Ancylostoma caninum (hookworm), 114
arthritis, 185
baby teeth, retained, 121
bites, **128**, 129
bleeding, 129
bones, broken, 129–130
breed-specific disorders, 120–122
cancer, 123
canine anaplasmosis, 119
canine cognitive disorder (CCD), 185–187, **187**
cataracts, 187–188
cleft palate, 55
congestive heart failure (CHF), 190–191
Ctenocephalides canis (flea), 117
Cushing's disease, 109, 188–189, **189**
dental problems
    baby teeth, retained, 121
    disease, 189
    gingivitis, 92
Dermatophytes (fungus), 117–119
Dipylidium caninum (tapeworm), 115–116
Dirofilaria immitis (heartworm), 114
diseases, 52–54
dog tick fever, 119
ear problems
    infections, 123–124
    mites, 119
ehrlichiosis, 119
entropion, 120
exercise and, 24, **113**
eye problems

cataracts, 187–188
infections, 124
fleas, 117, **118**, 121
frostbite, 130
general issues, 25, 122–124
gingivitis, 92
heart murmurs, 112
heart problems
congestive heart failure (CHF), 190–191
mitral valve disease, 120
murmurs, 112
pulmonary stenosis, 121
heatstroke, **130**, 131
hernias, 113

hip dysplasia, **123**, 124
hydrocephalus, 55
hypoglycemia, 55, **55**, 108, 188–189
hypothyroidism, 109, 189–190
Lyme disease, 52–53
mites, 119
mitral valve disease, 120
molera, 22, 55
motion sickness, 167
Otodectes cynotis (ear mites), 119
parasites
external, 117–120
internal, 113–117
patellar luxation, 121
poisoning, 131
pulmonary stenosis, 121

Rocky Mountain spotted fever, 119
seizures, 55, 121–122
seniors dogs and, 183–191, **190**
stings, 129
ticks, **118**, 119–120, 121
Toxascaris leonina (roundworm), 115
Toxocara canis (roundworm), 115
trachea, collapsing, 120
Trichuris vulpis (whipworm), 116
worms
Ancylostoma braziliense (hookworm), 114
Ancylostoma caninum (hookworm), 114

Dipylidium caninum (tapeworm), 115–116
Dirofilaria immitis (heartworm), 114
Toxascaris leonina (roundworm), 115
Trichuris vulpis (whipworm), 116
health resources, 201–202
The Healthy Dog Cookbook (Anne & Straus), 203
heart problems
  congestive heart failure (CHF), 190–191
  mitral valve disease, 120
  murmurs, 112
  pulmonary stenosis, 121
heartworms, 114
heatstroke, **130**, 131
Heel command, 135–137, **136**
hepatitis, 52
herbal treatments/medications, 126, 153, **153**
hernias, 113
hiking, **156**, 158–159
Hilton, Paris, 14
hip dysplasia, **123**, 124
history of Chihuahuas, 8–11, **9**
holistic foods, 106–107
Hollywood Dog (magazine), 14
homecoming, 37–38, **37**, 42–43, **43**, 81
homemade diets, 104
homeopathy, 126–127
hookworms, 114–115
housesitters, 169
housetraining
  accidents during, 66–67, **66**
  creates and, 28–29
  example of training routine, 65–66

indoor vs. outdoor, 62–63
process for, 63–65
schedule for, 64–65
time to start, 22, 71
Humane Society of Greater Dayton, 84
The Humane Society of the United States (HSUS), 173, 200
hydrocephalus, 55
hypoglycemia, 55, **55**, 108, 188–189
hypothyroidism, 109, 189–190

I
IAABC (International Association of Animal Behavior Consultants), 201
IAL (International Agility Link), 200
identification, types of, 41
infectious diseases, 51–54, **51**
International Agility Link (IAL), 200
International Association of Animal Behavior Consultants (IAABC), 201

J
Johansson, Scarlett, 14
jumping up, 149–150, **150**

K
Kennel Club, 200
kennel cough, 53
kennels, 169
kibble (dried foods), 101–102
kindergarten, puppy, 70–71

L
leash pulling, 147, 150, **151**
leash training, 29, 39, 70

leashes, 39–40
Legally Blonde (movie with Chihuahua star), 14
leptospirosis, 52
Levinson, Boris, 155
licenses, 41
life span, 20, 173, 179
lifestyle considerations, 23–24
lime sulfur dips, 119
litter boxes, 63
locating
  breeders, 33
  Chihuahuas, 33–37
  housesitters, 169
  kennels, 169
  trainers, 59
  veterinarians, 49
lodging while traveling, 168
Lola (Chihuahua), 14
long hair/coat
  brushing, 85–86, **85**
  characteristics of, 12–13, 21–22, **21**
  grooming, 24, **24**
lungs, care of, 112
Lyme disease, 52–53

M
Mabel (Chihuahua), 175
magazine resources, 203
male vs. female Chihuahuas, 23
Malta, history of Chihuahuas in, 10
Maricopa County Animal Care and Control, 175
mats (fur), removing, 87–88
Max Fund, 15
Mayan culture and Chihuahuas, 8–9
MBDA (Mixed Breed Dog Club of America), 165–166
medications, administering, 181

Mediterranean, history of Chihuahuas in, 9–10
Mexico, history of Chihuahuas in, 8–9, **9**
microchip identification, 41
Midget (Chihuahua), 12
Miller, Richard, 203
mineral supplements, 15, 99–100, 181, **182**, 191
mites, 119
mitral valve disease, 120
Mixed Breed Dog Club of America (MBDA), 165–166
molera, 22, 55
Moonie (Chihuahua), 14
Morgan, Diane, 203

motion sickness, 167
mouth, care of, 111–112
movie and television, Chihuahua's in, 13–15
multi-dog environment
adult dogs in, 76, **76**, **80**, 81
considerations for, 32–33, **32**, 81
feeding and, 104, 181
fleas and ticks and, 121
housetraining and, 67
introducing a new Chihuahua to, 176
leash pulling and, 147
puppies and seniors in,

177
puppies as gifts and, 29
schedules and, 43
seniors dogs and, 175, 176, 177, 184
vaccinations and, 25, 54
multi-pet environment, 27, **28**, 176

N
NADAC (North American Dog Agility Council), 160
NADOI (National Association of Dog Obedience Instructors), 201

NAFA (National American Flyball Association), 162
nail care, 91–92, **91**, 183
NAPCC (National Animal Poison Control Center), 131
NAPPS (National Association of Professional Pet Sitters), 169, 200
National American Flyball Association (NAFA), 162
National Animal Poison Control Center (NAPCC), 131
National Association of Dog Obedience Instructors (NADOI), 201
National Association of Professional Pet Sitters (NAPPS), 169, 200
National Dog Groomers Association of America (NDGAA), 95
natural disasters, evacuation plan for, 124
NDGAA (National Dog Groomers Association of America), 95
neck characteristics, 22
neutering, 47, 145
nipping, 150–151
noncommercial diets, 103–105
North Africa, history of Chihuahuas in, 11
North American Dog Agility Council (NADAC), 160
nutrition
   bargain brand foods and, 46
   carbohydrates, 99
   fats, 97–98
   importance of, 97, **100**
   premium foods and, 46–47, 97, 126
protein, 98–99, **98**
supplements, diet, 15, 99–100, 181, **182**, 191
water, 100, 181–182
Nylabone, 41, **41**, 94, 107, **107**, 147, 152, **202**

O
obedience training
   basic commands, 67–71
   importance of, 57–58, 133–135
   intermediate commands, 135–141, **135**
obedience trials and competitions, 165–166
obesity, 102, 109, 188
obtaining a Chihuahua
   considerations before, 31–33
   as a gift, 29, 36–37
   locating, 33–37
   preparation for, 37–38
odor neutralizes, 67
OFA (Orthopedic Foundation for Animals), 203
off-site adoptions, 175, **176**
Oliver and Company (Disney film with Chihuahua star), 14
online sales, 36
organizations, list of, 200–203
Orthopedic Foundation for Animals (OFA), 203
Osborne, Sharon, 14
Otodectes cynotis (ear mites), 119
outdoor activities, 155. *See also* activities; sports activities
outdoor environment, 38

P
Pancho (Chihuahua), 14
paperwork from breeders, 36
parainfluenza, 53
parasites
   external, 117–120
   internal, 113–117
parks for dogs, 27, 70–71, 159
parvovirus, 53–54, **53**
patellar luxation, 121
Pedro (Chihuahua), 166
Perro Chihuahueno, 9
pet quality vs. show quality, 31–32
pet sitters, 200
Pet Sitters International (PSI), 169, 200
pet therapy, 155–156
petit mal seizures, 121
pets and Chihuahuas, 27, **28**
physical characteristics, 20–23
physical therapy, 127–128, **127**
pills, administering, 179–180, 181
poisoning, 131
positive training method, 29, 58–59, **58**, 141
premium foods vs. bargain brand, 46–47, 97, 126
preparation for homecoming, 37–38, **37**
prescription diets, 105–106, **105**
professionals. *See also* veterinarians
   behaviorist, 144
   groomers, 94–95, **94**
   trainers, 59, 145
protective characteristics of Chihuahuas, 19–20
protein in diet, 98–99, **98**

PSI (Pet Sitters International), 169, 200
public transportation, travel on, 166
publication resources, 203
pulmonary stenosis, 121
puppies
    characteristics of, 19–23
    classes for, 70–71
    commitment requirements for, 31–33
    feeding, 45–48
    as gifts, 29, 36–37

grooming, 48
health care, 48–54
health issues, 54–55
homecoming and, 42–43, **43**
lifestyle considerations for, 23–27
locating a Chihuahua, 33–37
preparation for, 37–38
schedules for, 38–39
selection of, 35–36
seniors dogs and, 177

supplies for, 39–42
trainability, 27–29
training, 57–71
puppy mills, 34, 54
puppy-proofing, **37**, 38

Q
quantity, feeding, 47–48

R
rabies, 54
ramps, portable, 184

raw food diets, 104–105
Raynor, H., 12
rescue groups, 76–81, **78**, 173–175, **176**, 200
responsibilities of pet ownership, 20, **22**, 31
retraining adult dogs, 75
ringworms, 117–119
Rocky Mountain spotted fever, 119
Rohde, Bob, 15
roundworms, 115
Royal Society for the Prevention of Cruelty to Animals (RSPCA), 200

S
schedules
  feeding, 47, **48**, 108–109, 180
  importance of, 38–39
  multi-dog environment and, 43
  training, 64–66
seizures, 55, 121–122
semi-moist foods, 103
seniors dogs
  adoption issues
    advantages of, 173
    agreements, 176–177
    cost of, 177
    off-site adoptions, 176–177
  aging, signs of, 179–180, **180**
  breeders and, 175
  diagnostic tests for, 184
  end-of-life issues, 193–197, **194**
  food and nutrition
    feeding, 180–182
    supplements, diet, 181
    treats, 181
    water requirements, 181–182
  fostering, 175, 176
grooming
  bathing, 182–183, **183**
  brushing, 182
  combing, 182
  dental care, 183
  nail care, 183
health issues
  Alzheimer's disease, 186, **187**
  arthritis, 185
  canine cognitive disorder (CCD), 185–187, **187**, **190**
  cataracts, 187–188
  congestive heart failure (CHF), 190–191
  Cushing's disease, 188–189, **189**
  dental disease, 189
  diagnostic tests for, 184
  hypothyroidism, 189–190
  medications, administering, 181
  obesity and, 188
  preventative care for, 183–184
  vaccinations, 184
medications, administering, 181
multi-dog environment and, 175, 176, 177, 184
obesity and, 188
off-site adoptions and, 175
portable ramps for, 184
preventative care for, 183–184
puppies and, 177
rescue options for, 173–175, **176**
shelters/rescue groups and, 173–175, **176**
sleeping arrangements, 174, **186**
training, 191
traveling and, 183
vaccinations, 184
separation anxiety, 149, 151–153, **153**
shedding, 84–85
shelters, 76–81, **78**, **80**, 173–175, **176**
show quality vs. pet quality, 31–32
Sit command, 69, **69**
Sit-stay command, 140–141
size of Chihuahuas, 21
Skyhoundz, 164
sleeping arrangements, 43, 174
small-breed kibble, 46
smooth coats, 12, 21, **21**, **24**, 85
snacks, 107, 141
sociability, 25–27
socialization, 59–61, **60**
space requirements, 19
spaying, 47, 109
specialty diets, 105–107
sports activities
  agility, 157, 160–161, **160**
  conformation, 161–162
  flyball, 162–163
  flying disc competition, 163–164
  freestyle, 164–165
  obedience competition, 165–166
  preparation for, 159–160
sports organizations, 200
Spray, Ana Lee, 140
Stand command, 141
standards for breed, 20–23
Stay command, 137, **138**
stings, 129

strangers and Chihuahuas, 27
Straus, Mary, 203
The Super Simple Guide to Housetraining (Anderson), 203
supplements, diet, 15, 99–100, 181, **182**, 191
supplies, 39–42, 84, 88, 157
sweaters (clothing), 41–42, 64, **64**, **144**

T
Taco Bell commercial, 13
tags for identification, 41
tapeworms, 115–116
TDAA (Teacup Dogs Agility Association), 160
TDI (Therapy Dogs International), 40, 155, 201
Teacup Dogs Agility Association (TDAA), 160
Techichis, 8–9
teeth
  care of, 92–94, **92**
  health issues, 121
teething, 152
television and movie, Chihuahua's in, 13–15
Tellington TTouch, 127
Tellington-Jones, Linda, 127

testicles, care of, 112
That's So Raven (television series with Chihuahua star), 14
therapies, alternative, 125–128, **125**
therapy dogs, 40, 134, 155–156
Therapy Dogs, Inc., 201
Therapy Dogs International (TDI), 40, 155, 201
therapy organizations, 200–201
thunderphobia, 153
tick baths, 89
ticks, 52–53, **118**, 119–120, 121
Tito (Chihuahua), 14
Toxascaris leonina (roundworm), 115
Toxocara canis (roundworm), 115
toys, 41, **41**, **42**
trachea, collapsing, 120
trainability, 27–29, **29**
trainers, 59, 145
training
　adult dogs, 75, 79
　commands
　　basic, 67–71
　　intermediate, 133–141, **135**
　crate training, 28–29, 61–62, **62**
　doggy door use, 107
　housetraining, 22, 28–29, 62–67, 71
　importance of, 57–58, 133–135
　leash training, 29, 39, 70
　multi-dog environment and, 67
　obedience training, intermediate, 133–141, **135**

organizations, 201
positive training method, 29, 58–59, **58**, 141
retraining adult dogs, 75
schedules, 64–66
seniors dogs and, 191
socialization, 59–61, **60**
time to start, 28, **29**
training classes, 29, 59
traveling with your Chihuahua, 166–169, **167**, **168**, 183
treats, feeding, 107, 141
Trichuris vulpis (whipworm), 116

U
United Kennel Club (UKC), 200
United States Dog Agility Association (USDAA), 160
United States, history of Chihuahuas in, 11
US Food and Drug Administration Center for Veterinary Medicine (CVM), 203
US Freestyle Organization, 164
USDAA (United States Dog Agility Association), 160

V
vaccinations
　cautions prior to, 27
　DHLPP vaccination, 51–52, 70
　distemper, 52
　hepatitis, 52
　infectious diseases and, 51–54, **51**
　initial veterinary visit and, 25
　leptospirosis, 52
　Lyme disease, 52–53

multi-dog environment and, 25, 54
parainfluenza, 53
parvovirus, 53–54
rabies, 54
seniors dogs and, 184
veterinarians
　annual visits, 111–113, **112**
　emergency care and, 49
　initial visit with, 25, 52
　locating, 49
　preventive care and, **50**, 183–184
　relationship with, 48–51
veterinary resources, 201–202
vitamin supplements, 15, 99–100, 181, **182**, 191
volunteer opportunities, 77, 80

W
walking activity, 158–159, **158**
walking on leash, 70
wasp stings, 129
water bowls, 41, 159
water requirements, 100, 181–182
Watson, James, 11, 12
WCFO (World Canine Freestyle Organization), 164, 200
Wee-Wee Pads, 63, **63**
wet foods, 102
Wheelchair Willy (Chihuahua), 14
whipworms, 116–117
wolves, relationship to Chihuahuas, 7–8, **8**
World Canine Freestyle Organization (WCFO), 164, 200
worms, 114–119

PHOTO CREDITS

VETERINARY ADVISOR

Wayne Hunthausen, DVM, consulting veterinary editor and pet behavior consultant, is the director of Animal Behavior Consultations in the Kansas City area and currently serves on the Practitioner Board for *Veterinary Medicine* and the Behavior Advisory Board for *Veterinary Forum*.

BREEDER ADVISOR

Sherri Rohm
Chihuahua owner and breeder

DEDICATION
I dedicate this book to Arizona Chihuahua Rescue and the entire Phoenix rescue community for saving so many unwanted Chihuahuas, Chihuahua mixes, and other pets from abuse, misery, hunger, and hardship. You all make me proud. And I'm glad to be part of the gang.

ACKNOWLEDGMENTS
Special thanks to Chihuahua lovers Tina Eacret, Barb Rabe, and Joyce Mercer for their invaluable insight on living with Chihuahuas. I sincerely appreciate the guidance and input from Dr. Velvet Lynn Edwards of the Pecan Grove Veterinary Hospital in Tempe, Arizona (who also has Chihuahuas), and Scottsdale-based pet behaviorist and trainer Sam Kabbel. Shelley's Pet Grooming in Tempe, Arizona, provided helpful tips on grooming Chihuahuas.

ABOUT THE AUTHOR
After a long recovery after a pedestrian car accident in January 1994, **Debra J. White** redirected her life. She resumed animal shelter volunteer work and is currently with the Arizona Animal Welfare League in Phoenix. She is on the board of the Phoenix Animal Care Coalition. From 2001 to 2008, she and her adopted dog Luke were a therapy team with Gabriel's Angels. She volunteered for former Arizona Governor Janet Napolitano from 2004 to 2008. She is a member of the Dog Writers Association of America (DWAA), the Cat Writers' Association (CWA), and the Society of Environmental Journalists. She lives with three adopted dogs in Arizona.

NATURAL with added VITAMINS
Nutri Dent ®MD
Promotes Optimal Dental Health!

Visit nylabone.com
Join Club NYLA
for coupons &
product
information

360° Design
Cleaning Action!™

Dogs L♥ve'em!™
AVAILABLE IN MULTIPLE SIZES AND FLAVORS.

Nylabone®
Trusted For Over 40 Years

MADE IN THE USA